The L. Ron Hubbard Series

BRIDGE PUBLICATIONS, INC.
5600 E. Olympic Blvd.
Commerce, California 90022 USA

ISBN 978-1-4031-9884-6

Special acknowledgment is made to the L. Ron Hubbard Library for permission to reproduce photographs from his personal collection. Additional credits: pp. 1, 7, 25, 83, 117, 199, back cover Tribalium/Shutterstock.com; pp. 4–5, 7, 84, 85 National Archives; pp. 11–19, 88, 91–95, 97–98, 125, 149–151, 155–156, 159–161, 163–166, 169–170, 173–175, 177–178, 181–182, 185–186, 189–190, 193–194 Tatiana53/Shutterstock.com; pp. 12, 19 bioraven/Shutterstock.com; p. 13 pASob/Shutterstock.com; pp. 29–48 Blackbirds/Shutterstock.com; p. 52 Time & Life Pictures/Getty Images; pp. 51, 87–89, 136–145; EcOasis/Shutterstock.com; p. 89 optimarc/Shutterstock.com; p. 99 Mark Kauffman/Getty Images; pp. 101–105 Myotis/Shutterstock.com; p. 105 Jut/Shutterstock.com; p. 136 (upper right) NATALE MattA? © 0/Shutterstock.com, (lower left) Ulrike Haberkorn/Shutterstock.com, (lower right) Andrei Nekrassov/Shutterstock.com; p. 137 (upper left) Panoramic Images/Getty Images, (upper right) George Green/Shutterstock.com, (lower left) © Abuela Pinocho/Getty Images, (lower right) Liedo/Shutterstock.com; p. 138 (upper left) Richard Cummins/Getty Images, (upper right) Eric Gevaert/Shutterstock.com, (middle left) Kent Kobersteen/Getty Images, (middle right) De Agostini/Getty Images, (lower) Anibal Trejo/Shutterstock.com; p. 139 (upper left) Fotosearch/Getty Images, (upper right) Pichugin Dmitry/Shutterstock.com, (middle right) Ming Tang-Evans/Getty Images, (lower) David Salcedo/Shutterstock.com; p. 140 (upper left & right) Anibal Trejo/Shutterstock.com, (middle left) Miroslav Hladik/Shutterstock.com, (middle right) Diego Velo/Getty Images, (lower) Zbynek Jirousek/Shutterstock.com; p. 141 (upper left) Eric Gevaert/Shutterstock.com, (upper right) Philip Lange/Shutterstock.com; p. 143 (middle left) David W. Hamilton/Getty Images, (middle right) Buena Vista Images/Getty Images, (lower left) rj lerich/Shutterstock.com, (lower right) Achim Baque/Shutterstock.com; p. 144 (upper left) Pawel Kazmierczak/Shutterstock.com, (upper right) Dennis Macdonald/Getty Images, (middle left) rj lerich/Pond5.com, (middle right) AFP/Getty Images, (lower) Darren Keast/ Getty Images; p. 158 Serhat Akavci/Shutterstock.com; p. 180 Cristina CIOCHINA/Shutterstock.com; p. 192 Rui Vale de Sousa/Shutterstock.com; p. 201 (background) Brandon Bourdages/Shutterstock.com.

Article appearing on page 201 courtesy of *Maritime Reporter and Engineering News*.

The L. Ron Hubbard Series: Master Mariner—English

RON

The L. Ron Hubbard Series

MASTER MARINER AT THE HELM ACROSS SEVEN SEAS

Bridge

PUBLICATIONS, INC. ®

CONTENTS

An Introduction to

L. Ron Hubbard

AMONG OTHER CHERISHED ARTIFACTS AT A PORTUGUESE Maritime Museum in Lisbon is a faithful scale model of the *Apollo,* the last ship to sail under L. Ron Hubbard's command. It was presented to curators in the early 1970s, and stood among fixtures from fifteenth-century galleons and portraits of Vasco da Gama. Some

years later, in preparation of a commemorative room honoring exploits of the Sea Organization, former members of the *Apollo* crew attempted to secure a return of the model. Yet remembering the legendary status of that vessel and all her Commodore came to represent in the annals of modern seafaring, the Portuguese, understandably, would not relinquish it. Indeed, the very seawall where his Flagship docked on the Portuguese island of Madeira now bears a plaque to mark the site as historic.

So welcome to *L. Ron Hubbard: Master Mariner.* In this issue of our series dedicated to his life and work, we focus on the man

in a most adventurous capacity: as master of vessels across seven seas. Readers of related issues, may well recall the broader strokes of this story: how, as son of a United States naval officer, a young Ron Hubbard came to cross a quarter of a million sea miles before the age of nineteen, how he earned the rare license to helm any sailing ship on any ocean and how he headed a Caribbean Motion Picture Expedition aboard a last of the four-masted schooners. Then again, students of the man may well have heard tell how he further charted a treacherous North Pacific coastline in a 32-foot ketch, skippered

L. Ron Hubbard as Commodore
of the Sea Organization, 1969

hastily armed corvettes through the Second World War and codified all fundamentals of ship husbandry for now famed crews of the Sea Organization. Yet the greater story here requires a greater perspective, so let us proceed without fear of recrossing earlier water.

In fact, as son to United States Navy Lieutenant Harry Ross Hubbard, the young Ron had indeed walked many a "heavin' deck" before his nineteenth birthday. He had further called upon many an impressionable port between Asia and the Caribbean, charted many an unmapped shore below an Alaskan Panhandle, faced many a belligerent vessel through the war and, in short, logged enough miles under sail, steam and diesel to ten times circumnavigate the globe.

So our first crucial point is simply this: L. Ron Hubbard knew Old Man Sea as only a master mariner knows and that knowledge was inextricably a part of him. Thus, we find something of the sea in many an LRH short story and novel, in many an LRH technical essay and lecture, and much else bearing an LRH stamp or signature. Yet how Ron came to master this world of ships and sailing is not a generally known story, and so we present this publication.

In due course, we shall touch upon the whole of his life beneath the mast. We shall sign aboard tramp schooners to ply a South China coast; we shall brave typhoons off a still primitive Java; we shall watch the "whitecaps running like ghosts" along an inside passage to Alaska and cut a wake through hostile waters in times of war. Then again, we shall breast great Atlantic rollers and foil modern pirates; while through the course of it we shall taste of what finally inspired him to declare his everlasting love of the sea.

So let us weigh anchor on a seafaring history as L. Ron Hubbard both lived and wrote it. That it is a tale embracing all things nautical—ship care, ship safety, navigational arts and the volumes he authored on sailing fundamentals—only serves to underscore our title *Master Mariner*. That it is a tale very close to the heart of the man is all the more reason to embark in the spirit he himself sailed and the undiminished *"joy I take in the singing wind and sea."* ∎

The "heavin' deck" of a first L. Ron Hubbard command, somewhere in the Caribbean, 1932

Aboard such military transports as this one, a young Ron Hubbard embarked on his first leagues of nautical adventure

First
LEAGUES

First
Leagues

"HOW SICK I BECAME OF RIDING IN CARS. HOW GHASTLY to me appeared trains. But I loved the sea. I loved steamers and sailboats and surf and sailors. And I yearned and strained to the sea, always the sea." —LRH

Thus, L. Ron Hubbard began the story of his early life at sea and thus began a voyage of which the high-water marks run as follows: On April 30, 1927, the sixteen-year-old L. Ron Hubbard departed from a Dollar Steamship Line dock adjacent to the Ferry Building along San Francisco's Embarcadero. It would prove his first Pacific crossing and a welcome respite from highway travel between naval stations in California, Washington State and Washington, DC (ceaseless travel, one might add).

His vessel was a steam-turbine *President Madison,* accommodating 280 first-class passengers and otherwise providing most comforts of the era. The course was roundabout through Japan and China to Guam's Agana Harbor, where his father, Lieutenant Harry Ross Hubbard, then served with America's Asiatic Fleet. En route and under the tutelage of a second engineer, Ron wrote, "the great engines; the fireroom, so hot the plates were red

and the oil fire white, the metal 'Mike' which guides the ship by radio."

The return voyage aboard a no-frills USS *Nitro* proved even more instructive. He bunked with two young men of his then home port along the Puget Sound in Washington State. ("Dick Derickson and Jerry Curtis. Nice chaps.") He apprenticed beneath a no-nonsense

Below
A "no-frills" USS *Nitro* aboard which Ron sailed home from the South Pacific in 1927

executive officer by the name of Mr. Welden and an unnamed ensign. Included in the curriculum was small craft handling aboard a fishing punt and lessons from a chief engineer on the maintenance of oil turbines:

"These engines can turn out 20,000 H.P. (horsepower) and then some. The revs. of the prop. are 105 p/m. on the average making a speed of 13.5 to 14.7 (knots)."

Also from this voyage of the *Nitro* come evenings on the bridge for lessons in celestial navigation and a dizzying turn in the crow's nest:

"Lt. Brown said I might climb up to the lookout in the crow's nest. A moment later found me staring up the forward mast which looked ungodly high. I overcame a nervous tremor and climbed a rope up to the steel ladder. Nice prospect a fall was. The deck was doing all sorts of crazy things, as some sea was running. There had been quite a bit of breeze for days, but today it was awful. Going up it nearly blew me off twice. Scared? I hope to sneer."

There was more again on general seamanship and maintenance of berthing:

"Lieutenant Commander Welden, the exec, told us to appoint someone to take charge of the quarters. We appointed Jerry or rather sentenced him. I'm on tomorrow."

While as a closing note, he writes of easing into Bremerton, Washington, through veils of North Pacific fog:

"Ships all around us. Seems like a ghost sea."

His second Pacific crossing, commencing in June of 1928, proved an adventure of another sort entirely. All precipitously began when a then seventeen-year-old Ron Hubbard left the Hubbard seat in Helena, Montana, and boarded a USS *Henderson* out of San Diego. On yet again reaching Guam (much to his father's dismay), he signed aboard a China coast tramp christened the *Mariana Maru*. Two-masted at 116 tons, she was a fully working schooner registered out of Yokohama to haul "cargo of general merchandise" to Yokohama and the China coast. Her largely native crew was headed by three officers, and if Ron could not cite professional experience, he more than qualified on one count: "I could play an awfully nasty hand of bridge." And given the three *Mariana* officers were in desperate need of a fourth, "They made me a Supercargo and I went to Java."

Thereafter, he tells of mastering the ropes of seamanship in an utterly alluring world where listless colonials in white linen amassed small fortunes through illicit trade, where reprobate

missionaries went to seed in mosquito-ridden parishes, where sailors lost their hearts to half-caste girls in muggy bars. And while not every Shanghai lane led to an unmarked grave, these were nonetheless realms of high adventure as evidenced by all-too-unavoidable typhoons in an era before weather satellite warning systems.

"Talk about luck! Last night, we had a decided falling off of the barometer. About midnight, just as I went on watch, the typhoon broke. Powerless to do anything, we all held on while the old boat sunfished.

"All we could do was hold on because we were rolling 45°.

"Water boiled in the scuppers, threw itself over the bow. All ports were battened down as were the hatches.

"An hour after the thing started, we heard, between the intermittent screams of the wind through the tortured rigging, a resounding crackle and then a heavy bump on the deck.

"The typhoon played with us until three o'clock before the torrents of driving rain became less. Then the wind began to abate.

"At dawn, the world was warm and radiant. Light fleecy cirrus clouds scudded on the horizon. The sea was like glass.

"But My God! The upper mast was gone, water buckets were scattered on the deck, the radio antenna and its auxiliary trailed over the side into the blue water, wire lay over everything."

There is more, and it proved equally instructive. Between 1929 and the mid-1930s he writes of plowing keel aboard numerous vessels in various capacities. There was an auxiliary ketch christened *Vanity,* aboard which he served as chief engineer, and another ketch known as *Toughey,* named for the fact she was built for "gray rollers" in the Bering Strait. But for a sense of his progress and perspective through these years, let us return to an age when, as he so evocatively writes: *"sail ruled the sea."* ∎

As amply detailed in *L. Ron Hubbard: Adventurer/Explorer*, what amounted to a first nautical command came in the summer of 1932 with a now famed voyage of the *Doris Hamlin*. Last of the four-masted schooners, this was the ship aboard which Ron sailed his Caribbean Motion Picture Expedition. It was so named for the fact expeditionary aims included shooting newsreel footage of eighteenth-century pirate haunts, principally the Spanish Main stronghold of Edward Teach (also known as Blackbeard). It was further distinguished for the fact expedition members were largely college students in search of a last grand adventure before entering a largely jobless world in the midst of the Great Depression. As the *Hamlin* was "entirely innocent of auxiliary power" and her captain of record shredded both foresail and flying jib in high winds off Baltimore, Ron himself eventually took the helm. In said capacity, he not only steered a crippled *Hamlin* through an ill-tempered Sargasso Sea, he also augmented coastal charts along the Lesser Antilles. But what ultimately determined his course and filled imaginations just as trade winds filled the *Hamlin's* sails was that allure of piratical haunts.

There is something irresistible about canvas and clean keels, he writes. So it was when the likes of Henry Morgan weighed anchor for "empires won" and so it was when he penned what follows here as "Yesterday, You Might Have Been a Pirate." It dates from 1936 or when popular demand for L. Ron Hubbard tales of adventure kept him largely landlocked in Manhattan. Elsewhere, he would tell of continually hungering for the hiss of white wake even as he filled pulp fiction periodicals with such swashbuckling classics as "Under the Black Ensign." He would also tell of sinking profits from his literary works into a Puget Sound yacht and thereafter gleaning hard-won wisdom from arctic-born winds. But what follows here is something of the heritage and romance behind an ever-beckoning "lure of the tropics and salt spray."

YESTERDAY, YOU MIGHT HAVE BEEN A PIRATE

by L. RON HUBBARD

HISTORY HAS BEEN SINGULARLY unkind to the buccaneer. History tells us that, today, we have no buccaneers because of radio and steam navies.

But history is written—rarely enacted—by men behind cluttered desks who go home each night to a roast beef dinner and a double-spring mattress.

The historian has forgotten, patting his full stomach, everything except the fact that buccaneers used to scuttle ships and slit throats. The historian fiercely deplores this two-century saga of the sea, branding it with Teach, Morgan and l'Olonnais.

When the historian wants to travel aboard a liner far better appointed than his own home, for all the taste of the sea he gets, he might as well have put up a few nights at a local hotel.

As a matter of sober fact, if the modern steamer were less well appointed and if the crews still ate salt horse and dried peas and drank green-scummed water, we would still have buccaneers—radio and steam notwithstanding.

When we think of those yelling, cutlass-waving, plundering pirates and their black Jolly Roger, we fail to remember the times—those two centuries of imperial extortion, of blind rulers and enslaved people.

Of late, in researching the field, I have thought to myself that the buccaneer is certainly getting a lacing he does not deserve and he cannot rise up from Davy Jones's locker to answer.

Of course, if the pirates of the Main had ever thought anyone would try to apologize for them, they would have been amazed and even their stout hearts would have contracted with surprise. Because, I do not believe it ever occurred to a buccaneer that he was doing anything the later centuries would deplore.

I am sure that if I had followed the sea two centuries ago, I would have drifted into freebooting. Not for the romance of it, nor for the wild life, nor even for the fighting. I am one of the radical rabble who likes a little personal freedom, a fairly good meal and who dislikes punishment.

Yes, I would have undoubtedly fallen in with pirates and my heels would have swung, most likely, from some Execution Dock. Because I am certain that I do not possess the heart which was required of a sailor in those turbulent centuries.

"The buccaneer was akin to a privateer in that he stood up against one single nation—which he eventually drove from the seas."

A pirate may have had many reasons for existing, but a buccaneer, judging by contemporary standards, lived an unimpeachable life. You must understand that a pirate is not exactly identical with a buccaneer. In that far-gone day a buccaneer would have clove you asunder had you called him pirate.

In the seventeenth century there were few pirates and many buccaneers. The buccaneer was akin to a privateer in that he stood up against one single nation—which he eventually drove from the seas. The buccaneer was either English or French and his enemy was Spain.

At that time, Spain had the West Indies by the throat. It had taken the French and English many years even to discover the currents and prevailing winds—and they had learned by hard experience how to build staunch crafts with which to compete with Spain.

Thanks to the much overrated Columbus, Spain had been first on the ground. Adventurers under the flag of Castile and León had swooped down upon Hispaniola, Puerto Rico, Jamaica, Cuba and lesser islands, as well as the South and Central American mainland. The Indians who had lived there originally were eventually wiped out, almost to a man, by harsh oppression.

Spain, using mining methods which killed slaves by the thousands, was gutting the countries of their natural resources—mostly gold. Spain was interested in wealth and wealth alone. Spain wanted to humor its few noble families and its haughty captains. And Spain succeeded in ruining the West Indies.

Their loot was going home by the shipload. Their *commandantes* were becoming wealthy beyond an Arabian Night's dream. And England and France and Denmark and Holland were the little orphans out in the hurricane, without a smell of gold.

Eventually, the northern countries found the trade routes, managed to build adequate ships, managed to arrive in the Caribbean in some kind of force. Only to find that their lot was to consist of nothing more than a few moldy bones.

Now, if France and England had tried to build up their navies to combat Spain in that region, all might have been different. But the effort was half-hearted and the road was left wide open to the buccaneer.

Englishmen and Frenchmen, having no great support at their back, began to band together for their own

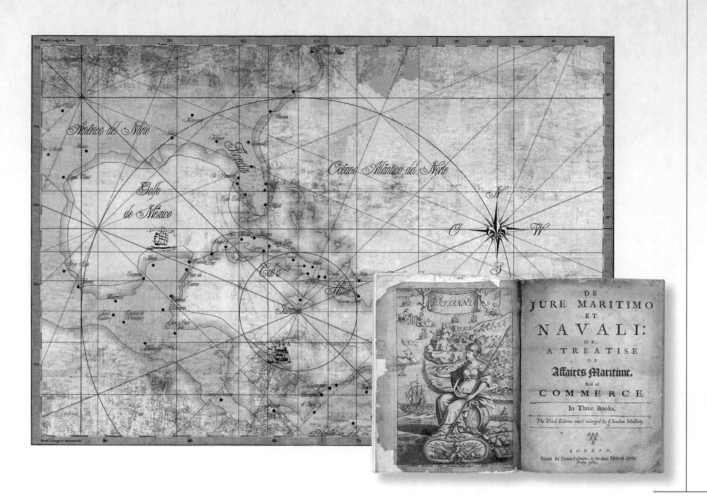

Above
The 1682 maritime law book as laughingly disregarded by Caribbean buccaneers

protection against the Dons. Thanks to a Spanish raid—and I won't bore you with details—upon the island of St. Kitts, the colonists at that place thought it best to seize and fortify another place against Spanish attack.

Tortuga (Turtle) Island, just north of Santo Domingo, was chosen for this purpose. The Island of Old Providence was also the scene of an English colonization.

But the Spaniards hated the thought of having all these Englishmen scattered about the Caribbean and the Dons thereby murdered all the people on Old Providence. Shortly after, the Spaniards made a second attack—and really committed suicide by it—upon Tortuga. There, they massacred the colonists.

By that time the English were thoroughly up in arms against Spain. Spain would not leave them alone. Spain had the West Indies all to themselves. Spain was hauling out Peruvian gold and all manner of rich cargoes. Spain was arrogant, unreasonable.

So the English there at Tortuga began recruiting. Men came to them from all over the Old World. Men who were heartily sick of home politics, men-o-war, merchant captains and fruitless religious warfare.

And the buccaneers began to become a real menace to Spain.

There are three phases of the buccaneer. From the massacre at Tortuga to the capture of Panama by Henry Morgan; the conquest of the Pacific, ending in 1685; and the decline.

After the buccaneer came the pirate—a lawless wolf of the sea, flying the Jolly Roger, respecting no country.

Henry Morgan and l'Olonnais were probably the greatest buccaneer captains. But they hold that notoriety because of their extreme cruelty and because of a fluke of fate which made Morgan the lieutenant-governor of Jamaica and because l'Olonnais once executed ninety seamen because they had been sent out to bring him in to Execution Dock. L'Olonnais also led an expedition against Venezuela and completely subjugated the Spaniards of three cities there.

Of the other buccaneer captains of this Morgan period we find but little. This is probably because they were a little more gentlemanly and quite a bit more conservative. Morgan's excesses removed the buccaneer from the circle of society and, from that period on, the profession slid and slid fast.

In the Pacific the buccaneering reached its height. Captain Cook sailed around the Horn with several hundred men to harass Spanish shipping. Cook died and the command went to the ablest buccaneer on record, Captain Edward Davis, who was seconded by a Captain Swan.

Davis strewed disaster in his wake. He plundered cities regardless of their armaments. He was making war against Spain and Spain alone and God knows Spain had it coming. As a consequence of this continual raiding, Spain's power began to slip and was almost destroyed by the end of the seventeenth century.

Now we come to the pirates and find that only one man is well known as such. And that because he was the cruelest human being who ever plotted a course. Captain Edward Teach was never a buccaneer. He operated off the southern United States, connived with the governor of South Carolina and generally made himself obnoxious. He was killed two years after he started pirating by Lieutenant Maynard of the Royal Navy in a sharp skirmish.

I list all this to show an incongruity—that over a period of two centuries—1630 to 1835—we know of only half a dozen buccaneers and pirates. And even the man who digs hard into the history of those two centuries cannot find more than two dozen men who stood out. And the two dozen were singled out for notoriety because they were bestial and greatly feared.

But what about the rest of these men? When you look over the tremendous lists of shipping taken in by them, you begin to understand that there must have been many thousands of pirates. And were all these pirates so thoroughly despicable?

My answer is no. The buccaneer and pirate were products of the day, most of them no harder than the average man of the period. They were driven into piracy by the conditions which surrounded their lives.

To understand just why a pirate became a pirate, one must understand the conditions of the sea at that time. It is impossible to go into the details, but a short sketch is sufficient.

Discipline—that god of so much hell—was enforced in the navies and merchant marines of the seventeenth and eighteenth centuries by several mechanisms, specifically the cat-o-nine.

This whip is, in theory, nothing more than nine thongs attached to a short handle. Even in this condition, it is wicked enough. But the military and merchant captains of the time did not think so. They sought to improve upon their discipline by taking copper wire and winding it around the tips of each thong. Then, sometimes, they affixed a lead pellet at the extremity.

> "To understand just why a pirate became a pirate, one must understand the conditions of the sea at that time. It is impossible to go into the details, but a short sketch is sufficient."

For forgetting to salute a midshipman, a sailor might receive fifteen lashes. You and I, in our modern way of living, could not have survived ten.

The British had a custom which deserves mention. If a sailor struck an officer—without regard to provocation—the penalty was "Flogging through the fleet."

The sailor would be taken in a boat from ship to ship and flogged at each gangway. Needless to say, no one ever survived the experience.

Any crime could be punished by flogging and very few of the commanders actually knew how many lashes a man could stand and still live—lashes given with every ounce of brawny strength behind them—brass-tipped thongs which left the back a raw pulp.

Complained about the food? Sixty lashes. Malingering? A hundred lashes. Failed to report on watch? Seventy lashes. And fifty was fatal, at times.

"Some years ago I went into the West Indies in a sailing vessel. We had some sixty men aboard a thousand-ton ship and we were terribly crowded and uncomfortable."

I do not speak of exceptional cases. This was the condition in every navy of Europe—and not many years ago it was the condition aboard our own *Constitution*. Can you visualize her decks redly spattered by the blood of flogged men?

The food was always bad, never plentiful. Men died from scurvy at an appalling rate. And even after the powers that were knew the cause of scurvy—lack of Vitamin C—they did nothing about it. Men's teeth rotted out, they wasted and were finally if the captain had time—rolled into canvas with some shot and pitched over the side. Usually they were merely pitched.

Water was always scarce, always putrid. Steam condensers were in the far future. Green scum in the kegs and under the scum a thousand crawling things. And no effort was actively made to find out that iron, instead of wood, transported water in better condition.

Some years ago I went into the West Indies in a sailing vessel. We had some sixty men aboard a thousand-ton ship and we were terribly crowded and uncomfortable.

But a few centuries ago, a hundred-ton ship carried around a hundred people. No dry place to sleep. Nothing softer than an oak plank. No effort made to supply the men with blankets or clothing to make their lives more endurable.

A navyman or merchantman rarely received any benefit of his pay. It was taken away by all manner of petty accounts and by moneylenders ashore—who were approached in the first place because a sailor could obtain not a penny in advance of his discharge.

No shore leave in either navy or merchant ship because the crew might walk off wholesale.

What about those colorful, romantic seventeenth and eighteenth centuries? How about the gallant boys who gave their all for king and country? Did they get compensation for wounds? No. Did they receive pensions? No. And did they get blown up often? I'll say they did.

Because the navies of that day were too cheap to buy lint, surgeons (ex-barbers) used sponges from man to man, a dozen men to the sponge, and a wound meant either a lost limb or lost life, heavy infection at best.

Those doctors used white-hot branding irons to cauterize wounds. They chopped off arms instead of setting a broken bone. And if the iron shot and chain shot and pikes didn't get the sailor's life, then the surgeon did.

Ah, yes, how about that romance?

The sailors did little joining in those days. They were gathered by press gangs which forced them, drugged them, slugged them, carried them off to a life of hell for country and king and the merchant marine. They couldn't even tell their families they were going. And even if they were making their twenty dollars a month on a merchantman, they were liable to be seized ashore and thrown into the navy.

In other words, they had no choice in the matter. They were impressed against their will. They were treated like cattle and they died like ants under a heel. They were flogged if they didn't work and fight and thereby died. And if they worked and fought, they died anyway.

"But through all this bitterness there is still something about the sea. Something which steam has lost to us. Something about sail and a clean keel and far countries which men could not resist."

But through all this bitterness there is still something about the sea. Something which steam has lost to us. Something about sail and a clean keel and far countries which men could not resist.

There was the lure of the tropics and salt spray and empire to be won. But these were not for the common sailor. The officers, yes. But an officer was usually of noble family and a sailor couldn't help it if he happened to be born on a hearth instead of a four poster. And history tells us truthfully that the most forceful men are those who have dragged themselves up through the ranks.

But to drive it home. How would you like to walk down to the corner drugstore for the air or maybe a pack of cigarettes and suddenly find yourself confronted by a band of armed men who scooped you up bodily and bore you to the harbor, where you would be thrown into a stinking, vermin-ridden hold with other wretches impressed like yourself? How would you like to be gone for years, beaten down as a slave, to return twisted of mind and broken of body to find everything you had known swept away by inevitable progress?

That's what the man of the past had to face.

Then, let's look at the brighter side of this picture. A sailor in the navy or merchant fleet didn't have a chance. Wasn't it natural that he would desert at his first opportunity? He'd brave the sharks in a foreign harbor at night to swim away from his floating hell.

He'd gladly ship with the first better ship which came along. He'd do anything to escape this living death.

And so, pirates were born.

It was a simple thing, this becoming a pirate. One day at dawn, your officers sighted a ship. Soon the vessel overtook yours and a short fight ensued. And then, when you were standing there, staring at these bearded hellions who had boarded you, you heard one of them say that any who wanted to be a pirate, step out.

You'd look at their splendid bodies, at the free and haughty way they held their heads. And you'd step out. Oh, yes you would, outlaws or no.

Or maybe your vessel was sunk on a reef and you had no place to go but another ship like her. And then one night, you walk into a tavern and see some loud-voiced bullies swilling their brandy. They look at you, testing your height and the strength of your arm, and then they ask you to join them.

Law? You're not thinking about law, you're thinking about a full stomach and a taste of sea life as it ought to be lived. You're thinking that here you'd get shore leave and here you'd be able to get good clothes and here you'd be able to hold your own against despotic officers.

Sure, you'd join.

"How would you like to be gone for years, beaten down as a slave, to return twisted of mind and broken of body to find everything you had known swept away by inevitable progress?"

A sea rover had it easy. He was overmanned and the work was proportioned well. He removed the captain when the captain became too rough. He put ashore whenever he needed water and to the devil with any set schedule or course. He ate well because he had the pick from the larders of the great cabins he captured. He could trade with the natives on any island at any time for fresh meat and fresh vegetables.

He didn't spend all his days at sea. He found a haven in St. Thomas or Culebra or—most anyplace which was warm and sheltered would do and the West Indies are plentifully supplied with coves for small ships.

He went to sea when he felt the need of exercise and plunder and stores. He sailed as you and I would sail if we had a fine yacht and plenty of time.

He was a demon in attack for two reasons. In the first place, a few cruel captains had given the pirate and buccaneer a name for bestiality. In the second place, if caught, the pirate would be swung up at some Execution Dock and left there to dry for months, even years.

That fact alone is a key to the times. Would you like to see a dried corpse swinging at the corner of 42nd and Broadway? No, of course not. But our ancestors must have liked it.

Today there are men who follow the sea because that is all they know. They understand the sea and they like it. They are restless unless they are afloat. Certainly the same is true of those adventurous times. Then how was a man to enjoy going to sea unless he was either a pirate or an admiral? And there were not many admirals.

The pirate company was not necessarily made up of cutthroats. You can see for yourself that they must have been very average sailors and their own laws show us that they had a taste for order and peace among themselves.

In fact, one pirate captain (one of the notorious ones who is known through his cruelty), named Kennedy, was despised by his men because in his youth Kennedy had been a pickpocket and was later a housebreaker. He ruled only because he was faster with a cutlass and pistol than any of his crew.

Their laws, regarded in the light that all pirates were fiends, are amusing:

I. Each pirate to have a voice in the affairs of the moment.

II. Every man to be called fairly by name and list in the doling out of prize shares. Every man allowed a suit of clothes from the prize. Marooning was the penalty for holding out so much as a dollar from the general fund.

III. No person to game at cards or dice for money.

IV. Lights to be put out at eight o'clock at night.

V. Pirates to keep their cutlass, piece and pistols clean and fit for service.

VI. No women to be allowed among them. And if any were captured, any man approaching her was to be executed.

VII. To desert ship in battle was punished by death.

VIII. No quarrelling of any kind aboard ship. Differences to be settled on the beach, properly supervised by quartermaster or captain. If combatants miss with pistols, they are to take cutlasses. Winner is the one who draws first blood.

IX. If any man shall lose a limb or become crippled, he shall be compensated to the extent of eight hundred dollars out of the public stocks. Lesser injuries in proportion.

"Today there are men who follow the sea because that is all they know. They understand the sea and they like it. They are restless unless they are afloat."

That certainly looks like a knavish crowd, utterly without heart. It is easy to see the wherefore of these articles. They are contradicting everything which went on aboard men-o-war and merchantmen. Even the sixth article was not the case in the regular services, as a quick glance at history will show. There are some very hideous instances regarding the conduct of navies and merchant marines with regard to article six.

The men banded together to free themselves from the real rogues of the time. The imperialists to whom human suffering was nothing and less.

With respect to the terrible reputations enjoyed by the buccaneers and pirates, outside of a few isolated instances—each accurately and laboriously recorded to prove their bestiality—I think there is one sidelight which has never cropped up.

When a merchantman saw the Black Flag burst from a truck, he usually struck his own colors without asking any questions. We know that from the pirate's own records. And yet the merchantmen were amply armed and manned for battle.

Upon boarding the captive ship, the pirates would take all the gold and silver, what provisions they needed, what powder they wanted and those trinkets which appealed to them. Once in a while, if they needed it, they would take the ship, but not often.

Upon returning whatever they thought returnable to the master of the captive, they let him go free.

Sometimes, of course, there were bloody orgies associated with such captures. But usually there was ample reason for it. Maybe the ship was from St. Kitts and the governor of St. Kitts had just strung up a dozen pirates at the Dock. Or perhaps the conduct of the captive had been treacherous. Or perhaps pirates had suffered from the master at some past battle.

The pirates knew they lived within a step of death and they were therefore prodigal with their funds. Why save it for someone else to spend? They at least were able to buy a good time and as peaceful sailormen (dying from scurvy, gunshot or gangrene) they would not even have had the price.

It is significant that we find few mentions of flogging among the pirates. With other customs then in vogue, they threw the cat-o-nine into the sea. Let them slay each other in duels ashore, let them die from gunshot, let them hang, but God spare them the lingering torture of the lash.

The only way you could escape the cat-o-nine (if you followed the sea) was to turn pirate.

As for surgery, the pirates had their own doctors. They had learned much from the Indians—and much from experience. They knew that rhum cured almost anything—and it did. They did not drink rhum, they drank brandy, Stevenson to the contrary. Rhum was issued by the British and French to their sailors. Did a pirate have to follow so unintelligent a practice? No! It was ban enough that the navies did it. Rhum and the tropics never mixed, but the British went right on serving up the ration.

No, rhum was only for a poor sailor. A pirate found that it cured infection. He didn't reason that it was germs and that the killing power was the alcohol. He therefore saved himself many limbs which a service surgeon would have sawed off (using one swig of issue rhum for anesthetic).

No, I do not believe in the historian's pirate. I believe that the ferocity was a name born of the cowardice of merchantmen who did not have the heart to stand up against the attack and who therefore invented the stories to cleanse their own honor.

I believe the pirate had a reason for existence. I know that if I were sent back into those centuries, I would have followed the more comfortable profession. I know the Caribbean to be soft and glamorous and kind and if I had had to turn pirate to enjoy it, I would have run a Skull and Bones up the truck.

And to hell with the navy!

The 32-foot auxiliary ketch *Magician* in Puget Sound off
Port Orchard, Washington, 1939

CHAPTER TWO

The Log of
THE MAGICIAN

The Log of
the Magician

"**A** FLOOD OF WATER HAS PASSED UNDER THE KEEL AND HERE we have another saga to write." —LRH

The log of the *Magician* chronicles L. Ron Hubbard's 1940 Alaskan Radio Experimental Expedition between the Puget Sound in Seattle, Washington, and the southern reaches of Alaska. As the expeditionary

title suggests, the voyage was primarily mounted to test a then novel radio navigational device (and, in fact, the antecedent of Long Range Navigational systems universally employed until the advent of satellite navigation). It was also significantly conducted under the hallowed flag of the Explorers Club, into which L. Ron Hubbard was admitted some months prior. That he additionally corrected imperfect charts for the United States Hydrographic Office likewise bears upon this account. But to begin where Captain Hubbard himself began, let us consider the 32-foot auxiliary ketch he evocatively christened the *Magician* and affectionately referred to as the *Maggie*.

Notwithstanding her forty years, she boasted the finest Washington oak and cedar. She further featured numerous LRH designed and directed modifications. Most notably, he removed the smaller of two masts and installed a larger mainsail for greater wind catch and ease of handling. He similarly altered her hull for greater speed and maneuverability. To improve overall sailing efficiency, he attached a canvas "sleeve" to the mainsail, allowing for a smoother airflow (a primary factor in sail efficiency).

To compensate for the lightness of her keel (displacing 80 pounds of water and thus considerably smaller than keels of commensurately sized vessels), he ballasted her with 500 pounds of strategically placed iron. In consequence, she cruised virtually upright to capture maximum wind for maximum forward velocity. Finally, he tested her in 28-mile-an-hour winds. With sails trimmed flat—a condition wherein most similarly sized

Captain L. Ron Hubbard at land's end
in Ketchikan, Alaska, 1940

vessels would have capsized—she heeled only modestly.

In consequence to all, she ultimately proved faster than any typical Puget Sound racing yacht and otherwise cruised with a surety all out of proportion to her size. She additionally boasted a 600-mile cruising range under motor power alone (all too necessary if becalmed) and a 70-gallon water tank to likewise extend that range still farther. Finally, and remembering her expeditionary purpose, she carried a then rare radio receiver (courtesy of RCA) to pinpoint broadcast direction.

Thus appointed and equipped, the *Magician* prepared to launch. That, on conclusion of the voyage, Captain Hubbard indeed earned a Master Mariners license to helm vessels of any size on any ocean makes for the perfect postscript. That what follows here is a contemplative dialogue hammered out topside

Below
A sea-battered *Magician* in the wake of Ron's Alaskan Radio Experimental Expedition, 1940

on a portable typewriter (affectionately dubbed the "Old Mill") is likewise entirely appropriate; for it is far more than a "ship's log" in any usual sense. It is an ode to the sea and deeply poetic narrative on a voyage through waters so chilled the very shadows seem to freeze in the wind. That he employs the plural throughout ("We proceeded at about five or six knots, boiling along so to speak") is both a reference to a deckhand as well as the *Magician* herself. The periodically mentioned *Stooge* (also known as *Three Sheets*) was a dinghy attached to the *Maggie*'s stern and loaded with navigation gear. The rest requires only an imaginative eye. ∎

LOG: CUTTER "MAGICIAN"

July 27, 1940

Departing Seattle for Alaska—Point No Point first stop—at about 4:30.

2:55 AM Passing Marrowstone Pt in the cold dark.

It's awful goddamn wet.

4:20 AM We ran and we ran and got wet and looked for an anchorage and finally wound up here in Port Townsend at the small boat basin. It rained and the motor had some water it couldn't digest.

July 28, 1940

Up at high noon to a foggy day and away from the yacht basin here at a few minutes after. But fog or no fog, after timing things last night, I feel fairly confident of the navigatorial ability.

All the ingenuity in the world seems to be required to run one of these Marine Engines. But relying wholly on luck as I do seems to work also.

Ground the valves in disgust when engine faltered and missed. Some carbon had collected in the head and some of it seems to have battered up a spark plug. I dunno. Anyway, it works.

We have just gotten under weigh again. We are somewhere out in the Strait of Juan de Fuca—a very fine place to grind valves.

Well, we ran and we ran and there was a tide. And we were astonished to find ourselves all mingled in with reefs en route to Cadboro Bay where one anchors at Victoria.

July 30, 1940
ROYAL VICTORIA YACHT CLUB TO BOAT HARBOUR

Up at the crack of dawn and got splinters in my eyes. Engine failing, five knot tide, no light and not much idea where we were.... Someday I am going to take up divination the better to navigate.

Having gotten veddy tired of the engine, for I found that by disconnecting a plug wire and then connecting it again I could get one

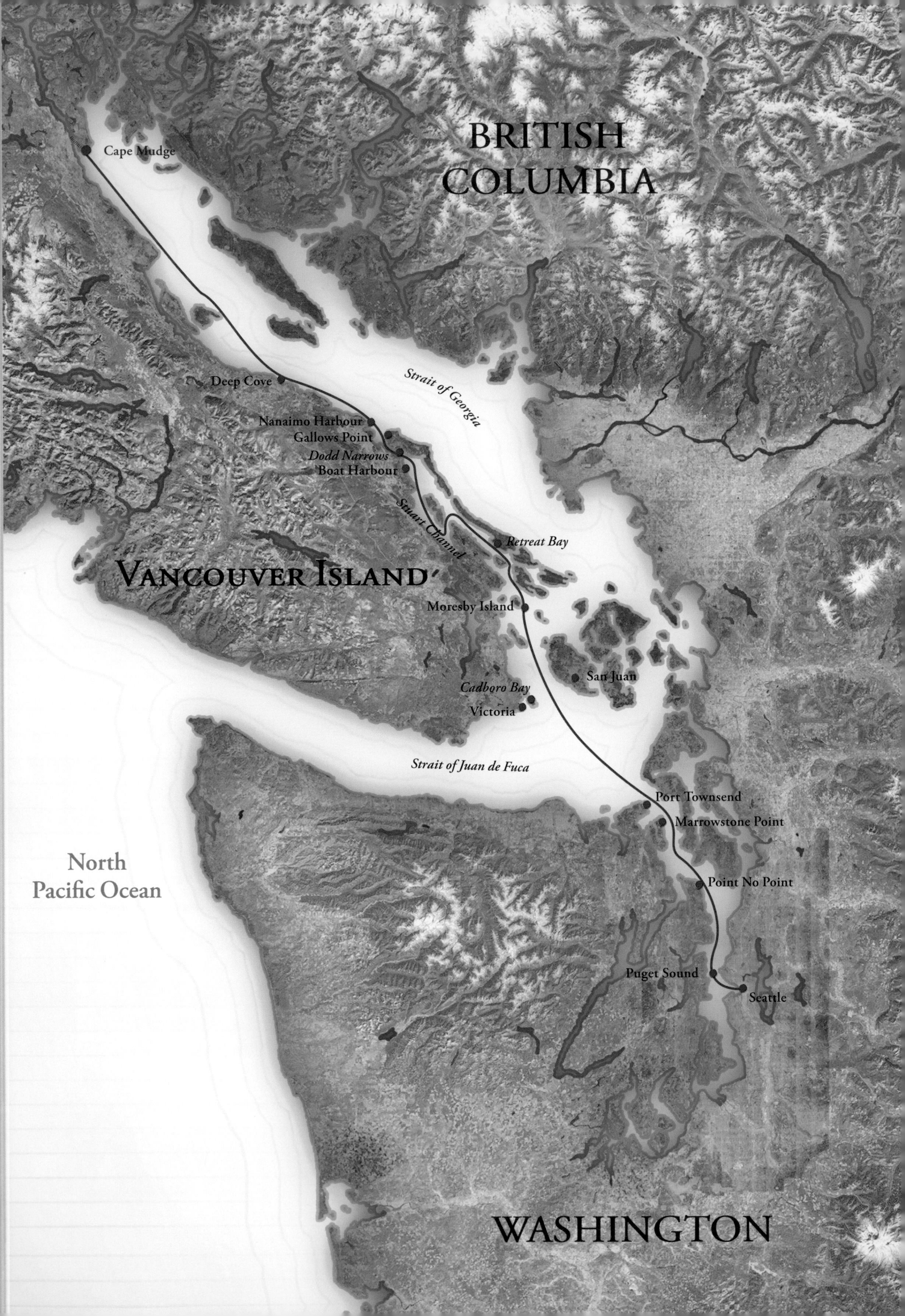

BRITISH
COLUMBIA

Cape Mudge

Strait of Georgia

Deep Cove

Nanaimo Harbour
Gallows Point
Dodd Narrows
Boat Harbour

Stuart Channel

Retreat Bay

VANCOUVER ISLAND

Moresby Island

San Juan

Cadboro Bay

Victoria

Strait of Juan de Fuca

Port Townsend

Marrowstone Point

North
Pacific Ocean

Point No Point

Puget Sound

Seattle

WASHINGTON

of two cylinders to hit and, having gotten five heavy shocks therefrom, got up sail. A fair wind up the bay and naught but the whisper of water under her bows. To hell with engines!

Poking through some lovely little islands near San Juan, taking out time to fish, ambitiously getting out the gaff as well as the line. Evidently fish dislike being gaffed.

Big steamers in this fairway which looks more like a series of little lakes than an ocean route. Charging full speed with their decks crowded with people in steamer chairs, swathed in blankets. Can't ever recall, in or out of the tropics, a steamer without people in deck chairs wrapped in blankets. They are always reading a book. Seems to be a lot of trouble to go to, just to read a book. Wonder if it is always the same book.

Took their swells hot off their sterns, swoosh, bam! Maggie doesn't mind.

Along about noon we got a fair wind again. We proceeded at about five or six knots, boiling along so to speak, up through tree studded islands along lengthy channels. Found that the Hydrographic Office publication on Moresby Island, etc., is strictly ballast.

We looked for an anchorage. However the anchorage at Retreat Bay is terrible, right out in the fairway with no protection from wind and so I decreed we go onward. Followed a spooky time for me. After finding charts wrong I had to navigate through submerged reefs in Stuart Channel. However Boat Harbour beckoned and, in a race against darkness under power, we surged for the specified anchorage, me reading all about it, tiller between my legs, cold and shivering for I had been twice soaked by thundering rains today already and now it was cold! The sailing directions tell about two buoys here at Boat Harbour anchorage, but as near as I can tell the seagulls must have eaten them. Sounded and sounded and then looked up and, to seaward! Saw seagulls sitting on rocks! We were going over a shoal that wouldn't float a toothpick!

Now know that Maggie has a steel plate keel as tender as a Polynesian's sigh and if she ever took a notion to scrape the top off a reef, we would probably sink or at least have to plow along with bent plates to a shipyard—of which there are so many up here. And so I furiously reversed her and then saw a boat and we proceeded, shoals or no shoals, onward. It was a boat, a cruiser of the Vancouver Yacht Club named the Sealeave, drawing perhaps four feet. Maggie draws a fathom. It was very dark by this time and I was even more skeptical than ever with my log and so proceeding and swing and proceeding again, mooched into the smallest little covelet I have ever seen. If this is a harbor I'll have it with wordage. But it is about three or four fathom and very well protected even if there are no buoys as stated and even if it is out of place from the chart.

The most amusing incident of the day was lying off a passage which appeared to be very gentle and reading that it was treacherous and dangerous and not to be navigated without local knowledge. Which meant, for a moment, that I'd walked us into a trap which we would have to retreat miles to escape. However, later saw that Dodd Narrows can barely be navigated at slack water (there really is no slack say the Coast Pilots) but which at run of the tide does seven knots.

July 31, 1940
LYING IN BOAT HARBOUR, B.C.

Up at ten to a spluttery lot of weather and a casual hello from the Canadian cruiser. More splutters. But now, at five twenty as this is being written, the sun, going down, starts to shine in faint apology.

There has been a farm up here on this point for as I sit at the table writing this I can look out and see, seventy-five feet away, a gnarled, hopeless apple tree. As I think I also see some fruit on it I am now going ashore. One to find a whisker pole for the jib (I have been using a wind charger blade) and two to get a stomach ache.

August 3, 1940

Still lying at the Nanaimo Yacht Club floats. Still blowing. Out in the Straits it must be tearing things apart for just behind an island here, fully protected, the whistle of it in the rigging is discouraging to any attempt to navigate the Straits of Georgia which are long and wide, a sea unto themselves, and where seas run high and wild in a blow.

I am learning how to run this mill for it is pretty still after using an electric machine for years. A little bit less effort to run it each day, however.

How much there is to keep straight on a boat! And how much time one can spend doing it! It isn't like a house in that on a boat a misplaced object can result in wrecking everything. Storm and night and no flashlight might spell disaster, for instance, and so one doesn't wonder vaguely where he has put said flashlight—if he is a good sailor. And so much gear in such a small space means that it has to be in order or there isn't room to sneeze.

Sunday, Monday, Tuesday, Wednesday

Why is it, may I rhetorically ask, that one allows a log or a diary to lapse? It seems that when nothing

The *Magician's* British-manufactured
Christie & Wilson barometer

is happening one writes in the log but when everything is flood tiding, never an entry gets made. The ratio would seem to be inversely proportional to the amount of material at hand. But then spare time is directly proportional to boredom.

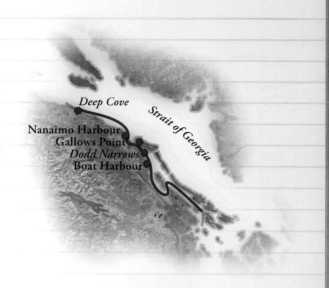

There has been, however, no boredom for the past many days. And so we begin the Saga of the Straits of Georgia.

One generally associates the name Georgia with honey chile drawl, lazy glances and time killed by the million years upon a store porch. But if one will deign to examine the charts of the region north of Puget Sound (and parts of Puget Sound) he will find that the fellows who first hung identification tags upon the gulfs and reefs possessed, uniformly, a sardonic sense of the fitting. And Georgia might fall under the same tabulation as Ripple Rock (over which tides throw ten feet of snarling spume).

For days we tried to plow forth across the Straits of Georgia. No storm warnings were up for the waves only came as far aft as the cockpit. But when one pounds the calking out of his boat upon the stony bosom of the deep he wants a better reason than mere anxiety to get going.

Out we went on Sunday. The wind was gusting and lusting and so we idled back to the floats and waited for Monday. Came Monday and, about noon, it seemed that the wind had dropped. On with the engine, off with the dock lines and off about noon to pass around Gallows Point and outward bound. The swells were heavy and grew worse. I had intended to bend on sail outside because of the gusts in Nanaimo Harbour and felt my way forward through the sting of spray. Maggie was lifting half her bow out and then dropping into the trough, for there was no regularity to the sea and nothing could keep her from slamming into it. Up bow, hover, slam, spray outward twenty feet on either side of her. With green water boiling up to my knees I essayed the sails. Finally I fought the sails onto her and somehow got aft. About then she began to heel and reel and the crash of things going to hell in the cabin was awful to my ears—and back we came.

The next afternoon, Tuesday, we set sail again for the wind had once more dropped. It seemed so calm, so easy, so gentle. Georgia lured us on like a lady and then scratched out our eyes like a bitch.

We ran into tidal current which cut down our speed to four knots over the ground, into a yelling wind which was like climbing a mountain to our suffering power plant. We had intended to make Deep Cove, thirty or so miles north but the night was ink and it

"These reaches and passages are long, narrow passes, wild and deep and straight" —LRH along the Inside Passage

On the eve of departure and under full sail, Puget Sound

seemed easier to stay out in the clear and keep battering away. Through a black night we took it heavy and wet. From two until five were lonely hours.

There is something magnificently terrible about a savage sea in the unwholesome green of half dawn, when the clouds draw down a heavy pall as though to keep out any possible rays of false dawning, when the headlands seem within inches and loom like tombstones, when the waves are sullen shadows leaping by. The ship is an unreal, fragile thing, full of strange groans, and engine and sails are dwarfed in their puny power when matched to all the countless horsepower in wave and wind and current. The whole world is an awesome threat. Alone, wet, hungry, hand cramped upon a tiller, a sailor knows more truth in those hours than all mankind in his millions of years.

And then how warm the sun! How glassy the sea! And a current with us and a steaming breakfast in us and there, at noon, is Cape Mudge. What an ugly name for such a welcome spot. And though the tide books say that many small boats are lost here in a flood tide when the wind is against it, how can one possibly imagine, of this place, anything but refuge.

And then——— That's like Old Man Sea. He gets you in a pleasant mood. You forget the waves and the wind and relax and then he sniggers and reaches out——— And the reverse gear failed as we were making a dock. Crash! No damage but the words which followed.

Twenty hours of important running takes too much out of a man and a day is too little to rest him, especially with SEYMOUR NARROWS just ahead.

This morning August 9, 1940, Friday

Reading about Seymour Narrows in the sailing directions is something like perusing the obituary column. One whirlpool there is supposed to have taken down a gunboat, the Gabriola, at a gulp with all her crew. And all up and down the northwest men talk about Seymour Narrows and tell tales. Last year four Americans in a fishing boat, about fifty feet, came through with the flood (southward) and became so frightened for their ship that they abandoned her, taking to their dinghy. Whirlpools and all, the ship came through without a soul at the helm. But the four Americans were drowned.

Seymour Narrows, say the Coast Pilot, can be navigated at night because the spray over Ripple Rock (nearly two fathom under the surface) is plainly visible for a great distance.

Up early, I secured everything topside. White line by the cable length! Everything wrapped and made watertight and stowed. And then, with a cup of coffee, hoisted anchor.

SEYMOUR NARROWS! The tide was running against us out of the Cove and up Discovery Passage for we were trying to make slack water. And for some reason we lost the eddy and fought the tide all the way. It was a greasy current, boiling and slick in alternate spots. And ahead———

The northern part of the Straits of that bitch Georgia drain through the incredible width about a few hundred yards at a velocity of from seven to twelve knots. In the center of the fairway, causing whirlpools to add to those caused by the torturous course of the passage, is Ripple Rock. SEYMOUR NARROWS!

We were nearly an hour late for slack water and already the current was running. We went scooting past Race Point. I had had so many conflicting directions on how to shoot the Narrows that I still was foggy on how I would do it.

And then———

A dingy Indian salmon boat was lying out by Ripple Rock. I was sure he was helpless and would sing out for aid.

But———standing boredly amidships, a hand was spinning for salmon. North another boat was so engaged. We came through without a single swerve of the helm and without seeing so much as one whirlpool. It was much worse getting to Race Point than through the Narrows.

Granted we were in the first hour after slack water, granted that we had good weather, granted all things. But it was still a bore.

I relaxed with a sigh on a full stomach, lounging in a deck chair at the helm. At last things had settled down. At last we would have an easy time of it———

And Old Man Sea said NO!

With a roar our muffler fell off!

I patched it up and, with open engine hatch smothering us with fumes, we somehow kept on going until we got to Salmon River (Kelsey Bay) the dock and Post Office of Sayward. We had to have an inch and a quarter pipe nipple and I had misgivings about ever finding one short of Victoria or Ketchikan and I was already dazed with the noise and smoke from the engine. But when we tried to get up to the salmon boat float we could not for lack of water and had to lie alongside a large ship on the outside of the dock. The Columbia of Victoria.

Captain Hubbard's well-traveled ship's compass

BRITISH
COLUMBIA

Queen Charlotte
Sound

Hope Island
Bull Harbour
Goletas Channel
Port Alexander
Christie Passage

Alert Bay

Blinkinsop Bay

Kelsey Bay
Sayward *Salmon River*

VANCOUVER
ISLAND

Ripple Rock
Race Point
Discovery Passage
Seymour Narrows
Cape Mudge

North
Pacific Ocean

She was a hospital ship and a hospitable ship as well. The engineer dug up an inch and a quarter nipple, advised on the repair and then did most of it himself!

There was no mooring there and so we came on to where we are now lying, Blinkinsop Bay.

Coming in, because I don't trust the charts, I went ahead of Maggie in the Stooge, putting slowly to examine the water. We anchored in ten fathom (groan as I think of hoisting those hooks in the morning).

You know, it's a worse strain running a small boat than a big one, for in the big one the Captain has time to breathe and examine his charts. And when he has anchored it is up to his mate. But here we are, lying over mud and here I am listening to every sigh and feeling with question every lurch, wondering if her anchors are holding in this running tide, wondering if the wind will freshen———

It is dark and spooky in this place. I feel like I did when I was a kid and slept out one night in the Olympic Mountains, hearing cougars snarl and then seeing the tracks of one fifteen feet from my camp the next morning. This is wild, wild country. Tall and steep. The chart carries the line "Apparently a large valley."

Saturday, August 10th

Blinkinsop. All night the tide ran past, just outside, with a roar which sounded like seven lionesses having cubs. And most of the night I sat around wondering what the holding power of an anchor might be in mud so soft that it was merely dirty water. Shelves in there of the same constituency are most unpredictable. The Coast Pilot says that it is a fine anchorage. Same being a matter of opinion or taste as the old lady said, kissing the cow.

We had a fine run down to Alert Bay. Passed a nice night withal and hied away Sunday to the rolling hoops of sound, church bells ringing.

Hope Island
Bull Harbour
Christie Passage
Goletas Channel
Port Alexander
Alert Bay
Blinkinsop Bay
Kelsey Bay
Sayward
Salmon River

Sunday, August 11, 1940

This is being written in Bull Harbour. Tidal currents, according to the tables, were very nicely with us. The wind was favorable. We made about four knots all day. We wanted to be across Queen Charlotte Sound (for the lady would appear, what with fog, to be the better bitch than Georgia) but about three we found ourselves no more than entering Christie Passage, less than twenty miles upon our way. Accordingly we scanned the Pilot for an anchorage and found that one, "Port" Alexander, had had the best press agent. But after spending an hour and a half poking about Port Alexander in an attempt to obviate the necessity of anchoring in the indicated hundred and twenty feet of water, we gave it up. I led Maggie in with the Stooge, skeptical because an island was misplaced on the chart and reasoning that if an island could be mislaid God knows what had been done with the submerged rocks. This heart in the throat navigation is a sure way to reduce—if there is any truth in the thinning effect of worry.

At five, then, having left Port Alexander to the bears, with dark coming on, a sou'wester brewing and no place to go, we hauled wake outward to plow down Goletas Channel. Hope Island was some twelve miles away and off our course and beyond Hope

"A few bear, deer, birds, blue sky, countless trees, mountains and long, long, long reaches of water bound in like silver rods on flounced green cloth" —LRH

ALASKA

Ketchikan

Revillagigedo Channel

Nakat Bay

Chatham Sound

Dundas Island

Duncan Bay

Indian village

Metlakatla Channel   Prince Rupert

Dixon Entrance

BRITISH
COLUMBIA

Herbert Reefs

Cardena Bay

Stuart Anchorage

Queen
Charlotte
Islands

Baker Inlet   Morning Reef

Klewnuggit Inlet

Lowe Inlet

Grenville Channel   *Wright Sound*

Whale Channel

Graham Reach

Tolmie Channel

Nowish Cove

Finlayson Channel

Milbanke Sound   Ivory Island

Main Passage

New Bella Bella   Bella Bella

Lama Passage

Camp Island

Fitz Hugh Sound

Safety Cove   Canoe and Paddle Rocks

Hannah Rock

Cape Caution

Queen Charlotte Sound

Hope Island

Bull Harbour

North
Pacific Ocean

was Siberia as the next stop. Down, down, down came the night. Up, up, up came the wind.

Here we are at the jump-off to infinity. I bank we stay here tomorrow. I don't know why except that we are halfway to Alaska. If I don't die of apprehension and reef fever we'll arrive. Yea, we'll arrive.

Raining and blowing out on the Pacific. Just raining in here. Gosh what a solace, a good anchorage!

Monday, August 12, 1940

Bull Harbour
Rain
Wind
Zzzzzzzzzzzzzzzzz

Tuesday, August 13, 1940

BULL HARBOUR with the rain still pouring down. This place is so named because of an odd rock formation about thirty feet high on the eastern side of Indian Island. The natives think it resembles a bull and so have painted in his eyes, nose and mouth.

Thursday, August 15, 1940

Up from Safety Cove for a long and dull run until we were well inside Lama Passage, just east of Camp Island about four when the shaft took a notion to twist itself off. We had been much awed by the rocky and torturous course of Lama Passage but we sailed her most of the way to Bella Bella, taking her in the last few hundred yards with the tender.

Friday, August 16, 1940
NEW BELLA BELLA VILLAGE

Waiting for the turn of the tide to get through Main Passage where, 'tis said, the wreck of the "John Drummond" is awash at low water. It is very narrow through the passage and there are numerous rocks. I hope they have found them all. Survey work or not I dislike finding rocks with Maggie's keel.

Got through Main and past the reefs and thence into a tough nor'wester all the way to Ivory Island in Milbanke. Milbanke was doing tricks and it was very late, so late that by the time we were halfway across this open Sound we were favored

The Log of the Magician   41

by the brilliant light of a full moon. There was some northern twilight left—how long it lasts! And we had a chain of rocks and reefs to navigate, mainly unlighted and so, with the wind on the port beam we upped sail and kept the power on full and went boooooooming through at about ten to twelve knots, the wind sharp, the moon huge, the waves restless. When we were in the clear the engine had developed some more weird noises and, gently, we went into Finlayson. This channel had lots of darkness in it and we poked along looking for Nowish Cove. Having no topographical sketch we failed to find it and one just doesn't leave the helm like the quartermaster in the Capital Ship and so we ran into Tolmie Channel. Coming up to a light—one of about three in miles and miles of torturous going—we had the uncertain feeling of tide rips under us and in this country tide rips are sudden and swift. On through the blackness into Tolmie Channel.

"All one sees, league upon league, is an occasional fishing boat scooting along to a better ground" —LRH

Saturday, August 17, 1940

These reaches and passages are long, narrow passes, wild and deep and straight. The sharp, unmapped scarps march in column on either side, some of them glacier chilled and frosted with snow, most of them ragged with slides and mighty with cliffs. Anchorages are far between unless one has a few hundred fathom of line. The shores are merely a dingle of trees almost in the water, no beach. A mile down and a mile up. All one sees, league upon league, is an occasional fishing boat scooting along to a better ground, sometimes four or five fish boats all lashed together, gunwale to gunwale, so that one man only has to steer. The winds come snarling down these highways and short seas combine with millrace tides to make seamanship a fine point of business. Now and then there is an opening into which one can duck and perhaps a bar surrounded with rocks on which one can anchor. The unknown secret of the sea here in the position of rocks, invisible lurking monsters, starved to tear the guts out of a ship. A few bear, deer, birds, blue sky, countless trees, mountains and long, long, long reaches of water bound in like silver rods on flounced green cloth.

We got into Lowe Inlet quite late and made anchorage by moonlight, exhausted from a nonstop run too many miles to count up on two charts.

Sunday 18, 1940

Is it bad luck to sail on Sunday?

We left Lowe Inlet and plugged against a tide which was supposed to be running the other way. We had a head wind which zoomed and boomed. And when we got to Morning Reef Light—a real light, it is, the only one for miles both north and south—we found Grenville Channel growing wide and the wind growing stronger. It was almost as choppy as Georgia and so we hurriedly scanned the coast for an inlet and reached with the jib at fourteen knots into an anchorage so peaceful that we forgot all about the storm.

Morning Reef

Grenville Channel

Klewnuggit Inlet

Lowe Inlet

August 22, 1940

Here I sit in a cabin a-reek with gasoline fumes, dogfish tired and cold, trying to appease my conscience by bringing this log up to date.

We are in Prince Rupert, ready to step off into Alaska from British Columbia, providing we can swing our departure.

Boats!

Why do men so love boats that they will mortgage their energy for years to come? Merely a statement advanced without hope of answer for I go right on loving boats. I have nursed an ailing engine for hundreds of miles and now it has faded away to a splutter of its old self.

We have had, despite the difficulties of piloting in these vaguely chartered waters, playing tag with rocks and guessing at the Coast Pilot, very slight casualties. Just before we got to Lowe Inlet we banged into a log which knocked the stem askew a bit and we ran aground in Nanaimo to possible injury of the keel and now the propeller shaft won't track, but we'll get along. We have to.

To bring this up to today isn't difficult for events have been very mild.

We came bowling up from Klewnuggit Inlet where we had refuged from a yelping nor'wester and found that Stuart Anchorage was much too exposed. We tried to get into Baker but the spread nets of seine boats barred the way. I decided to run all night. We came up to Herbert Reefs Light with an angry red sun setting behind a curtain of moltenly glowing fog pouring across a sea of gore. I came below for a little while and happened to see that an island offered what appeared to be an anchorage. On looking it up I found that Cardena Bay, hard on our starboard beam at that very moment, was a waiting ground for fogbound vessels. We suddenly had a home and swerved out of our course to drop the hook on good mud about a half mile from shore. We were well protected there and safe, though a racing tidal current made us appear, when anchored, like a vessel under a full throttle.

So here we are. Maybe, tomorrow, the engine runs again. If not then it's up sail and to hell with engines. I've always felt that way anyway.

Chatham Sound

● *Duncan Bay*

● Indian village
● *Metlakatla Channel*
● Prince Rupert

August 30, 1940

Days have passed and a flood of water has passed under the keel and here we have another saga to write.

We had the crossing of Georgia, then of Charlotte the harlot and, finally Chatham, Dixon Entrance and Revillagigedo Channel, which are rather large bodies of water with the Pacific behind them and Japan the next stop. These are added to one another in such a way that if one doesn't get you the next might and no breathing allowed between.

Prince Rupert allowed us to get our shaft aligned again and we sailed abortively last Sunday to get no further than the Naval Examination vessel in Metlakatla Channel where the engine wearily coughed up the ghosts of its horsepowers. Ignominiously we came back and, Monday and Tuesday, had the engine out of the ship and cleaned. The crankcase was full of salt water and all valve springs were broken in one or more pieces. Then, despite weather sitting down upon the already morose Prince Rupert we assayed to sail Tuesday evening, planning to anchor at the other end of Metlakatla Pass, near the Indian village, and take off early Wednesday morning. And there the storm found us. About a hundred yards in which to swing with reefs to port and starboard, ahead and astern within spitting distance and no protection from a wind which whooshed and howled until Maggie trembled hard enough to rattle the dishes off the table The rain millraced down until the Three Sheets was nearly sunk in less than twelve hours—in truth she was nearly gunwales under, which would require a fall of some ten

"The unknown secret of the sea here in the position of rocks, invisible lurking monsters, starved to tear the guts out of a ship" —LRH

Ketchikan

Revillagigedo Channel

Dixon Entrance

Nakat Bay

Dundas Island

Chatham Sound

inches. Weather on the water, eyes on the barometer. There was damned little sleep for Maggie, having no room to swing, required constant watching though all her hooks were down. It was a matter of fighting forward against such ferocity of speeding air that a raincoat became a willful kite, to slack off on the lines and then, again, to take them up again. All day Wednesday after all Tuesday night. All night Wednesday. Seventy-two hours of yelling wind and drenching downpour. And we finally became so desperate that, visibility or not, we decided to tackle Chatham the moment the gale abated. And so, Thursday about noon, with a brisk sou'wester behind us and slate colored houses ominously indefinite above us, we sallied out.

The passage from Prince Rupert to Metlakatla is for small boats only and is much beset by rocks and reefs so that one corkscrews through it, imitating what fish boats are in sight. The exit into Chatham is worse for the buoys suddenly give out and leave one amid reefs and islands. There is another bay besides Metlakatla and it is possible to cross over a bar at certain stages of the tide. Abruptly confronted by the last of the channel buoys and without time in a tideway to find out if there was water, we dived over the bar and into Duncan Bay and so, shakily, out into Chatham Sound.

Thursday was one long chain of appeasement to the hunger of the sea. First the jib sheet slipped from the rail and went into the wheel there to stick so solidly that no amount of chopping would free it. We were in the middle of Chatham as it happened with a large sea running and I had no liking for hanging on desperately, seas running green over my face and when I had tried three times and come up soaking and so exhausted as to have difficulty in getting back aboard, I quit. We had the main up and so, cracking on the jib, said it was sail or nothing. And Northward Ho! We gradually found a steady wind, fair, and got along at about five knots despite the seas. We said we would anchor at the north end of Dundas Island but we didn't dare for that was a lee with a sea running. At dusk we had to pass up Nakat Bay at the side of Dixon Entrance for it was too many miles in the lee to be run with the sea that was rolling there. And so with a long Pacific swell, heightened by wind on our beam and a cross swell from Chatham, wind driven, and a tide running obliquely to both, we fought our way into the night and U.S. waters again. We took a bad shaking up for bilge water climbed, in the tossing, over the floor boards, making the cabin deck a minor sea in itself. Not a thing on the ship, it seemed, stayed dry or in place. But the wind blew on and the darkness was gray with rain and the tiny bits of light which were our only guides would vanish for minutes at a time in the downpour and blackness, leaving us without any idea of direction for the wind was caroming off headlands and the tidal currents were uncertain and the reefs were many.

Without doubt Neptune was getting even with us. He snatched away my cap and let it float until I almost swamped us coming about and was in the act of reaching for it when it sank lazily out of sight. With a shattering snarl our whisker pole flew into fragments and over the side. A belaying pin went by the boards. Hour in and hour out we lost things and could do nothing about it but weep.

"We arrived in Alaska. And maybe tomorrow we will even go ashore." —LRH from Thomas Basin, Ketchikan, Alaska

All in the ink save for occasional glimpses of wholly unfamiliar lights, worn out from hours at the helm with the sea banging it about, we won through the night. Ninety miles under sail through heavy seas and ink. The dawn grayed, showing us the torturous courses of our channel. The rain was coming down with renewed violence. But Ketchikan was in sight, we were ghosting along in the calm waters of the narrows with a tide with us for a change. I anchored and lashed up. The town, despite rain, was awake. Ketchikan we have won. We arrived in Alaska. And maybe tomorrow we will even go ashore. *Ron*

A perfectly preserved sextant and yacht's ensign
from Ron's 1940 Alaskan expedition

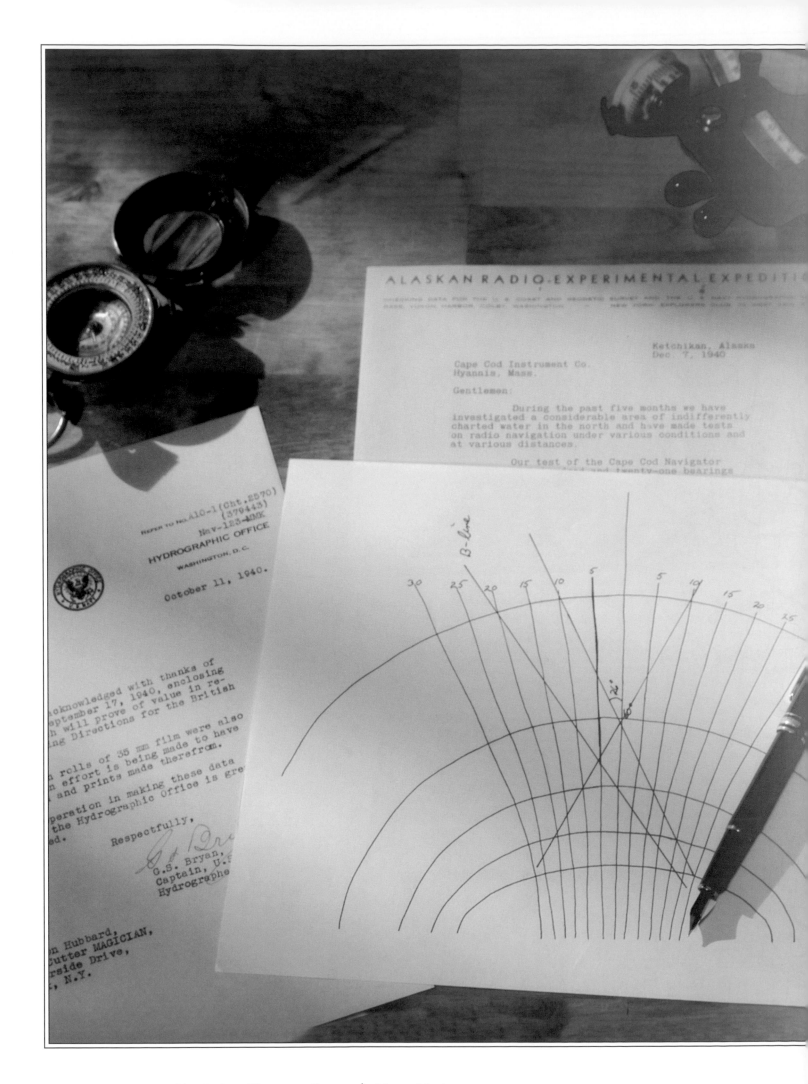

ALASKAN RADIO-EXPERIMENTAL EXPEDITI

Ketchikan, Alaska
Dec. 7, 1940

Cape Cod Instrument Co.
Hyannis, Mass.

Gentlemen:

During the past five months we have
investigated a considerable area of indifferently
charted water in the north and have made tests
on radio navigation under various conditions and
at various distances.

Our test of the Cape Cod Navigator
and twenty-one bearings

REFER TO NO. A10-1(Cht.2570)
(379443)
Nav-123-4RX
HYDROGRAPHIC OFFICE
WASHINGTON, D.C.

October 11, 1940.

acknowledged with thanks of
eptember 17, 1940, enclosing
h will prove of value in re-
ing Directions for the British

rolls of 35 mm film were also
n effort is being made to have
and prints made therefrom.

peration in making these data
the Hydrographic Office is gre
ed.

Respectfully,

G.S. Bryan,
Captain, U.
Hydrographe

n Hubbard,
Cutter MAGICIAN,
rside Drive,
, N.Y.

Radio Navigation

"In spherical trigonometry it should be possible to obtain an unknown position from two known positions in terms of latitude and longitude." —LRH, January 1940

So it was, in conjunction with mathematics professor E. L. Vernon, that L. Ron Hubbard advanced radio navigation well beyond the age. It was no inconsiderable feat and no less than Rear Admiral Chester Nimitz would eventually request an audience with Captain Hubbard to hear more; for here indeed was that legendary antecedent of the LOng RAnge Navigation system (LORAN) employed along all air and sea lanes well into the twentieth century. Here, too, was the universal formula by which mariners/aviators could swiftly determine positions without complex and time-consuming calculations; for here, in short, was the original Position Nomograph.

By way of a few ancillary notes: the beauty of the Nomograph and accompanying formula lay in the fact that, owing to Earth curvature, radio navigational calculations were habitually in error 3.5 miles for every hundred miles. There were, of course, compensatory formulas, but calculations typically took a prohibitive ten minutes. Moreover, the requisite charts required ample space. Hence, the ample "chart tables" to draw long intersecting lines from radio station beacons to a fix far out at sea.

In highly convenient contrast, then, we come to L. Ron Hubbard's description of the Position Nomograph. It dates from March 1940 and was drafted amidst other predeparture correspondence concerning canvas, engines, fuel tanks and all else necessary to ensure that *even if we get blown to China we'll still arrive somewhere.*

"This is a simple celluloid instrument which, when the arms are crossed properly, give out the position of the vessel, once the sights are known on two radio stations. The way this is done today is to contact Station A, which gives out a bearing. Then one contacts Station B, which says the ship's bearing from there is so-and-so. Then the navigator on the ship draws his graph lines and computes a formula for correction (which depends on the accuracy of his ded-reckoning) and, after a couple hours' work, has his position. With this one, we take two bearings, move the arms, read the position directly in terms of longitude and latitude. It is revolutionary in navigation because it may be as accurate as a sextant shot and it is certainly more simple to work out.

"A yachtsman needs know nothing about navigation now to navigate except the way to twirl a dial and move those arms. It is accurate within half a degree on the instrument (half a mile) and the sighting shot, with a half degree error at a thousand miles from the station, would be ten miles. However, stations are seldom more than three hundred miles, which considerably reduces the maximum error. Two shots at different stations will give an average. A sextant error is about three miles and this error is just about the same. Further, Leo Vernon figured out a graph which gives the distances of arcs between any longitude and latitude and any other longitude and latitude upon the surface of the Earth. These two things have never been done before!" ∎

The Mail Buoy

On the heels of landfall in Ketchikan and in light of the fact his Alaskan voyage evinced considerable prowess, Captain L. Ron Hubbard was invited to share his "marine authority" through a series of radio broadcasts entitled the "Mail Buoy." Airing from KGBU Ketchikan and hosted by stationmaster James "Jimmy" Britton, listeners were called upon to submit written queries for LRH consideration. Broadcasts were avidly followed up and down the Alaskan Panhandle as Ron was soon heard discussing all manner of seafaring subjects—quite literally from rigging sails and ventilating engine rooms to selecting anchors and propellers, not to mention his "special broadcast" on radio reception. That he also speaks of employing his radio direction finder to nab a Nazi saboteur is another tale entirely, but roughly parallels the story of how British spy-catchers pinpointed enemy agents through 1939 and 1940.

Presented here are transcripts of six Ketchikan broadcasts that once riveted seamen to their radios in anticipation of that on-the-air announcement: "Here now is Captain Hubbard." ■

BROADCAST FROM KGBU RADIO; KETCHIKAN, ALASKA

MUSIC: "The Alaska Chief"

BRITTON: KGBU radio brings you the "Mail Buoy," a program especially designed for Alaskan boatmen. It is the hope of this station that the exchange of information regarding sea and ships will be found of benefit to those who wish to brush up on their calling, to those who wish to study the fine art of fighting the sea and to those old-timers who can help the world to remember how to make all things shipshape and Bristol fashion by keeping close tally on the data contained in this presentation. Captain L. Ron Hubbard, whose sailoring and engineering and writing have carried his keels through the seven seas, is here in command. Captain Hubbard, himself a marine authority, has taken every way of authenticating this material, checking it vigorously against the best-known authorities. Questions sent to him in care of this station, if accompanied by a self-addressed, stamped envelope, will be answered either by mail or on the air, free of charge. Here now is Captain Hubbard.

MUSIC: "The Alaska Chief"

SOUND: Four bells and a jingle.

HANDLING YOUR HULL

And so, fishermen tall and small, yachtsmen rich and poor, dock loafers tired or argumentative and armchair navigators, we hope sincerely that we will hear from you in volume. Call us liar, thief, wise man or fool, confirm or condemn. The microphone, through your letters, is yours.

I picked up, for this first broadcast, a puzzle down on the docks the other day. A young fellow who had hauled out his rowboat was gazing at her in sorrowful accusation. The boat was a very sweet round-bottomed, carvel-built craft of some sixteen feet in length, powered with an outboard.

"Look at it," he said. "It's ruined!"

And it did look very bad. The sight of a two-hundred-dollar boat with the cedar hull frazzled and torn was a sorry one. Shreds stuck out of the planking at all angles. Deep gouges ran athwartship and fore and aft. It seemed as if someone had been working on it with a combination ax and vegetable grater.

When asked what he had been doing to it, he maintained with violent gesture that it had never touched a reef, that he had used it only as transportation to and from his camp. Further inquiry elicited the information that his beach was rocky and that he had been in the habit of dragging his boat over it. As any sailor knows, that is a fine way to start a boat to the graveyard.

It would have been easy for him to have anchored a raft seaward from the low water mark and attached a pulley upon a three-foot mast. A line reeved through this would have served as an outhaul. Thus, at any stage of the tide, he could have run his boat to the beach, unloaded her and then hooked her to the line and, by hauling on the other one, sent her to a secure mooring. A roller or two on the landward side of the float, and making a lip or ramp, would have allowed the boat to have been pulled up on the float where it would be dry, though its owner is ashore, a hundred yards away. Getting her off is just as simple, for one merely pulls upon the stern line.

The young man thought his boat's ragged bottom was the greatest part of his worries, but it had been well built, with thick planking and a plane soon took out the scars. However, this was a small part of the damage. Teredos had seized upon that bare wood, for wherever there is a break in antifouling paint, even though that break be but of microscopic size, the teredo can find his way in. The small pinhole which marks his entrance is always found to be backed with twisting tunnels through which he had devoured his way.

Even then it was not too late to save the boat. When she had been scraped and sanded, the young man went and purchased a can of copper solution. This is a green or colorless liquid which penetrates dry wood deeply and

Voice of Radio Alaska, KGBU—James "Jimmy" Britton

not only kills off everything inside the wood but also prevents future invasion, dry rot and waterlogging as well.

After the boat was painted, a coat of copper paint was added and a close observer could not have seen that anything had been wrong with the boat.

It was fortunate that he dragged it out when he did, for his boat would have been a ruin within another three months and it would have cost him the price of a new one. And now his will last him many a year to come.

He maintained that it was too much trouble to build a float at his camp. That seems very shortsighted when one remembers that it took him two days of hard work to undo what damage he had done to his boat and it would have taken him an equal amount of time to have built the float. Some men seem to like work so much that they will do a task over and over rather than remove the cause of the labor.

I knew a fellow once who, each day when he started for the grounds, had to spend an hour or more bailing before he could cast off. He was asked why he didn't plug the leak, which was, after all, very apparent. "Well," he said, "I was going to get after that last year, but somehow I can't see the sense of it. Some day this danged fishpot is going to sink and think of all the time I would have wasted fixing her up." He's still bailing.

BRITTON: Send in your questions and problems to the "Mail Buoy" and they will be answered free of charge if accompanied by a self-addressed, stamped envelope. The foremost marine architects and authorities will be consulted. Comment and criticism is invited. The "Mail Buoy," with Captain Hubbard, will be heard regularly over this station. ∎

Alaska Radio & Service Co., Inc.

KGBU

"The Voice of Alaska"

BROADCAST FROM KGBU RADIO; KETCHIKAN, ALASKA

CLEARING THE AIRWAVES

BRITTON: We will now take you to our remote reception station, where L. Ron Hubbard has assembled some data for you in the interests of good radio reception. The many questions which we have received concerning our method of getting radio programs from the States and the many complaints which we have had about local conditions, we hope you will find answered in this special broadcast. Take it away, Captain Hubbard.

HUBBARD: Here we are at the KGBU remote line station at Mountain Point in the midst of the equipment which enables KGBU to pluck programs from the atmosphere and relay them into your homes.

As the only chain broadcast station in Alaska, it is mighty important that KGBU receive these programs, especially at those times of the day when the highly magnetized and humidified air of this region resents being plucked by crackling and hissing instead of throbbing and crooning. To achieve this, Jimmy Britton, some time ago, put out a considerable chunk of change to obtain a twenty-four-tube Super-Pro receiver, a remote station here and a telephone line seven miles into town. Jimmy, like the good radio engineer he is, exerted the fullest extent of his wide knowledge to make this reception as nearly perfect as possible.

The plot of this pickup station is simple. An aerial tuned to the wavelength of KOL and pointed straight down the channel at KOL's broadcast station on Harbor Island in Elliott Bay takes the Mutual Broadcast System programs out of the atmosphere and brings them in to this professional receiver, which is tuned to a hair's width on the wave. A Tork Clock automatically turns this receiver on and off at the proper times. The Mutual program is then whisked through the phone wire to KGBU and through the Collins transmitter there and so is again released into the atmosphere with power behind it so that Alaska can have the best programs manufactured in the States without having to reach the States to get them.

A short time ago I came out to the station here to write a few stories, availing myself of the quiet and the distance from fascinating occurrences and Mr. Britton asked me to see what I could discover about the poor quality of the reception which had been his lot of late. Because I had been doing some radio experimental work on beacon signals for the Navy Department, Fisher Research Laboratories and the Cape Cod Instrument Company, I chanced to have some radio direction finders of high sensitivity. Some weeks ago, though I am not permitted to tell you the details, these direction finders played an exciting part in a slight adventure with a Nazi saboteur, for they are so precise that a source of interference, even if slight, can be spotted at a distance of half a mile.

For instance, a sewing machine motor, unfiltered, will send out a radio signal strong enough for these direction finders to intercept and bracket, leading one to the house in which the motor is running and then into the room of the house. Not, of course, that one uses them to find seamstresses, but only as an illustration of their sensitivity.

Playing with these scientific instruments, I chanced to make three minor discoveries. No credit to myself, for when one has the equipment, the task is simple and, so far as I know, these are the first instruments of this kind to be so employed in this country.

The first thing they found was the existence of a type of set evidently still in use here in Alaska which spoils reception for one and all.

These sets are old-timers, not much in advance of the crystal set era, and they have two advantages in that they get long-distance reception and are cheap. They have a decided disadvantage in that they put out a signal of their own.

Have you heard that monotonous squeal on your dial? Or a howl like a wolf full of pins? Well, those howls are caused by the regenerative receiver. Such a receiver takes in the station signal and, like the pack rat, always leaves something in trade. They regenerate the signal as a banshee scream and, within half a mile of one, any other set, instead of getting that station clearly, gets the howl and the station and, as a result, no reception. These sets proved so annoying to reception that the government no longer tolerates their existence and, when one is found to be in use and attention called to it, the government puts the owner someplace and throws the key away.

New portable sets, ranging from seven to thirty-five dollars are too

"The many questions which we have received concerning our method of getting radio programs from the States and the many complaints which we have had about local conditions, we hope you will find answered in this special broadcast. Take it away, Captain Hubbard." —Jimmy Britton

easy to operate and too cheap to buy for any listener to keep on spoiling his neighbor's reception with a regenerative radio receiver, vintage 1928. The owner of such a set knows he has one when he can hear the howl himself when getting on a station. His set howls and then the howl vanishes when he gets on the exact wave of the station. But it only vanishes for him. All the time he is sitting on that station, some poor devil, with just as much right to the air in his vicinity, is having to stay wide of that spot on the dial.

That accounts for part of bad reception. These instruments have located seven such sets in Thomas Basin and two at Mountain Point, but of course it does not happen to be KGBU's business to pick them up. Law enforcement agencies are far between in Alaska and it takes some little time for them to act.

The next point of reception interference which a listener might find of interest, but which he probably knows already, is that an electrical household appliance is a miniature transmitter itself. An electric refrigerator, grinding away, throws a signal into the radio set in the house. A light switch, going on and off, sparks and does the same thing. Of course when one is listening to a strong signal such as that of KGBU within a few miles or a few hundred, this domestic interference does not bother one's radio too much. However, when one tries to get a faint signal from the States, his set is strained to the point that he is liable to get household noises to the exclusion of a program.

KGBU Ketchikan transmission tower

All this leads up to an experiment we have rigged for you at this remote line station.

I have here at hand a small Philco portable radio. It is an extra-good portable, but it is not, of course, to be ranked with large sets. It operates on both its own batteries and on house current. By taking a plug out of the back of it and putting it into the 110-volt house current, its own batteries are cut out and it is operating on public current from the power lines, just as your set is probably doing.

Now we turn up this battery set on KGBU. Give us a record, Mr. Britton.

MUSIC

That is clear reception, is it not?

Now we go into the second part of our song and dance. This plug here at the back of the set, when pulled out, cuts off the batteries. We plug this extension into the public power line just as we would a bridge lamp and as your radio is plugged in. It is not now operating upon its batteries, but upon public-utility juice. It takes a moment for this to warm up. We chose this part of the day for this demonstration because so many appliances are in use that the juice on this line is particularly dirty.

MUSIC WITH SQUEAL

There. We switch it back quickly to its own batteries because if we listened to that very long, we would go nutty as a fruitcake.

Want to hear it done again? There, we have disconnected the batteries and the set is running on public-utility electricity, not its own battery current. Now here it goes on the power line again————

MUSIC WITH SQUEAL

There. During the past week two people have witnessed this experiment. Anyone is free to examine this Philco.

If you want to perform this experiment yourself, get a battery portable with 110-volt connections and notice that at those times of the day when your reception has been bad the little radio will raise the devil himself with "static."

But this static we are getting is *not* static. It is dirty juice. The electricity which is being pumped into the Ketchikan home is so full of interference that it is a wonder anyone ever hears anything.

The question arises whose fault this is. Well, all I know is that big-town electricity is not dirty.

About eight months ago in New York City I lived up on Riverside Drive. I was doing my work on a full electric model of an International Business Machines typewriter which is run by one-sixtieth of a horsepower motor. One-sixtieth.

This little motor made no disturbance upon my own radio on the broadcast band and so I thought nothing about it. Well, I opened the door one day to find a Consolidated Edison man there. He was carrying an interference locator. He came in and set down his pickup beside my machine, where it whirred and crackled. He sighed with relief.

"For two weeks," he said, "I have been on the lookout for that interference source. Thank God I've found it."

"But," I said, "I don't think it ruins any reception. My radio works with it going."

"Yes, but there are a lot of refugees in this neighborhood, sir, and they get Europe on their shortwave sets and this is just enough interference to throw them out in the afternoon. Here is a filter for your typewriter."

New York's power company, Consolidated Edison, is just that strict and accurate about its power. Any modern light plant is that strict.

If the electricity in a big town was dirty with domestic noises, then radio reception in the midst of millions of appliances would be impossible. But there *are* those appliances in a big town, connected in to the same power which runs radios and there is *no* interference in the power lines from those appliances. It seems that if one wants good radio reception, he has to go into the center of millions of electrically animated horsepower to get it, for in big cities, public-utility power is properly filtered and led.

If this juice at Mountain Point were clean, then it would be possible for KGBU to give Alaska chain programs *all* the time with clarity comparable to those programs emanating from KGBU's own studios. It is nearly impossible to run a receiver of this size on batteries or to receive programs with a smaller set.

Some of our listeners have advocated lynching people for letting this interference continue. However, we think this is extreme. All we want and need is clean juice. If KGBU has that and if you have that for your own radio, the quality of your reception can be trebled.

Thank you. ∎

Southern Alaska's salmon trawling fleet at anchorage in the Ketchikan basin

Alaska Radio & Service Co., Inc.

KGBU

"The Voice of Alaska"

BROADCAST FROM KGBU RADIO; KETCHIKAN, ALASKA

MUSIC: "The Alaska Chief"

SOUND: Four bells and a jingle.

FIRE SAFETY

HUBBARD: Greetings, mariners, and thank you for the response to the first program of this series. If all these questions were answered, it would take several such hours and so I think it is best to take a single group.

From J.R. at Ketchikan comes the query "I was told yesterday that I had to have firefighting equipment aboard my boat even though it is only a small outboard runabout, fourteen feet in length. I got to wondering, after that, just what I would do if the motor did catch fire and what I ought to have to put it out." And as there are several others on the same subject, let's talk about it.

J.R., you are being very smart, for very few sailors ever wonder just what they would do in case of fire. Instead they comply with the law and suppose that in time of emergency they will be able to meet the situation.

Of course there are quite a few around who have already met Old Man Fire at sea and Old Man Fire has filled them with such a wholesome respect that the boats owned by them are so arranged as to provide for nearly any eventuality. These, sorrowfully enough, are in the minority. If you have ever awakened to find yourself aboard a fiery coffin with green gouts of flame leaping hungrily between yourself and the hatch, you won't take any chances in the future. It is a soul-blasting experience, particularly when the fire-extinguishing equipment is on the other side of that companionway. Men who have had such an experience have seldom lived to yarn about it and Uncle Neptune has been served up with roast sailor.

Fire at sea is a theme which has made up fully as much material as reefs and storm. Fire is the most unexpected of accidents, for it flares up at the least likely times and follows a course with a hunger which is assuaged only when an entire vessel has been consumed. To be aboard a vessel with fire in her hold is to be on the brink of Old Nick's stokehold either from nerve reaction or actual, spectacular demise. Fire eats and eats and gnaws and chews and turns a vessel from well-fitted and shaped planks into a cloud of smoke drifting over an empty sea. For violence and guile, fire holds all records.

Uncle Sam, in his anxious interest in his seagoing citizens, is very tough where fire is concerned. He issues bulletins and makes researches on the subject and has a number of stiff laws to enforce. If these laws are not obeyed and if the Coast Guard, when inspecting, finds that this is the case, heavy fines are imposed. No matter how small or how big the boat, it must be suitably equipped to prevent and fight fire.

For such a boat as J.R.'s, which comes under Class I, it is merely stated that the craft must be equipped with the means of extinguishing a gasoline fire, which means must be ready for immediate use. Most commercial fire extinguishers have been approved. The gun type is a cheap and efficient extinguisher and will serve J.R. very well. It should be placed amidships where he can get at it in case of fire, not aft, near the motor, where he is liable to get scorched reaching for it.

If J.R. has any trouble with fire in his outboard motor, it will be because he has slopped gasoline around while filling it in a seaway and has either ignited the gasoline with a spark from a damp plug when starting it immediately after or because he has gotten gasoline into his bilge and has then allowed a passenger to smoke before the fumes have evaporated. A can which has a long, flexible snout will help to confine the gasoline to the tank.

But, relatively speaking, fires in such small craft as outboard motorboats, are not particularly dangerous or usual. Only when we get into larger, cabin vessels do we have much fatality from fire.

Every year a number of such vessels blow up or burn. I have seen the entire stern of a thirty-foot yacht spray fragments fifty feet in the air. Up here in Ketchikan hospital are two men, right now, victims of fire. The epitaph of such boats is usually "dirty bilges," but this is not always true. A vessel with a bilge clean enough to wash clothes in can still become a haven for gasoline fumes.

Any builder who would design a boat with inside vents should be soaked in benzine and ignited. As you know, every gasoline tank must have such a vent, as required by law, and sometimes these vents are made so that they lead from tank into the cabin. If any man has such an arrangement on his boat, his wife may well begin to dream about how she is going to spend his insurance. He may get by for years and then, someday, BLOWIE—toasted crab meat. Some boats have originally been built with inside tank vents and some thoughtful soul has made them into outside vents by attaching a rubber hose and leading them to the open air. I have seen several seine boats so rigged. In fact, the *St. Joseph,* which blew itself to seiner heaven last summer, was so fixed.

Rubber hose is rarely proof against gasoline, for gasoline dissolves it. The hose thus slowly disintegrates, dropping lovely little line pluggers into the tank and making ready for an engine failure, come some stormy night. The hose will eventually guide gas fumes no more but allow them to settle down into the bilge, where they lie in wait for a spark. A man might as well fish from a war-headed torpedo as from a fumy-bilged boat. The most enjoyable part of the subsequent explosion is that it doesn't hand out a nice, quick death but often traps some poor devil in either the galley or engine room, giving him a slow roast until well done.

Of course even a well-vented tank may leak. Unknown to an engineer, a fitting may be faulty. Some flaw in a petcock or a copper line may give way to a jar or corrosion and flood the bilge. Vibration will chafe a copper gas line through unless such spots are taped and if that happens and the engineer's first cigarette of the morning is accompanied by a roar and crash, then it's too late to worry about prevention. And if the cure isn't right to hand, it's goodbye boat and often crew as well.

On larger vessels of Classes II and III, it is required by law that they carry, as in Class I, effective means of quenching fire.

However, insurance companies generally demand that boats of Class II—over twenty-six feet in length—carry both a gun extinguisher and a foam type carrying two-and-a-half gallons. The foam type will mix up soda and acid when inverted and expand two-and-a-half gallons into fifteen gallons of smothering foam. These are very effective. Occasionally there is a failure of one of these foam-type extinguishers, for often a boatman forgets that they have to be loaded once a year to guarantee results. The process of filling is simple. Half of the guns I have seen around have either been half or completely empty and it is generally good practice to carry a refill. It is easy to put into the gun and there is slight excuse for having an empty gun around unless one uses it to fill stove tanks or some such thing.

Letters from dedicated listeners of Captain Hubbard's "Mail Buoy"

I have seen several boats carrying five and six cans of refills, placed here and there about the vessel, at both ends of the engine room and near the wheel. It is not necessary to have a gun at each vantage point, for that is expensive. The can is knocked open with an ax and thrown at the base of the fire. However, it would seem to be better sense to refuse the risk of not having an ax handy and transfer the contents from tin can to glass bottle—whiskey bottle or whatever—when purchased. These bottles, which can be found in Thomas Basin any Sunday morning, when filled can be shied at the fire and even if they don't break instantly will blow their corks under stress of heat.

The principle of fighting fire is, of course, the robbing a fire of its oxygen. Once a free supply of air is shut off from the blaze, it will go out. Throwing a blanket over a flame achieves the same purpose, though one would rather use an extinguisher than more expensive and less efficient blankets.

There is also the carbon tetrachloride bomb. This is a glass globe filled with its red fluid and suspended near a place where a fire might start. The heat of the fire releases a pin which breaks the globe and the fire is put out, whether the owner is aboard or not. A light globe filled with carbon tetrachloride and suspended from the wall with picture film will serve the same purpose, though I have seen these come crashing down, fire or no fire, in a seaway, much to the consternation of a strangling engineer.

Near a bunk especially, either a bomb, a foam type or a gun type should be kept. Even the bottles I mentioned, if placed around a boat at strategic points, will cut down the risk of getting trapped in a burning boat. Firefighting equipment, where it can't be reached, might as well be down at the local store, gathering dust on the shelf, for all the good it will do the beleaguered boatman.

Some boats have a sprinkler system rigged with pipe running to all parts of the vessel. A series of holes no bigger than a sixty-fourth of an inch are drilled in the pipe. There is a central tank which can be reached from deck or cabin which is filled with five or six gallons of extinguisher fluid. By air pressure on the tank the fluid can then be made to spray out all through the boat, not only localizing a fire but fireproofing the rest of the vessel. Though the boat will smell of the fluid for a time, it will eventually evaporate. And it is better to have a boat on top of the water than one under it.

There are many means of extinguishing fires and, when compared to the loss of a boat, even the most expensive is dirt cheap.

Davy Jones is just sitting down there waiting for guys who have thought it cheaper to buy either inferior fire equipment or none at all.

BRITTON: Thank you, Captain Hubbard.

Send in your questions and problems to the "Mail Buoy" and they will be answered free of charge if accompanied by a self-addressed, stamped envelope. The foremost marine architects and authorities will be consulted. Comment and criticism is invited. ∎

The Ketchikan waterfront where many a heedless
mariner let his canvas rot and cordage fray

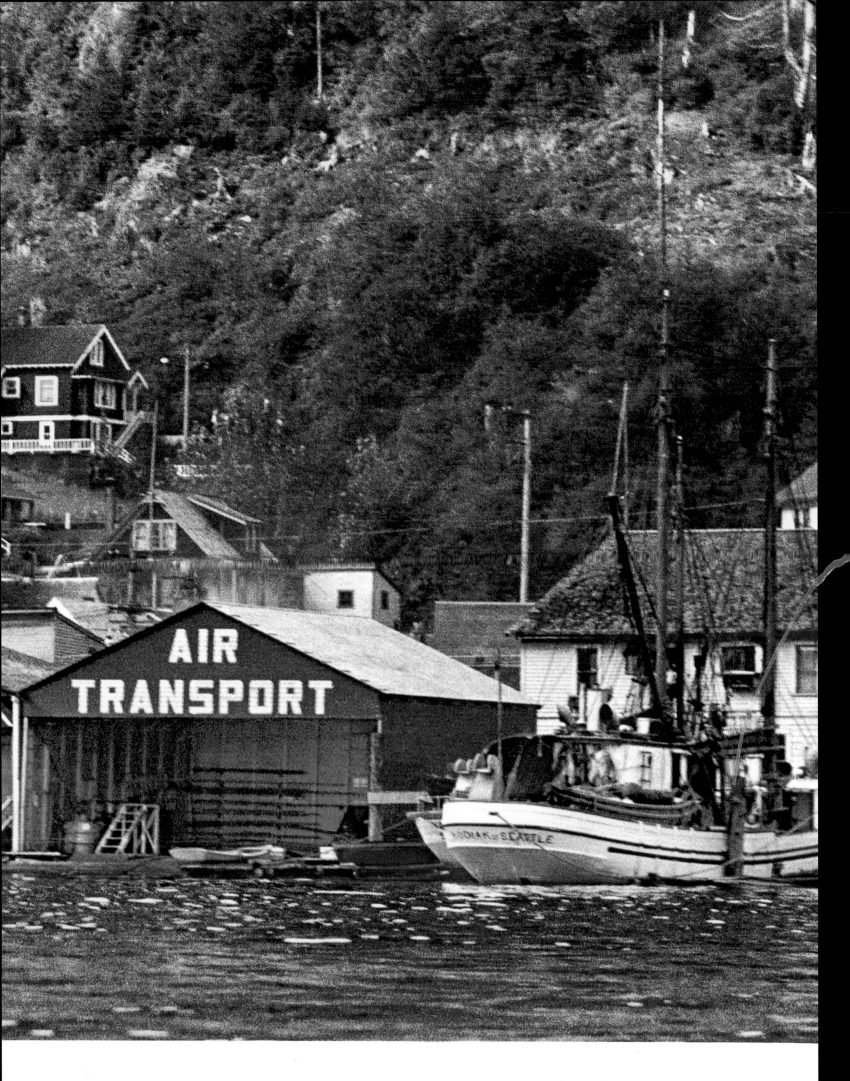

BROADCAST FROM KGBU RADIO; KETCHIKAN, ALASKA

MUSIC: "The Alaska Chief"

SOUND: Four bells and a jingle.

SAILING A TRAWLER

HUBBARD: Greetings, mariners, and thank you for your response on the last program, especially for the requests of additional advice on fire prevention and equipment. I am collecting other data on the subject, much of it from your letters, and checking it over with underwriters and other authorities and at some later broadcast will again take the subject in tow.

My interest, however, is at present caught with a query received yesterday on a subject which is very close to my affections, sail.

A fisherman at Craig wrote as follows:

"I always was told that if I put a sail up on my trolling mast, when I ran into a rough sea it would steady me and keep my boat from rolling. She rolls pretty badly and, the first few times I used the sail, it steadied the boat. But off Chacon recently I ran into a blow and the sail just about foundered me. Here is the drawing to show what kind of a sail it is. Maybe if I rigged it differently, it wouldn't do that. I don't know much about sails and would appreciate some advice on the subject."

He shares his lack of knowledge with most of the fleet on the subject of sail, for it has been thirty-five or forty years since sail was extensively employed in fishing and despite the fact that gas boats, even now, break down, only these balancing sails seem to be employed. This would seem to me to be an oversight on the part of those skippers who cruise offshore.

Sail, like a gas engine, is motive power. It possesses certain attributes which a gas engine does not, just as a gas engine possesses attributes which a sail does not.

Sails are of no use when there is no wind and engines are of no use when they either break down or run out of gas. The sail is the best possible motive power in a bad sea for it will drive and steady a boat when a screw would thresh wildly, a third of the time out of water. Neither means of driving a boat is, in my opinion, satisfactory by itself. Sails were once helped by engines and now engines can be helped by sail.

Lying out in a wild sea with the wind yowling, many a gas boat has had engine failure. Water, long untroublesome in the [fuel] tanks, will accumulate in earnest when the tanks are sloshing and the result is a dead engine. Cleaning out filters and carburetors while a boat is lying in the trough of a bad sea is a risky business. Exhaust pipes are usually still hot and many a sailor has gotten a bad burn while undertaking this simple repair under unfavorable conditions.

A cruiser, crewed by some fellows of my acquaintance, once had this happen in the Straits of Georgia and the task of clearing out the water was so difficult that it had to be abandoned. One broken head and one sprained wrist dissuaded further effort. The cruiser, the *Tanus,* lay out all night, drifting perilously close to a reef, thrown about in a sea which broke continually over the pilothouse. The Coast Guard saved the *Tanus* only by accident for a patrol plane, off its course, passed over and sighted them at dawn.

A sail could have given the *Tanus* enough way to have brought her into port early in the evening, waves or no waves, and yet not so much as a tarp was aboard and her crew, products of a gas-boat age, could not have rigged it had they had it. That experience almost cost them their boat and perhaps their lives, but the *Tanus* has yet to be equipped with any kind of a sail.

But, to return to our fisherman at Craig, a poorly rigged sail can be as much a liability as a help. I see by his sketch that his sail, a small triangle of rigidly secured canvas, is much too high. Its foot is well above his pilothouse. Now, the way the wind comes whooping around some of these points, thus redoubling its velocity, a high sail may resist [the wind] sufficiently to overturn the boat. Ballast, of course, can help this, but we will take up ballast at some future date. The point here is, the fisherman's sail, if it can be called that, is no more than a fin.

Sails, as carried by most trolling boats, are useless. The center of gravity of the boat is so high that the arc of swing is slight and the steadying effect scarcely noticeable unless the fisherman has a good imagination. However, if the boom or after corner—the clew—of the sail could be controlled, the vessel could be made to run and reach across the wind and materially aid the engine.

All the fisherman has to do is put a sheet to the clew of his sail, thus controlling his boom, and his sail will get down and slave for him.

The power which can be gained from a sail like this, even if small, will sometimes put two and three knots on a boat's speed and will allow her to be sailed, even against the wind, to port should a breakdown occur. Because the sail is small, a boat could troll with it, engine off, when on the fishing grounds, thus saving considerable money in gasoline.

There's little excuse for a boat to fail to take advantage of a following wind to or from the grounds, for again this means dollars saved. A little experimenting and an eye on the tachometer will teach a fisherman about sail in a surprisingly short time.

There is no reason to pay out any large sum for a sail for a man handy with needle and palm can make one without much work, work which might eventually save his life and which will undoubtedly save him dollars in fuel consumption.

A few yards of canvas can be gotten cheaply at the marine supply store along with fittings. A coil of three-eighths-inch cordage and three blocks will complete the rig. Even if one has a sail made at the sailmakers, it is best to purchase the canvas and gear for it, for only in that way can one be sure of high quality fittings. The practice of putting leather around grommets is not safe, for leather in Alaska rots quickly.

Because a sail would get little attention on a fishing boat the best precaution is to have it mildew proofed. Otherwise a sail will only last a very short time.

A walk through Thomas Basin ought to prove to a man that it is good policy to take care of his canvas by carefully drying them and stowing them each time they aren't in use for there isn't a square foot of fishing boat canvas down there which would stand up to a sneeze unless somebody has bought a new sail since I was last there yesterday.

A sail is horsepower in reserve. Your tank can be empty, your crankshaft broken and your engineer drunk and you can still get home.

And, as for our fisherman at Craig, unless you make some provision for handling that sail of yours, you had better save it to wrap fish in, for it's a menace. Either a sail is there to work or it's not there at all and there's no halfway point whatever.

BRITTON: Thank you, Captain Hubbard.

Send in your questions and problems to the "Mail Buoy" and they will be answered free of charge if accompanied by a self-addressed, stamped envelope. The foremost marine architects and authorities will be consulted. Comment and criticism is invited. ∎

KGBU

"The Voice of Alaska"

BROADCAST FROM KGBU RADIO; KETCHIKAN, ALASKA

MUSIC: "The Alaska Chief"

SOUND: Four bells and a jingle.

ANCHORS

HUBBARD: Greetings, mariners. For the fourth time we open the pouch of the "Mail Buoy" to see what we can do to keep ships on the sea and sailors on top of it, and in it we find an aggregation of questions which stretch from the best method of coldcocking a cook to the worst method of hoodwinking a prospective buyer of a dry-rotted fishpot. Unfortunately the marine supply store isn't having any bargain sales in blackjacks just now and it doesn't sell the wherewith to get the prospective buyer so drunk he won't know a strake from a herring rake, but perhaps we can find other ways of furthering this fight against Old Man Sea. Besides, I didn't think there existed a sailor in Alaska ignorant of the main methods of making a sap or the best places to buy the worst liquor.

Digging down, we pull out three queries regarding anchors and as that is the most of any one type of information present, suppose let's read the longest one and see what we have.

"Dear Captain Hubbard. I have a forty-foot trawler. Last summer I was anchored in Metlakatla, BC, harbor and got caught in one of these sou'easters. I had a ninety-pound patent anchor out on sixty feet of chain and a sixty-pound patent anchor on my hawser and I dragged so that I had to hold her in place with the engine or go aground on a reef just behind me. Ever since that time I have been wondering about the selection of another weight or type of anchor for next season. T.N."

Well, I suppose, T.N., that a bad anchorage in Metlakatla, British Columbia, is better than being out in Chatham—but not much. The way a sou'easter swoops across that bay is apt to make a man wish he'd dived for it an hour or two earlier and gotten himself into Prince Rupert. But of course a man would rather make a night anchorage anywhere than try to run Metlakatla Passage in the black of a howling gale.

About your anchors. Ninety pounds for your heavy on a forty-foot boat should be more than enough, especially when stretched by chain, and sixty pounds for the light would appear to be entirely too much for a man to haul up from ten or fifteen fathoms. I see that you have *two* patent anchors and I wonder a little bit, for the light one might better be a kedge. A fifty-pound kedge or a seaplane anchor should do all the anchoring you ever want.

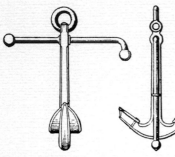

Kedge

You also say that you had them out on two lines and that is probably one of the reasons you dragged. The other reason is that you starved your hooks for length.

Perhaps the best procedure in this matter would have been to have taken the lighter anchor and lashed it about five fathoms up the chain from the heavy anchor, thus putting them both on the same line. This process is known as kelleting and is far more effective than having out two anchors on two lines. With the heavy anchor all the way out, any picking up would have been done on the nearer, lighter anchor, if the kelleting process had been used, and the heavy anchor could then have dug in and stayed there.

Herreshoff

Sea, not wind, breaks out anchors. The lifting tendency or a sea-sprayed bow will let an anchor work itself along the bottom, particularly a patent anchor. Chain is some check on this but not enough to warrant all the use of chain one sees on small boats. A patent or stockless-type anchor depends for its holding power, not on its weight so much as its length of rode. A patent anchor may be very nicely stowed and all that, but it has only 60 percent of the holding power of a Herreshoff or what we commonly refer to, if erroneously, as a kedge.

Sixty feet of chain might as well have been twenty for all the holding power it was giving that ninety-pound patent anchor. There is one rule of anchoring which very few boatmen have heard about or will follow or believe and that is the seven times rule. If you anchor in four fathoms of water, in order to get all the holding power out of your hook, let out seven times as much line as the water has depth. Four times seven is twenty-eight fathoms, or one hundred and sixty-eight feet of line. T.N. had out sixty feet, or only half enough to permit a kedge to hold and only about a third enough to hold a patent anchor. The patent anchor requires some ten times the line as there is

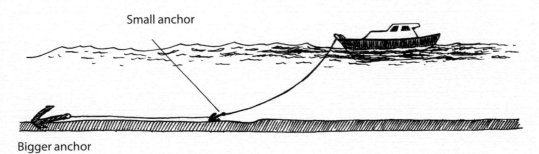

Small anchor

Bigger anchor

depth. Chances are if T.N. had let out a hundred and fifty feet of line in his four fathoms of water, he would have swung to his ninety-pound patent very nicely.

The patent anchor has its advantages and disadvantages. On deck it is easy to have around. On the bottom it requires more line and weight than any other type. It has been stated that a patent holds better in rock than a standard Herreshoff or kedge, but this is open to question, for I have never seen anything which would hold decently on a rocky bottom and, if it did hold, could easily be gotten up again.

Down the centuries there have only been a few types of anchor invented which were any good and every type seems to have some disadvantage peculiar to itself. A kedge will get the line wrapped around its upright arm and so let itself be pulled out. A folding anchor will sometimes decide to fold up when put out to work. The folding stock kedge as invented by Herreshoff and the stockless patent anchor are fairly modern improvements. However, in recent years, another type of anchor has come into being.

Seaplanes need anchor and no plane is going to carry any more weight than is wholly necessary. Accordingly engineers worked out a new type of anchor, the seaplane. This anchor will hold as much as a patent anchor several times its weight and has the advantage of being easy to hoist and easy to stow.

The sea is very slow to change and the sailor, because his life depends upon a conservative outlook upon new invention, is very slowly accepting this new anchor, but he *is* accepting it.

When I first saw one and had a chance to use it, I did so with great caution. I let it out in a calm harbor and uneasily inspected it every few hours during the night. By daybreak it was still holding. But that was no real test. Later on, I had occasion to anchor down in Cardena Bay where the tide zips through at a considerable pace from Telegraph Passage. The bank there being very wide and long with much room to swing, I let the anchor out. I was much too tired that night to inspect it and by next morning I found, to my relief, that I had not shifted more than ten feet all night, though a fast tidal stream had been running under the keel both ways, fast enough to shake the anchor line and make the ship vibrate considerably. Once again the seaplane anchor had held. Of course I had given it much line and there had been no great amount of swell. I like it and use it mainly because it is easy to bring up and easy to stow.

But in using one of these anchors, it is well to remember to use lots of line. That is a good rule with any anchor, of course, but particularly with the lighter seaplane. By putting a couple fathom of chain to it and by letting it have lots of rode, I think the right-sized seaplane anchor for the boat will hold in almost any condition. Of course one should have a heavy anchor as well for unusual conditions.

An ideal anchor combination would be a light anchor, a kedge anchor of medium weight for the boat and a very heavy patent anchor for use on rock bottom in bad weather. If of the right size for the boat, these anchors will take up any stress to which a vessel is subjected in an anchorage. If seven times the depth is put out in rode, or fifteen times the depth in unusually bad waves, any one of these should hold in good ground and the patent in indifferent ground.

It is a beautiful feeling to be able to go to sleep, depending completely on the anchor to hold, come what may. And it's a terrible thing to drift reefward, dragging all the hooks that are aboard. Lots of line and good, reliable anchors are worth ten times their cost in security.

This anchor combination is good because, in extreme conditions, one can tip the line with the light anchor, then twenty feet up from it fix the kedge and then twenty feet nearer the boat than that and, on the same line, place the heavy patent. Allow from seven to fifteen times the water depth from the bow down to the patent. There isn't anything short of a tidal wave which can shift this combination of double kelleting if they are of the right weight for the boat.

BRITTON: Thank you, Captain Hubbard.

Send in your questions and problems to the "Mail Buoy" and they will be answered free of charge if accompanied by a self-addressed, stamped envelope. The foremost marine architects and authorities will be consulted. Comment and criticism is invited. ∎

Alaska Radio & Service Co., Inc.

KGBU
"The Voice of Alaska"

BROADCAST FROM KGBU RADIO; KETCHIKAN, ALASKA

MUSIC: "The Alaska Chief"

SOUND: Four bells and a jingle.

PROPELLERS

HUBBARD: Greetings, Alaskans. The old mail pouch is reeking, these days, with inquiries about propellers and from all the interest shown in these, it would seem that nearly every man in the fishing fleet is convinced that his boat would go faster and better if it weren't for his present wheel. A wheel is, of course, a very handy thing on which to blame speed, but I thought that it was the boat racer who was most interested in those.

Speedboat men, you know, are highly skeptical of their craft's performance and because speed is of the essence, the ardent enthusiast is forever trying to get another sixteenth of a knot out of his boat by changing the wheel diameter or pitch. It is common to see three or four wheels, some of them unnicked, in a speedboat man's kit. And it is perfectly true that one can only find the ideal wheel through much experimentation.

There is, too, much confusion about wheels. Most mariners know, of course, the theory underlying the selection of a propeller, but now and then one comes across a chap from whom we heard and contacted. He wanted to know why he wasn't getting more speed out of his boat and so we asked him some questions on the subject. How fast does your motor turn?

"A thousand, I think."

But that is a converted automobile engine you have there and most of those turn up from two to four thousand rpm.

"Well, I guess maybe mine turns up two thousand, then."

What size of wheel are you swinging now?

"Well, I don't know exactly. Eighteen-inch diameter I think. Or maybe fourteen."

What is the pitch of your present wheel?

"Pitch?"

The Mail Buoy   75

How many inches does it bite off at each revolution?

"Gosh, I don't know that."

What speed are you getting now?

"Well, a fellow I had with me the other day looked over the side and said he thought she was making seven knots. I figured it ought to go faster."

Of course, with all that information it was simple to calculate what he needed. One guessed at his horsepower, guessed at his rpm, guessed at his speed and then did the best he could.

Getting the horsepower of an engine is easy. A hand tachometer will give a man the revolutions per minute—and one can borrow a hand tach in most machine shops. Getting the resistance of the boat is something else again. Very few marine architects have ever guessed the speed of a boat with any accuracy before a test. However, there are set rules of experience which sum up very well. A heavy work boat, for instance, would not get above ten to fourteen knots if it were powered with the largest engines made. Up to a certain speed, as we all know, a boat pushes easily, but from that point onward, the drag of the boat mounting by the square while the speed advances but unit, faster driving eats up gasoline or diesel all out of reason.

Hence we select our wheel's pitch in accordance with the speed the vessel can reasonably make and the revolutions per minute which the engine can maintain without struggling or laboring. If an engine will race under additional throttle when under weigh, the pitch of the wheel is too slight. If an engine heats and refuses to get up to speed, then the pitch is too great. Somewhere between the two lies the reasonable pitch. It is highly doubtful if any boat has the exact pitch for it in its wheel, for that is arrived at by the owner under test. By luck he may get it right the first time.

The best way to keep a check on a wheel is by having a tachometer installed, for it will then reliably report any lag in speed and will materially assist in selecting a wheel as well as eventually navigating the vessel. For every revolution reported by the tachometer, the boat is advanced so many inches and when slip has been calculated, the skipper can accurately judge his speed, whether he has to throttle down for a head wind or has a following wind and can drive harder. The speed by ear method of the old-time standard is not good enough when applied to a modern marine or automobile conversion engine.

When a sailor stops to remember that the wheel is the motive force of his boat and that his engine and boat is just as strong as his wheel is weak, he'll turn aside from the secondhand chunk of second-grade brass which he had thought of putting on his brand new engine and invest a small sum in a good propeller.

Wheels are not expensive. The finest grade propeller, if of the proper size, will pay for its difference in fifteen or twenty hours of running time and it is not risking the boat.

The amount of force exerted by a wheel on the water is tremendous. The entire useable hp of an engine is centered on two or three slender blades of brass. When Sir Malcolm Campbell was testing out one of his speedboats, he broke up several special wheels. The driving power was so great that the blades were bent straight back as though they had been made of putty. A solid steel, one-piece casting was finally made and that alone stood up. And it doesn't make any difference whether a man is cruising a boat at ten knots or a hundred, his wheel is under a terrific strain. If it is wrong, it may last just long enough to get him into serious trouble. Even a good wheel, improperly matched with boat and engine, can wreck itself. A propeller wrongly matched may last a thousand hours, true, but in the end something has to give way. A bad propeller, badly matched, even though its price was only twenty dollars, can ruin a two-thousand-dollar power plant.

In other words, the sailor who is practicing economy on propellers is putting his power plant and all attended repair expense to a great strain.

There is an idea extant that a slow-turning engine is the best engine. Perhaps they have certain virtues, perhaps not. Certainly the virtue does not lie in the propeller speed. A hydroelectric engineer, one of Westinghouse's key men on turbines and blades, once told me that he was of the opinion that a big wheel with a slight pitch, turning at great speed, was far more efficient than a steeply pitched wheel turning at a slow speed.

This is borne out by figures advanced by the propeller company. A slow workboat wheel, turning at four hundred rpm, slips 30 to 35 percent. In other words when it has turned three revolutions with, say, a fifty-inch pitch, it has only advanced the boat a hundred inches. Under perfect conditions it would have advanced the boat a hundred and fifty inches and so is only two-thirds efficient. On the other hand, a wheel of, say, ten-inch pitch turning over at the rate of two thousand rpm has only a 20 percent slip. When it has turned fifteen times, it has driven the boat a hundred and twenty inches. Assuming that the hp was equal, the boat would be gaining twenty inches on every hundred of the slow-speed wheel. There isn't anything which a slow-speed engine can do which a high-speed engine won't, *providing* their true horsepowers are equal. BUT it is easier to make an error selecting a high-speed than a low-speed wheel. The slow-speed wheel, getting a greater reach out into good water and doing less vibrating if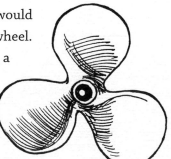

wrong, can put up a fine show even if it is in pitch error. But a slightly pitched high-speed wheel can also have diameter. The *right* high-speed wheel, in other words, can do more work than the right low-speed wheel.

If a man wants a boat to go ten knots and thinks he has the correct power plant for her, he then takes an easy cruising rpm for his engine and multiplies it by sixty to get the revolutions per hour. If high speed, he subtracts 25 percent, if low speed, 35 percent of this last figure. Taking one thousand rpm as a basic, he gets sixty thousand revolutions per hour, less, roughly, a third, or forty thousand revolutions per hour. He wants ten knots and his pitch in inches. Therefore he divides the above forty thousand into the number of inches in a nautical mile, or seventy-two thousand nine hundred and sixty times ten knots, and the answer will be in inches of pitch required. If you want to take that formula down, here it is in symbols. PITCH equals SPEED IN KNOTS TIMES TWELVE TIMES 6,080 divided by the rpm × 60 times effective percent slip, which is to say, about 70 percent. If you put this down, you can get a constant from which you can always work out your speed for any revolution per minute your engine is making at the moment. You need such a scale when using your tachometer. You can reason out this equation very easily by remembering that pitch means the distance a wheel drives a boat for every revolution, less the amount lost by slippage.

Be sure your wheel is of the proper pitch or you may pay for the error with your engine or your speed.

On the matter of wheel diameter, your rpm should go down quickly when the boat is meeting resistance. If you get kelp or a board across your bow and your engine does not slow down, even though your boat does, then your wheel is of too small a diameter.

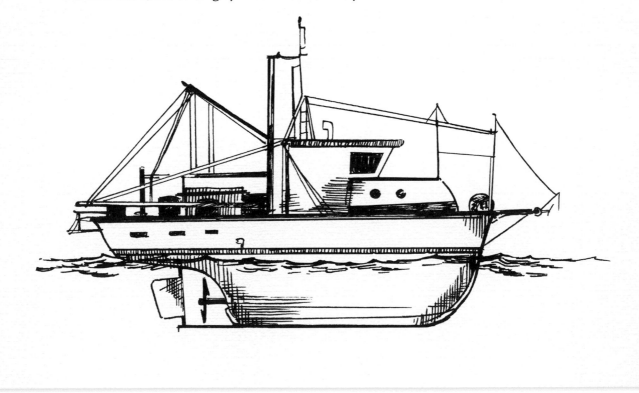

Excessive diameter is not common and the only thing an overestimate of diameter will do will increase the friction area of the blades beyond an efficient point. Diameter is usually regulated by the builder's provision for a wheel more than by any set rule. If a manufacturer says that a certain engine will swing, say, a 22-inch wheel, then there is some reason in putting a 22-inch wheel on the boat. But manufacturing specifications for pitch should always be eyed with askance, for the engine builder never sees the boat into which his plant is being installed.

If a boatman wishes to get maximum performance from his engine, he has to have a propeller of the right pitch and a propeller which is balanced and strong. A wheel of inferior metal, of an unknown brand, may also be off in weight so that it will jump under load, setting up vibration enough to knock the pillow block off the shaft or the stuffing box out of the sternpost with a leaking and laboring ship to show for it.

Another point to keep in mind is that a wheel is hard to realign after drift or reef has knocked it out. Every year or two a boatman ought to buy himself a new wheel and save himself the grief of slowly decreasing efficiency due to nicks and bends. Wheels are too cheap to economize on. For even a propeller of the very best costs less than a new engine or a lay-up right when the fish are running. And the difference in cost between a cheap, inferior wheel and a quality wheel is a matter of a dollar or two.

It's common fault to swear at an engine company when one should be swearing at an error in selecting a wheel.

BRITTON: Thank you, Captain Hubbard.

Send in your questions and problems to the "Mail Buoy" and they will be answered free of charge if accompanied by a self-addressed, stamped envelope. The foremost marine architects and authorities will be consulted. Comment and criticism is invited. ∎

Lieutenant

L. RON HUBBARD

Commissioning Day for the *PC-815* antisubmarine patrol craft: Ship's Captain
L. Ron Hubbard (center and rear of fellow officers), Portland, Oregon, 1943

Lieutenant
L. Ron Hubbard

"**I** AM THE LAST PERSON IN THE WORLD TO ADVERTISE WAR. I served the US Government and then the US Navy for several years, was honorably discharged as an officer and really don't care to say much more about it." —LRH

Nevertheless, if we are to appreciate the larger story of LRH at sea, then certain things must be said, beginning with the events of December of 1941....

Within months of a United States declaration of war, Atlantic seaboard residents were regularly peering out to an evening glow of torpedoed freighters. By June, or concurrent with then Lieutenant L. Ron Hubbard's arrival at Boston Harbor, estimated Allied shipping losses exceeded eight hundred thousand tons. And with no significant loss to the submarine fleets, U-boats prowled ever closer to the mouth of American harbors.

In hasty reply, and in lieu of specialized convoy escorts, a collection of civilian vessels was assembled for conversion to corvettes. Popularly known as the "Donald Duck" navy, this motley armada of fishing boats and motor yachts comprised as ragtag a fleet as ever put to sea in time of war. Although most were

reasonably seaworthy, few could match a U-boat's submerged running speed of 7 knots, much less the 17-knot surface speed. And lest captains still displayed confidence, crews were not only untrained, but frequently criminal—all but scraped from brigs to save regular seamen for the properly fitted vessels. Thus, the felonious sailors serving impromptu escorts after assurances, as Lieutenant Hubbard so pointedly phrased it, they would "not immediately kill an officer." And thus his inaugural briefing to a first command in the North Atlantic theater.

The details are these: upon mustering his crew on the foredeck, Lieutenant Hubbard summarily announced all previous service records were cancelled. The counts of insubordination, the dereliction of duty, the assaults on officers, the theft, battery and destruction of government property—all was effectively null and void. Moreover, all the

Portland naval yard, 1944

YP-422
antisubmarine
patrol and escort
off the coast of
Massachusetts,
1942

record would thereafter reflect was each man's service to the ship; for should anyone fail to perform assigned duties, so the vessel was that much less "a valiant mechanism in which to breast the deep." Whereupon he commenced an altogether rigorous training program.... Until, by the end of thirty days, those previous misfits were suddenly standing watch in their undress blues if only because "they thought it would look better."

His next command was a converted Grand Banks trawler retrieved from Boston's Lawley & Son's shipyard on June 25, 1942. Originally christened the *Mist,* she was best described as sturdy but clumsy. Nevertheless, and notwithstanding limitations of speed and firepower, as the *YP-422* escort she indeed kept torpedoes at bay. She also distinguished herself according to all other naval standards; hence the unqualified recommendation from a succeeding Lieutenant Francis A. del Marmol upon Captain Hubbard's assumption of higher duties:

"It is with considerable pleasure that I find this ship in such excellent condition and discover that her stores and hull and machinery are in a state of high operating efficiency, superior to that of the other vessels of this division. It is with considerable

gratitude that I receive from you a well-trained crew."

Thus acknowledged and commended, Lieutenant L. Ron Hubbard advanced to an elite Navy Submarine Chaser Training Center in Miami, Florida. Established the previous March and expressly for "waging war on enemy U-boats," the Center occupied a two-story, white stucco complex on Miami's Pier 2. Instruction was altogether cutting edge under famed subchaser theorist Lieutenant Commander E. F. McDaniel. Trainees, particularly officers, were selected for intelligence and prowess under fire. At least a hundred of those in Lieutenant Hubbard's class "had from one to three ships shot out from under them," or so reported the *Miami Daily News.* In addition to general antisubmarine techniques, officers were expected to gain proficiency in all principles of spotting, sonar detection, navigation and weapons management; while in emphasis of the risks, an orientation lecture was conducted beside a bullet-riddled lifeboat.

A newspaper article celebrates Lieutenant Hubbard's next command. It opens with an appropriately two-fisted description of his arrival at an Albina shipyard in Portland, Oregon, to helm a sixty-man, state-of-the-art

subchaser christened the *PC-815*. She was honed to an exquisite point, with a formidable complement of "K-gun" depth-charge launchers. As such, she was a veritable godsend to Pacific Northwest communities then living in terror of enemy submarines shelling coastal cities. It was, after all, the first time United States shores had suffered foreign bombardment since 1812 and all the more unsettling given guns were trained from waters just north of Los Angeles.

As it happened, the *PC-815* indeed encountered submarine action in the spring of 1943. In point of fact, the *815*'s victory over two marauding vessels at the mouth of the Columbia River was among the most regionally celebrated engagements of the war. But to a captain who regarded every seaman's life—whether friend or foe—as sacred, what best reflects Lieutenant L. Ron Hubbard are the letters from those beneath his command. ■

PC-815 at the mouth of the Columbia River off Portland, Oregon, 1943: It was in these waters she would encounter and engage two enemy submarines

Letters of the PC-815

Excepting Ron's own missive to the mother of a despairing sailor, what follows here trailed in the wake of his interim assignment to a combat-bound attack-transport. Although self-explanatory, the rarity of the sentiments expressed in these letters cannot be overemphasized. ∎

Dear Madame:

I am writing with regard to the morale of your boy, Robert.

Some days ago I noted that your son was blue and when I questioned him he gave me to believe that he was upset at not hearing from home. He made no statement about it but I believe his blues are directly connected with his failure to receive mail, as I have not seen his name on incoming mail.

The morale of naval personnel is vital. On it, depends our fate in this war. You who are at home and far from the scream and crash of bombs and shells, well removed from the tigerish ferocity of the sea and the enemy, probably fail to realize the terrifying responsibility of those you have sent into the zones of bloodshed.

Your son is a seaman second class in the Navy of the United States, a respected member of an honorable service. He needs your help. And because he is my man here, I need your help.

Please write your boy often. He loves you or he would not worry about you so. Please send him the letters which are such a large factor in sustaining his morale in the face of the glorious Task he must perform.

Sincerely,
L. Ron Hubbard,
Lieutenant, Commanding

PC-815 captain, L. Ron Hubbard, and his executive officer, Thomas Moulton, at Portland's Albina Shipyard, 1943

July 1943

Dear Lt. Hubbard:

I haven't forgotten the last time we talked and you said you would try to get me back aboard your ship. I certainly miss you and the fellows and I wish you could get me back there as soon as possible. No matter what ship I am transferred to and what skipper I get, the 815 will always be my ship and you will always be my Captain. So please try and get me back as soon as you can. I'll promise you that I will be one of the best sailors you have ever had under you.

Yours very truly,
RGT

The Commissioning pennant of the *PC-815,* initialed and presented to Captain L. Ron Hubbard by ship's crew and inscribed: *"TO A REAL SKIPPER AMONG HIS MEN"*

7/July/43

Dear Captain,

This is by no means a letter adhering to strict naval form, rather it is just a friendly letter very far from formality.

I never have been able to say much at times like these nor am I in any way able to do any better by pen and paper but I do feel that I owe you a tremendous debt of gratitude, first for your acquaintance, secondly because you have portrayed to me all the attributes of a "storybook" naval officer. I can see for myself that you were an officer and a gentleman long before Congress decided so.

It was indeed a blessing that I should have begun my life at sea on board a ship that had the good fortune to have been under your command. I can well remember the first day at sea with the PC-815 and the very poor showing I gave as a mariner. Then, unlike I feel now, I was totally helpless, green and very disillusioned. However barely four weeks after that date I find myself, and much to my surprise, developing sea legs. Yes I now feel like I have a leg to stand on. Without your guidance, patience and personality I'm sure I never would have achieved the foundation I now have.

I'm not the only one on board who feels that way, you well know that. As long as the PC-815 remains afloat and anyone who served on her remains alive you will always be our "Captain."

Strickland is grieving himself as though he has lost his best friend. After you left the ship and he went back to the wardroom to straighten things up, I walked in on him and found him in tears. I asked Strickland what was wrong and he said, "I have nothing against the PC-815, but my Captain has left the ship and I want a transfer." His one statement can easily be applied to us all, but since that can't be, all of us who remain aboard will keep her the best ship of her class. The 815 has not yet begun to fight.

Happy sailing Captain—I'm still for being your cabin boy when you become 1st officer.

Sincerely,
LN

Among other maritime essays from L. Ron Hubbard's years at sea through the Second World War comes "Courtesy" and "The Care of a Ship." These essays are but two of several instructional works authored between 1941 and 1945. To cite but two more: while a United States Army enlisted the future Founder of Dianetics to develop a means of "prebattle mental conditioning," a United States Navy enjoined the leader of the Alaskan Radio Experimental Expedition to develop radar operator training techniques. Yet regardless of subject, the intent throughout was the same: he deeply regretted loss of life in "the thunder and passion of war" and tirelessly strove to guarantee the safety of those with whom he served.

RESTRICTED

ORGANIZATION BOOK
U.S.S. PC815

Commanding Officer's Copy
Do Not Remove or Use

METERS

COURTESY

by L. RON HUBBARD

"COURTESY" HAS BEEN DEFINED as the lubricant of civilized machinery. A barbarian, requiring another portion of meat, hits his brother over the head with a club and takes the meat. A civilized human being says, "Please pass the meat." The latter is less strenuous and less liable to eventual retribution.

Courtesy and good manners are synonymous. One seldom feels deeply endeared to a companion who wipes his nose on his sleeve and carelessly spits into one's coffee. In better-civilized circles such action is considered discourteous and one who uses such manners is considered careless of his associates and even disrespectful.

In the military world courtesy takes a form slightly different from the civilian and failure in major courtesies of a military nature stamp as a barbarian he who blunders. Some civilians, entering the service, fail to understand the meaning and purpose of military courtesy and have been heard to state that it is "demeaning." Such civilians in uniform are the butt of many military jokes, for their discourtesies and repeated breaches of military etiquette demonstrate that they are ignorant and fresh caught. Those who have served a little longer and still blunder are considered stupid and generally hopeless by all hands.

Naval courtesy is as old as ships themselves. Before men had discovered how to make a compass, they had been bludgeoned by the fact that men, crammed into boats and ships without room to swing, had to be governed by certain rules of conduct or everything would degenerate into a hell of a mess. Some crew began to yell suggestions at their officer, who was deeply concentrating on keeping them all off the rocks. The confusion became such that the lookouts and orders to set sail could not be heard and the ship hit the rocks; the officer thereafter made a rule that no one would henceforth address him without permission and, in some such way, rules of naval courtesy began to be born.

If men fail to be courteous to each other in close-packed ships, irritability and bad feeling will result and everyone will be miserable. If men fail in courtesy to their petty officers, they interfere with their petty officers' execution of orders and bring about a necessity for harsh measures of discipline. If men fail to be courteous to their officers, they are imposing disharmonious facts upon brains already occupied with keeping those men fed, clothed, dry and afloat. And if a crew fails to be courteous to its captain, then, of course, that crew is thrusting a number of irritations, needless chatter and excess work upon the one mind they must keep clear. For Old Man Sea, war or no war, is a full-rigged adversary and the lives and fortunes of every man jack on a ship depend upon the calculations and decisions of that captain.

There is no single naval custom of courtesy which is without background and that background is rooted into ten thousand years of Man's battle against the Sea.

It is much to expect of a fresh-caught boot to imbibe the elementary outward forms of naval courtesy. In the first place the boot is stunned and bewildered by the immensity and the strangeness of the seagoing civilization into which he has enlisted. He is told to do things for which he can find no reason, for he cannot reason without information and his horizon, before he enlisted, was narrowly bounded. The boot seeks to retaliate and fails to see the ridiculousness of pitting his puny individuality and his unschooled wits against the millions, even billions, of seafaring men who lived and died before him. The boot's most common tack of rebellion is disrespect, for he conceives

"There is no single naval custom of courtesy which is without background and that background is rooted into ten thousand years of Man's battle against the Sea"
—LRH

courtesy as compulsion, not necessity. He never reasons that the long lives and vast experience of people like Barbarossa, Nelson, Drake, John Paul Jones, and admirals and men as great but long forgotten, composed naval courtesy out of naval necessity. He does not rationalize that he, one fresh-caught boot, is disagreeing with all the minds the sea has ever known. No, the boot is going to start a new philosophy of naval behavior all by himself and be, with great originality, discourteous.

Officers and leading petty officers are greatly aided in the performance of their duties by respectful courtesy. And that courtesy is not the "right" of any *individual,* but is distinctly due to the office that individual may hold as a part of the necessities of that office. Therefore courtesy displayed is a token of understanding.

Any experienced sailor takes considerable pride in his knowledge of courtesy and his ability to display that knowledge, for he has come to recognize that the rendering of courtesy is an art, not easily acquired. Courtesy, he knows, is as necessary to the safety and efficiency of a ship as the soundness of her hull.

A few basic naval courtesies follow:

1. Enlisted men, when seeing an officer for the first time that day, salute that officer briskly and wish him, "Good morning, sir." The officer salutes the enlisted man and returns the greeting.

2. When an officer comes near to seated enlisted men, they rise respectfully. If the officer addresses one of them, that man salutes to acknowledge the designation. Unless the officer says, "Carry on," all the other men remain standing. The man addressed, on the conclusion of the conversation, salutes the departing officer, who then salutes the enlisted man.

3. Before one speaks to an officer about routine affairs, one salutes and says, "Permission to speak to you, sir?" When informed that it is granted, and not otherwise, one states his business. When that business is concluded (having been conducted with the greatest possible brevity), one says, "Will that be all, sir?" When informed that it is—and not until—one salutes and goes on his way.

4. When addressing an officer or leading petty officer, a man keeps his hands out of his pockets, removes the cigarette, if any, from his mouth and assumes a military appearance. An enlisted man seeking to address an officer should not be smoking, and should not, through mental discomfort, slouch and squirm.

5. Enlisted men at work, playing games or eating do not stand or otherwise remark the presence of an officer unless they are addressed by that officer. If so addressed, they (or the man designated) cease work and stand as above.

6. The proper form of address to an officer is "Sir." This prefaces and ends all conversation as regularly and inevitable as capital letters and punctuation. "Sir, my inspection of…" and "Will that be all, sir?"

7. "Yes sir" is agreement or token of understanding. Otherwise, the Navy lets the Army have the phrase. The receipt and understanding of an order is "Aye, aye, sir." From one enlisted man

to another who is relaying an order, the reply is "Aye, aye." "Okay" was excavated by an army officer from the Cherokee Indians and the Navy has never heard of it.

8. A junior never uses the phrase "Very well, sir," or "Very good, sir," to a senior. "Aye, aye, sir," is the *only* answer. A senior's reply to a junior is often "Very well" or "Very good."

9. The proper way to address all officers below the rank of lieutenant commander is "Mister" except a commanding officer. A lieutenant commander is generally addressed as "Commander" out of courtesy. A commanding officer of any rank except admiral is addressed as "Captain" out of courtesy. Third person, when speaking to a commanding officer, is customary; such as "Would the captain..." Not "you." First person is customary except to high ranks. The use of third person to an officer is, however, a mark of respect. Officers address enlisted men by their rates or their last names only, never by their first names.

10. An enlisted man addresses his leading petty officers by their last names or rates, unless their rating is equal or nearly so. The use of the names like "Boats," "Flags," "Sparks," etc., is resented as a token of patronage or undue familiarity.

11. An officer, entering the mess compartment when the crew is eating, removes his hat. A sailor entering the wardroom country also removes his hat. Not long ago—in naval history—sailors removed their hats instead of saluting. The British Navy shortened the formality by introducing a touching of the hat, which eventually became a salute. Hence, the extreme form of courtesy in the removal of the hat.

12. Enlisted men overtaking an officer going the same way on the deck (or street) and desiring to pass, salute and, holding the salute, say, "By your leave, sir," and only pass when the salute is returned.

13. Any enlisted men seeing an officer or leading petty officer trying to get through a crowd of men should sing out "Gangway!" and clear a passage.

14. The senior member of a party, officer or petty officer, is always last to enter a boat and first to leave it. All others must assume that such is the intention of the senior and wait, patiently and quietly, until this has taken place. In starting up ladders, entering doors or passageways, the senior always goes first and all others stand aside to so permit him unless it is obvious that a way must be cleared for him.

15. An enlisted man seeking use of a gangway or a ladder and seeing an officer upon it or about to step upon it should back off, leaving the gangway or ladder clear, even though the enlisted man may suppose that there is room for both.

16. When desirous of leaving the ship at the dock or in the stream, even for a brief absence, a man requests permission from the Officer of the Deck or Watch Officer, saying "Permission to leave the ship, sir?" The answer is "Permission granted" or "Permission refused." There is no discussion beyond that unless the man is under orders which take him from the ship, at which time he briefly states the order.

   When returned to the ship, the man seeks out the Officer of the Deck or the Watch Officer and reports his presence with "Reporting my return aboard, sir," to which is answered, "Very well." Officers desirous of leaving the ship, if only for a few moments on ship's business, must request, with the same formula, that permission from, on small ships, the commanding officer. They must also report their presence aboard when returned.

17. An officer or enlisted man salutes the colors and the quarterdeck on entering a ship and the quarterdeck and the colors when leaving a ship. This applies when the colors are flying. After sunset, only the quarterdeck is saluted.

There are many other small points of courtesy and custom in the naval service. They are not designed to have political significance or to give a senior any more than his office entitles him. The senior present, by virtue of his years, his experience, as well as his rank, always has the responsibility and this applies even to seniority of two months between two seamen second class.

It should be plain, then, that courtesy is a means of expediting and safeguarding the requirements of the service.

That is the Navy.

THE CARE OF A SHIP

by L. RON HUBBARD

A SHIP HAS ALWAYS BEEN considered as a demanding, feminine personality, which requires constant grooming if one would secure her best.

The reasons for this are quite obvious. The sea itself is a mighty opponent and unless the ship is always at her best, then she may surrender, partly or wholly, to the sea, spitefully bringing disaster to those who failed her.

Therefore it is important to care for a ship as a valiant mechanism in which to breast the deep.

And then, what is personally important to a sailor, a ship is a home.

In these guises she requires care, care of a meticulous kind which a landsman does not begin to understand.

If you have ever been caught in the unlighted wrath of a storm and had to have a hammer or a wrench to keep the ship afloat, you will appreciate how vital it is that every article aboard have its place and, what's more, be in that place. Only in this way can one find things which, in emergency, are vital to existence. Hence, a ship must be orderly, each thing in its proper place.

If you have ever tried to read a chart made illegible by oil smudges, if you have ever found cockroaches in your potatoes, if you have ever been shipmates with disease, or if you have ever attempted to dress for liberty in clothes stained by a dirty deck, then you won't ask why a ship must be clean. A sailor of experience swerves from a dirty ship as he would from a woman covered with filth and sores, for he knows them both to be deathtraps.

From this understanding the sailor who has been afloat knows his responsibility to the ship to be responsibility to himself.

The theory of cleaning is twofold: first, to prevent dirt from getting aboard and, second, to drive that which does back out of the ship again.

"Shakedown" cruise of the *PC-815*,
Columbia River, 1943

It is not enough to clean the obvious places, for dirt and flotsam are sly stuff which crawl into unlikely places and await a chance to come out and soil whatever is at hand. Dirt beneath a radio cabinet is only waiting to end communications with the shore or spoil the log. Dirt in the seams of an overhead joins eagerly with moisture to come down and smear the bulkhead. Dirt on the decks, behind the bitts, under the flag bag, is waiting the rain which will let it draw long black marks on the superstructure and hull. And dirt in the bilges, if allowed to remain, happily waits for the hour of disaster when it can plug the pumps and watch a ship drown.

It is not enough to put gear out of the way where it can be readily found. The sea likes to play ball with loose or improperly lashed gear. Stand a new ship on her beam-ends and almost always the ensigns' scented shaving lotion winds up in the black reek of the engineers' coffee pot and the chronometers crunch musically underfoot. Whatever gear is stowed, it must be kept stowed even when the seas pile her over forty-five degrees.

To keep the gear where it belongs, to keep the ship clean, to keep running what should run and whole what should be whole, these are the responsibilities of one who would live at sea. It is toward this that inspections are directed, for a ship which isn't groomed won't live. ∮

That Captain L. Ron Hubbard would set sail aboard a free-roving schooner in the wake of the Second World War is only too appropriate. That he would do so in quest of pirate lore is altogether poetic. By way of a few ancillary notes to what appeared in the Miami Daily News on the 30th of June 1946: his "trim little schooner" was the second of two vessels he skippered through that postwar summer. Aboard the first, weighing anchor from Miami on the 15th of June with a crew from Honduras and the Bahamas, he indeed searched out buccaneer legends in and around Havana. Immediately thereafter, he sailed to Catalina off the coast of California and there directed the Catalina Island Yacht Club while writing of "screaming combers wild with wind."

MIAMI DAILY NEWS

MIAMI 30, FLA., SUNDAY, JUNE 30, 1946

The World's HIS OYSTER

By MIKE SCHINDLER
(Miami Daily News Staff Writer)

A FEW DAYS AGO A TRIM LITTLE SCHOONER over at Miami's Howard Bond yacht basin let go her lines, used her engine to back away from the dock, swung gracefully into the stream and blew her siren for the open-bridge signal at MacArthur Causeway. Half an hour later she was well along in Government Cut, her trim little forefoot and her sturdy jib boom pointing eastward—seaward....

A little later her white wings began to flutter aloft, her sheets were trimmed in on the starboard tack and under all plain canvas the schooner *Blue Water II* began reaching her forefoot into the Gulf Stream, her questing nose adventure-bound among the storied West Indies....

Skipper Ron Hubbard was peaking his halyards, coiling lines' ends, getting his little ship snugged down

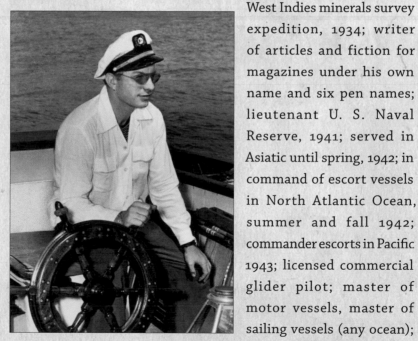

Sits at the wheel as the schooner leaves Miami for pirate islands in the Caribbean

for a nightlong reach to the south and east. First stop, Havana.... Next stop? *Quién sabe?* Anywhere—everywhere, in quest of pirate lore.

Who is Ron Hubbard?

Who's Who in America replies:

"Hubbard, Lafayette Ronald, author, explorer, officer U. S. Naval Reserve: Born, Tilden, Neb., March 13, 1911; ... graduate Swavely Prep School, Manassas, Va.; B. S. in civil engineering, George Washington U., 1932; commander Caribbean motion picture expedition, 1933; commander, West Indies minerals survey expedition, 1934; writer of articles and fiction for magazines under his own name and six pen names; lieutenant U. S. Naval Reserve, 1941; served in Asiatic until spring, 1942; in command of escort vessels in North Atlantic Ocean, summer and fall 1942; commander escorts in Pacific 1943; licensed commercial glider pilot; master of motor vessels, master of sailing vessels (any ocean); licensed radio operator; past president American Fiction Guild, member Author's League of America, Explorers Club, Theta Tau, Phi Theta Xi. Author: *Buckskin Brigades* (1936). Co-author: *Through Hell and High Water*, 1941. Contributor

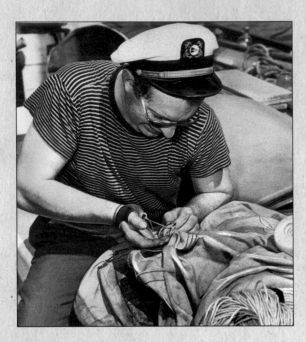

Sailmending: Author—Captain Ron Hubbard mends sail in preparing his schooner for the cruise

of articles and fiction to 72 magazines, mostly action books, adventure, sea stories and fantasy. Considers his greatest achievement is having scaled Mt. Pelée in Martinique at night. Home: Explorers Club, New York, N. Y."

CAPTAIN STORMALONG

Hearing that Hubbard was in Miami, unheralded, this writer grabbed a cameraman and laid a course for the Bond basin to beard him in his cockpit. We found him busy making ready for sea.

"Just got out of the navy," said he, "and after a bit of loafing around I decided to carry on with my character old Captain Stormalong. He stormed along in the Caribbean, and so that's where I intend to go looking for his ghost. Going to make Miami my base for an indefinite period."

Captain Stormalong, by the way, is Hubbard's latest book, based on 17th century Caribbean legends, ballads and folklore

he picked up on previous sashays into the Romantic Isles.

"And do you know," said he, "research has now proven that Stormalong is more than a legend. He was a fact. Actually lived and stormed his way through the West Indies."

Hubbard had just bought the *Blue Water II* here and was in the throes of getting a "new" ship ready for sea—and for an extended, indefinite voyage, at that—which is no small task. So while he was working, I talked and the photographer photographed. (A few of the myriad chores that are musts on the eve of a voyage you'll find illustrated on this page.)

Hubbard is also the author of "Dive Bomber," printed in a national magazine and later filmed by Warner Brothers.

"Who played in it?" we wanted to know.

"I don't know," said he. "Never saw it."

Navigation: Overhauling the sextant, octant, chronometers, barometers. Octant is rare type.

Motive power: Engine is checked and all parts gone over to make sure of future reliability.

WEST INDIAN LEGENDS

And while the little schooner and its questing skipper are nosing through the warm blue waters of channels in and out of the Indies looking for more data on old Stormalong, there are other legends and facts that will be gathered and catalogued for future use.

"For instance," said Hubbard, "I'm going to try to locate Henry Morgan's grave. Henry was the boy, you'll remember, who ploughed his bloody way through these seas, and then decided to try for a pardon. He was successful, and the king, thinking perhaps the best way to catch pirates was with a pirate, made him Sir Henry, and the governor of Jamaica. Then the old buzzard turned out to be as thorough a disciplinarian on the righteous side as he had been in maintaining his bloody rule over the buccaneers. He got rich in a few years by using the death penalty, tricing the pirates up in chains, selling slaves to the plantations and seizing pirate craft right and left. He is supposed to have died in Jamaica, but no one knows for certain, and certainly no one knows where he's buried.

"Surely a man who cut such a mark on the history of his day would not have been buried in an unmarked spot."

THE BUCCANEERS

Hubbard wants more information of the buccaneers l'Olonnais, Ringrose, Teach, Vane,

Seamanship: The serving or splicing of lines, reeving of halyards. Sisal rope is used here.

Checking compass: Smoothness of operation of the binnacles keeps compass level in seaway

Hornigold, Burgess, Rennes, Fife, Martel and the pirate who became a Church of England clergyman, Sam Speed.

"There was a fellow for you," said Hubbard. "Old Samuel Speed: He was the rascal who quit buccaneering at the right time, went home to England, joined the church and became a well known pastor, and later, during the war with the Dutch, he became famous as a chaplain aboard one of the men-o'-war...but his fame didn't stem from his preaching to the sailors. When his ship laid alongside a big many-gunned Dutchman and the going was tough, this rascal Sam Speed tossed his Bible and his churchly garb over the side, grabbed a cutlass from a dead man, and yelling and cursing fierce enough to scare the poor Dutchmen to death, he led the crew of his ship in boarding the Hollander and slashed his way through the enemy with such piratical skill and abandon that the day was won for the British ship. Yes, I'd like to know about that fellow, all right."

And that, in a nutshell, may be said about everything in the Caribbean insofar as it touches Ron Hubbard:

He wants to know more about it.

And that's where he is now—booming down the old trail, the trail that is ever new...the trail of adventure and romance...romance of the Then and Now. ☸

Washington, DC

Between helming a first Founding Church of Scientology in Washington, DC, and a thousand and one administrative duties incumbent upon him as Scientology's first International Executive Director, L. Ron Hubbard kept a small flotilla at a neighboring Capital Yacht Club. Moreover and not withstanding incessant demands as he charted the course of Scientology across three continents, he still found an occasional day to ply blue water. Indeed, logs from these years tell of voyages to the Florida Panhandle and excursions along numerous Potomac river tributaries. Moreover, amongst his trio of motor vessels was a decidedly classic Chris-Craft and a last in the line of mahogany Cruisers (with a high-compression V8 power plant no less). Also found in logs of the era are passing references to wild inlets and alligator-infested marshlands, followed by a wry description of navigation as that: "time-honored profession of keeping water under a keel."

But the overarching point follows from the fact of Scientology's meteoric growth and the consequent fact that he and his Cruisers rarely strayed far from home. Accordingly, and while his boats may well have yearned for open sea, some time would pass before a long voyage on truly open seas would present itself.

Top
Ron's 22-foot Express Cruiser, christened *Dixie Belle* and boasting a 200-horsepower V8 engine. It was expressly owing to the problematic nature of her engine, however, that he eventually traded the Cruiser for a Chris-Craft.

Bottom
A 36-foot Chrysler Cabin Cruiser dubbed *Apache,* aboard which he fought contrary tides along the Florida Panhandle, while noting in the logs: *"Give me my gas back, Father Neptune!"*

Washington, DC

Potomac River

Hampton Roads

Pamlico Sound

Cape Fear

Charleston

Port Royal

Savannah

St. Catherines Sound

St. Andrew Sound

St. Augustine

Daytona

Titusville

The *Apache* as she appeared when Ron took her helm at Titusville,
Florida, and embarked for the Potomac some 850 miles north

Apache

A Sunday in October 1957

504 Making my ETA at Daytona
(5:30P) on time without even
staggering.

506 - A lovely rainbow
behind me. One ahead
of at once! The rest of
the sky lowering, yet sun is
shining Rather spectacular
evening I must say.

Sky - wind or current - this
old baby sure holds a
course intended. Like an
iron Mike.

530 On time at Daytona Boat
Works Yacht Harbor.

Stopped at Texaco station
for gas just south of northernmost
bridge in Daytona Beach.

Finished with engines for
today.

Above *Dixie Belle* at dock along an inland Florida waterway where the "unreliable character" of an Express Cruiser engine would soon make itself manifest

Below *Dixie Belle* upon safely arriving home at Washington's Capital Yacht Club

Wednesday Mar 12, 1958

Yacht CSS Dixie Belle?
Enroute Jax to Key West.
Up well before dawn.
Breakfast and waiting for
sunrise. Some 50 mins for
before sunrise there was
light to travel.
Fixed windshield wipe.
Beginners Luck. It now
works.

0610   Underweigh. Palm Valley.

0740   Stopped St Augustine for
       picture and hot chocolate.

0825   Underweigh. Know St.
       Augustine. Cloudy, mild.

0930   Matanzas Inlet abeam.
       Turned over wheel to steward
       on long easy straightaway ahead.
       N & S St Augustine a
       snake would be ashamed of
       himself for such a winding
       series of tracks.

       Arrived Daytona Beach.

       3 mi N A Daytona, engine
       cut out and was coaxed

The 30-foot Chris-Craft, *Husky I,* with twin 130-horsepower engines and full seagoing capabilities. This was the vessel aboard which Ron plied Potomac tributaries some 50 miles south of Washington's Capital Yacht Club. But she ultimately waited in vain to taste the open Atlantic.

Washington, DC

Aquia Creek

Potomac River

Chesapeake Bay

CHAPTER FOUR

The
COMMODORE

The Commodore

WHILE MUCH HAS BEEN SAID ON L. RON HUBBARD'S greater progress beyond 1966 and his formation of a Sea Organization to safeguard Scientology far into the future, let us consider these matters from the purely nautical perspective. That is, let us leave his greater philosophic voyage (across those "tumultuous oceans

of data") for another issue of this series and tell the comparatively simple tale of how he returned to the sea.

In an early statement of intentions, he spoke of a ship as a kind of retreat—a floating research base where work might progress undisturbed by all but lapping water on the hull. Home port initially lay at Las Palmas in the Grand Canaries and the vessel in question was a 60-foot Bermuda ketch—originally christened *Enchanter,* later rechristened the *Diana.* The next to appear was a seasoned North Sea trawler—then *Avon River* but remembered today as the *Athena.* She was dark and hulking. Ron himself would describe her as "fishermanned into a filthy mess," with a hold and boiler house still reeking of cod blood and oil. She had additionally suffered a mishap

while making her way down from Aberdeen and so badly begged for new rear plates. But his first and keenest concern lay with the seventeen original Sea Organization recruits on the still blackened *Avon* decks—one formerly from the merchant marines, two more with a smattering of nautical experience, the remainder with barely a league of it.

As a word on what followed, we are told that to simply walk a deck with L. Ron Hubbard—to watch him inspect a frayed cable or fractured plate—was to watch a man who might have spent his whole life at sea. Similarly, we are told of his uncanny knowledge of all other things nautical—right down to the rusted railings and overworked engine bearings on the *Avon River* or a faulty rudder he eventually redesigned himself. Finally, we are told that while no nautical

Rechristening the *Royal Scotman,* whereupon she was ever after known as the *Apollo,* the Greek Isle of Corfu, 1968

college will certify a seaman as competent with less than four years of training, the texts upon which those colleges depend were then both incomplete and inadequate. Consequently, even the most diligent student might miss "essential bits" of nautical know-how, including the substance of this irreducible first lesson to the Sea Organization from its Commodore:

"The difference between sailors and landlubbers is as follows: The landlubber doesn't have to put the land there. And so he very often comes to sea without an awareness that the platform on which he is standing has to be put there and continued to be put there, and he is there to move this platform around and keep it in place and keep it afloat.

"Now, when the landlubber goes to sea and doesn't know this very important fact, that he now has an additional action which is 'putting the land there,' you get the damnedest things you ever saw in your life. It is the most remarkable mess.

"If you look around very carefully in any yacht harbor, you will see some examples of it. Somebody has bought himself a boat and he is now going to put out for a cruise. Well, it is a very, very remarkable fact that the anchor goes down, won't come up, won't go down, the sails

won't go up, won't go down and the net result of it all is 'Yacht in Trouble' becomes a standard news story."

To ensure no Sea Organization vessel ever became that standard news story, he next spoke of codifying all seafaring fundamentals. If the statement seems in any way pat, it is not. Indeed, when considering the contents of L. Ron Hubbard's instructional materials, beginning with his illustrated *Sea Watch Picture Book* and *Ship's Org Book,* one is looking at a most concise summation of all shipboard know-how—quite literally from swamper to skipper, from oiling main engines to washing clothing. Of special note is the LRH distillation of navigation (an essentially simple subject made complex, owing to an "assumption that one can't confront where he came from or is going or where he is").

No less significant was his Watch Quarter and Station Bill. It is fairly unique beyond naval circles and most simply defined as a system to indicate for every member of the company "where he berths, what his title and duties are as per the Ship's Org Board, what his position and duties are for every evolution and activity and drill of the ship." The point—and it's particularly crucial on Sea Organization vessels—here was a system to ensure a sufficient complement of crew-maintained ship operating systems, while the remaining filled administrative posts. Moreover, here was the assurance in times of threat, emergency or high activity that all hands were at the ready.

As another word on shipboard operations in total, all was predicated on three degrees of operation: Dangerous, Threatening and Peaceful. To effect swift and smooth transitions from one condition to another, he conducted regular "billing and drilling" under a heading that read: "I don't usually have emergencies, but I like to have drills for them just in case." Said drills were routinely stopwatched to hone response time and performed with full simulation—hoses laid out, hydrants opened, fire suits donned—and all at a dead run.

With Watch Quarter and Station Bill in place and a refit of the *Avon* more or less complete, training continued across open sea. Specifically cited were the short sprints along a North African coast, where those demonstrating the most maritime promise were afforded opportunities to skipper the *Enchanter*. Although following a misadventure with her diesels and a tearing of the stern plate, the Sea Organization's Commodore allowed only sails when he himself was not aboard. His

Above
The 60-foot Bermuda ketch *Enchanter,* latterly rechristened *Diana,* 1968

point here: inexperienced sailors "will take all kinds of risks with a sailboat if they think that at the last minute they can turn on the power and get out of there." The greater point: In a world where advancement through rank is so often dependent upon seniority or favor, here was an organization of truly rare equality. Indeed, here was a maritime organization where one waited not ten or more years for retiring officers to vacate a post, but only long enough to master a skill and demonstrate competence.

What amounted to the culmination of these days came with the purchase of a third Sea Organization vessel: the 3,200-ton *Royal Scotman,* remembered today as L. Ron Hubbard's Flagship *Apollo.* She boasted a long and distinguished heritage, replete with service as a British operations vessel through the Second World War. She featured what was described "a *very* thick hull of excellent hard steel," an "imposing bow" and her decks were of the finest teak. The Commodore himself received her at Southampton and set out with a skeleton crew for what amounted to a shakedown cruise on the 28th of November 1967. If her subsequent adventures were few and far between—and rightfully so on a vessel intended to provide a "distraction-free" environment—we might nonetheless recount a few sea tales of the era.

Somewhere off the Sicilian coast, a "dogwatch" espies a distress flare coursing through an otherwise blackened night. As noted in ship's log: "Swept into a streak by the growing wind, it seemed to come up from behind the ridge of rocks which stood to seaward of a narrow channel." To which the First Officer adds: "By chart reckoning, we knew a vicious series of rocks grew out of the choppy sea about three quarters of a mile ahead." Yet presuming a yacht indeed had floundered on said rocks, we next hear tell of the Commodore steaming into that narrow pass "without a second thought."

In fact, however, he may well have entertained a second thought, or at least a fleeting memory of tales from the Cornish coast, where wreckers once lured ships to the rocks with terrible regularity. What the *Scotman* encountered was hardly less calculating: a Sicilian fisher boat, tucked into a rocky outcrop and fitted with lights atop spars to suggest a vessel in distress. If and when some Samaritan yachtsman grounded on the shallows, one can only presume the worst.

In reply—and one can hardly improve upon eyewitness accounts—we hear of the Commodore leaning from the bridge wing to better view a darkened pirate's vessel before ordering a deafening blast from his ship's resounding whistle. Whereupon: "As the echoes of that outsized blast faded into the night wind, panicked would-be pirates scrambled to their deck to see what had come up on them in the night. The sight of that giant bow so close to their hidden spot must have raised their survival level somewhat; and the sound of an electric bullhorn, blasting Italian at them, demanding to know what they were doing seemed to produce a sudden realization. They never answered the question, but the false lights blinked out and the

Right Rechristening ceremony, Corfu, 1968: *"Goodbye old Royal Scotman. I finally learned your habits and then you disappear and become the Apollo."* —LRH

puny one-lung diesel coughed into action for a fast retreat. And the small yachts who might have answered their treacherous signals cruised without incident that night, not knowing they had been helped—or by whom."

Additionally from these days when L. Ron Hubbard helmed his Flagship comes his altogether daring escape from high winds off the Azores. It was by then late October 1970. His yacht lay off Ponta Delgada and directly in the path of what is remembered in Atlantic annals as "Hurricane Ten." As a wave-driven *Apollo* draws ever closer to a rocky shore, the Commodore directs his crew on raising the ship's three anchors, without catching them in the propellers, while simultaneously heading out to open sea (a most delicate maneuver that requires playing out anchor chains like kite strings to yank the ship on course). If then reasonably safe at open sea, we next hear

of propellers actually lifting from the water when cresting thirty-foot rollers, i.e., "You'd hear the engines roar, feel the shudder and all of a sudden the bow would rise again." Upon finally reaching the eye of the storm, she waited out the winds in an unreal calm and provided sanctuary to gale-tossed gulls. On returning to a devastated anchorage two days later, the docks were lined with villagers who turned out to marvel at a ship any lesser captain would have lost.

There is more and it tells us a lot. Notwithstanding her bold lines and proud heritage, the *Apollo* was nothing approaching a twenty-first-century vessel. She lacked modern storm-tracking equipment. Her propellers were fixed-pitched, which meant the shaft must come to a complete halt before reversing, so necessitating upwards of 1,500 feet to stop. In consequence, one had to stay at least ten

Replica of *Apollo* presenting all salient details

moves ahead of the game, which is why Ron established a tradition of billing and drilling quite unique in maritime realms. (As a matter of fact, only elite naval units are commensurately honed—carrier flight-deck teams, for example, or nuclear-submarine crews.)

Beyond 1969, Sea Organization signature drills were generally conducted in the evenings and from those evenings come quite specific memories of L. Ron Hubbard demonstrations: how one adjusted radar for detecting small craft at sea, how to take bearings on waves in blackened night and ways by which a Helmsman might steer without a compass, while bridge personnel steered with only engines. As a note on the brand of competence ensuing from such drilling, the Commodore directed that a long-stemmed glass, filled to the rim with water, be placed atop the radar. Thus, proud was the bridge watch team that

completed a voyage so free of "roll and pitch" nary a drop was spilled.

There is more still and it likewise speaks volumes of the Commodore: he could read wind and tidal changes as few can in this age of electronic dependency. Then again, he knew what clouds signaled, what barometric pressure foretold and even knew what knowledge gulls carried. But the summary point is simply this: In ages past, there may have been others of his ilk. Yet rare it is to find a modern mariner who lived on such easy terms with Old Man Sea—and rarer still that he imparted all he knew to leave an enduring nautical legacy. ∎

As an introductory word to L. Ron Hubbard's own words on the Apollo, it might be further mentioned she originally entered British Admiralty service as a supply carrier in October 1940. By early 1941, however, she went entirely operational as an infantry transport for amphibious landings. In precisely that capacity she indeed served then British Prime Minister Sir Winston Churchill—specifically at the Allied liberation of Southern France in August of 1944. Upon war's end, she sailed the Irish Sea until November 1967; whereupon the Commodore took command of her helm and sailed her into history.

THE YACHT APOLLO

by L. RON HUBBARD

T HE *APOLLO* IS THE third-largest yacht in the world. The *Britannia* is 12 feet longer and the *Atlantis,* launched in July '74, is 3,400 tons.

The *Apollo* is 3,278 gross tons, 320 feet, is powered with two Harland and Wolff diesels delivering 5,200 brute horsepower. She makes 19.5 knots but ordinarily cruises at 13. She carries from 300 to 350 crew.

The ship has a glorious history. Built in Belfast for Irish Sea service in 1936, the finest steel and workmanship were used. She was rebuilt in 1945 and again in the late '60s and has been kept modernized in every respect.

During World War II she took part in many campaigns over the world as an Operations flagship. She successfully carried US Rangers in the North African landings. At the Salerno landings she was the headquarters vessel in 1943. She was Sir Winston Churchill's command vessel for Operation Anvil in the Mediterranean.

Her captains and engineers were decorated for their service over the world.

In 1968 she was purchased by Operation and Transport Service and was used for a floating management center in the European area.

She has been chartered by the Church of Scientology of California.

A vessel with a brave and romantic past, her adventures continue in a modern world, serving the causes of humanity and peace.

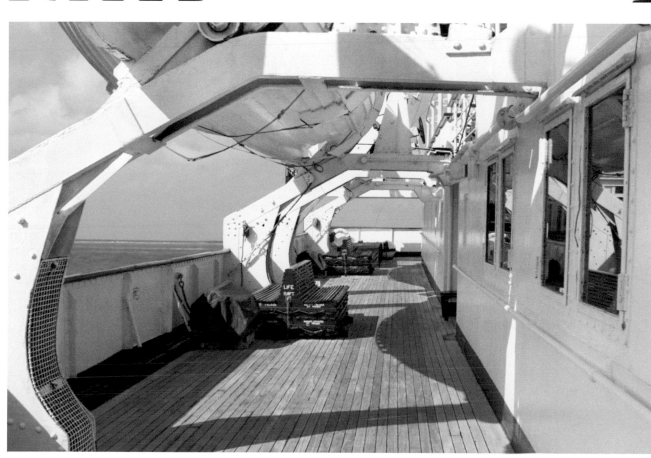

Far left
Commodore's inspection along the Promenade Deck, starboard side

Above
View from the Crow's Nest looking aft

Left
Starboard Promenade Deck adjacent to the LRH Research Room and Office

Bridge wing, port side   Chart room

Apollo Bridge

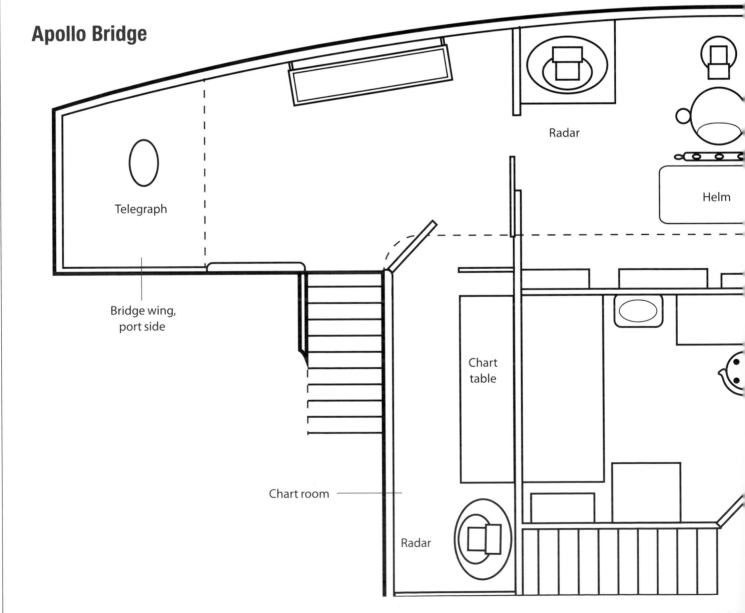

Telegraph

Bridge wing,
port side

Radar

Helm

Chart
table

Chart room

Radar

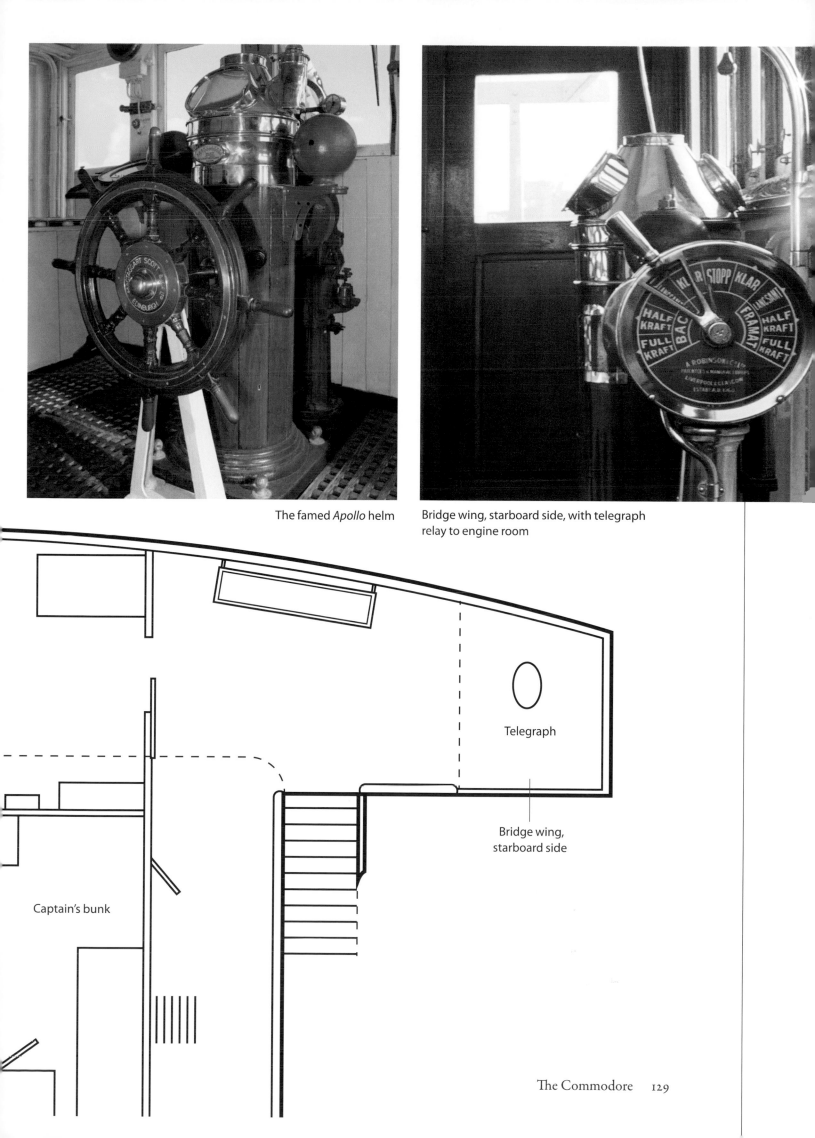

The famed *Apollo* helm

Bridge wing, starboard side, with telegraph relay to engine room

Telegraph

Bridge wing, starboard side

Captain's bunk

Right
Promenade Deck Stairway with Art Deco flourishes

Below
Main Foyer on B Deck

Left
Officer's Dining
Room

Below and inset
Commodore's
Dining Room
and Lounge

Right
Corridor to the legendary LRH Research Room

Far right
At the mantel of his Research Room fireplace for a photograph known to Scientologists world over

Principal Ports of Call

"This certainly is a beautiful coast and the moon shining over the fog banks seen from high in the mountains was a breath-catching sight." —LRH from the Portuguese harbor at Setúbal

ALSO OF NOTE, SETÚBAL IS BUT ONE OF fifty ports of call named in *Apollo* logs between the Mediterranean, North Atlantic and the Caribbean. Likewise of significance was Las Palmas amidst the Canary Islands and where, for all intents and purposes, the Sea Organization was born. Then came Corfu, just off the Greek mainland and where his Flagship *Royal Scotman* became the *Apollo* in November 1968. There was another again at Agadir on the southwest shores of Morocco and where no seaman of old ever entered without a muttered prayer to Neptune. There was still another at Valencia, where he wrote of watching a "whole empire of tradition" sinking in his lifetime. Thus his nod to early mariners who sailed so utterly "off the chart" and thus the drilling of the Sea Organization to standards not seen in five hundred years. There were still more

again at the regularly visited Funchal, on the Portuguese isle of Madeira, and where he would fondly bid farewell with this: *"We leave these shining waters and beaming faces to go to bigger places."*

With an Atlantic crossing in October of 1974 came yet another array of *Apollo* ports scattered across the Caribbean. There was Santo Domingo, where he wrote of finally planting feet firmly on the earth and watching "wild sea waves hammering the coast." Then again, there was Kingston, Jamaica, with a passing salute to the glory of Horatio Nelson, and Curaçao in the Netherlands Antilles, where, as we shall see, the LRH legend similarly continues to this day. But the overriding point simply follows from the fact that wherever he made landfall through these years so remains a memory of the Commodore's *Apollo*. ∎

Lisbon harbor, 1972

"In every port the Sea Org leaves, there are lots of tears and fond farewells. And new ports get to love us very soon."

—L. Ron Hubbard

La Coruña
Vigo
Oporto
PORTUGAL
Lisbon
Setúbal
Terceira
Ponta Delgada
Horta
Cádiz
Santa Maria
Tangier
Casablanca
Madeira
Safi
MOROCCO
Agadir
Tenerife   Las Palmas

Corfu, Greece (1968, 1969)

Cagliari, Sardinia, Italy (1967, 1969)

Marseille, France (1968)

Monte Carlo, Monaco (1967)

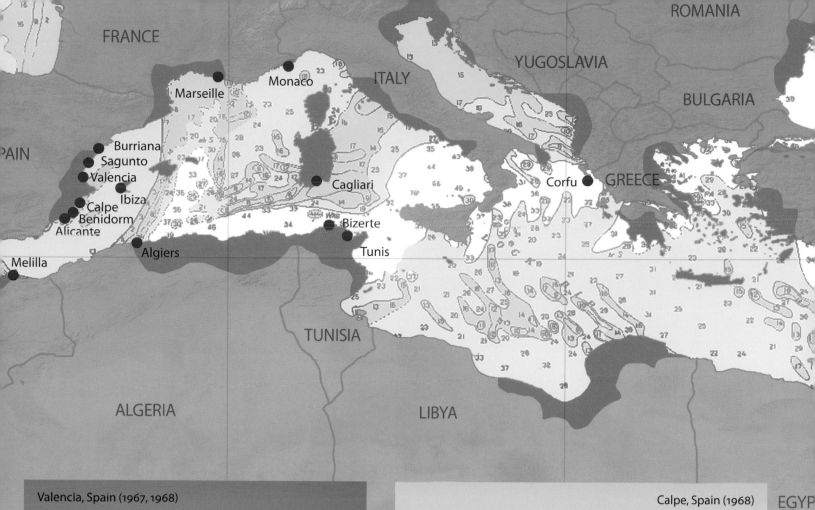

FRANCE

Marseille

Monaco

ITALY

YUGOSLAVIA

ROMANIA

BULGARIA

PAIN

Burriana

Sagunto

Valencia

Ibiza

Calpe

Benidorm

Alicante

Melilla

Algiers

Cagliari

Bizerte

Tunis

GREECE

Corfu

TUNISIA

ALGERIA

LIBYA

EGYP

Valencia, Spain (1967, 1968)

Calpe, Spain (1968)

Burriana, Spain (1968)

Benidorm, Spain (1968)

Melilla, Spain (1968, 1969)

Ibiza, Spain (1969)

São Vicente, Cape Verde Islands (1969)

Dakar, Senegal (1969)

Safi, Morocco (1969, 1970, 1971)

Tunis, Tunisia (1968)

Algiers, Algeria (1968)

Bizerte, Tunisia (1968)

Tangier, Morocco (1969, 1970, 1971, 1972)

Cádiz, Spain (1969, 1970, 1973, 1974)

Santa Maria, Azores (1970)

Terceira, Azores (1970)

Port of Horta, Azores (1970)

La Coruña, Spain (1974)

Funchal, Madeira (1969, 1970, 1971, 1972, 1973, 1974)

Las Palmas, Canary Islands (1970, 1973, 1974)

Tenerife, Canary Islands (1970, 1973, 1974)

Oporto, Portugal (1970, 1972 ,1973)

Setúbal, Portugal (1970, 1971, 1972, 1973, 1974)

Lisbon, Portugal (1969, 1970, 1971, 1972, 1973, 1974)

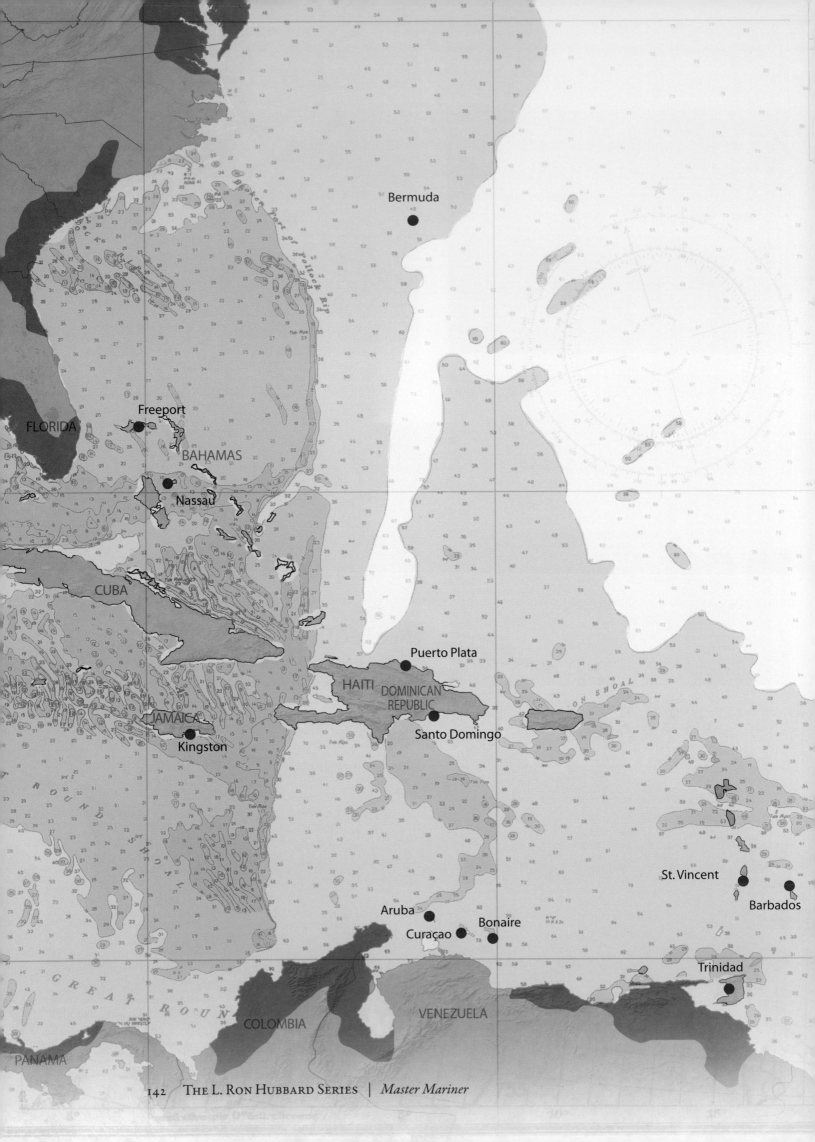

Bermuda

Freeport

FLORIDA

BAHAMAS

Nassau

CUBA

HAITI

DOMINICAN
REPUBLIC

Puerto Plata

JAMAICA

Kingston

Santo Domingo

St. Vincent

Barbados

Aruba

Curaçao

Bonaire

COLOMBIA

VENEZUELA

Trinidad

PANAMA

Willemstad, Curaçao (1975)

"New islands and warm summer seas never fail to delight."

—L. Ron Hubbard

St. George's Island, Bermuda (1974)

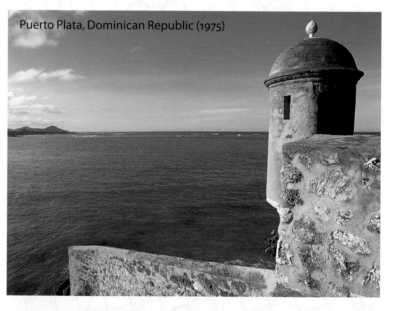

Puerto Plata, Dominican Republic (1975)

Oranjestad, Aruba (1975)

Kingstown, St. Vincent (1975)

Kingston, Jamaica (1975)

Bridgetown, Barbados (1975)

Santo Domingo, Dominican Republic (1975)

Chaguaramas, Trinidad (1975)

Nassau, Bahamas (1975)

In 2011, in honor of both his Centennial Anniversary as well as his legendary prowess as a mariner, the Portuguese Island of Madeira placed this commemorative plaque at the very place where L. Ron Hubbard's Flagship once docked in the port of Funchal

L. Ron Hubbard (1911 - 1986)

and his	e o seu
Motor Vessel *Apollo*	navio *Apollo*

In commemoration of the centennial of his birth on this 13 of March 2011, the friends of L. Ron Hubbard are proud to mark the location where the MV *Apollo* often moored at Funchal. This plaque is in recognition of the dedication of Mr. Hubbard, as a Mariner, Humanitarian and Philosopher to the arts and culture of the people of Madeira while navigating these seas from 1969 to 1974.

Esta placa foi colocada pelos amigos de L. Ron Hubbard neste local onde atracava o *Apollo*, para comemorar o centenário do seu nascimento, no dia 13 de Março de 2011. A presente foi colocada em reconhecimento da dedicação do Sr. Hubbard, como navegador, filantropo e filósofo, às artes e cultura do povo da Madeira, quando sulcava estes mares de 1969 a 1974.

Apollo, Willemstad, Curaçao, 1975: *"A vessel with a brave and romantic past, her adventures continue in a modern world, serving the causes of humanity and peace"* —LRH

The Diana (Enchanter)

As noted, among the first vessels in Sea Organization history was a 60-foot Netherlands ketch, initially dubbed the *Enchanter* and latterly rechristened *Diana*. She served as both an auxiliary vessel and training craft between 1967 and 1975. She was also the ship aboard which the Commodore conducted his legendary Mission into Time whilst the *Apollo* was under refit and readied for service. Consequently, and most historically so, this was the ship he helmed when testing whole track recall by tapping memories from former lifetimes to unearth archeological wonders and so furnish incontrovertible proof of past life existence.

She presently sails with the *Freewinds*, providing crew and passengers a sense of sailing aboard a vessel that demands the finest in seamanship. She has further enjoyed a loving restoration to her original splendor and so vividly recalls the days when L. Ron Hubbard so gracefully steered her through towering swells and under cloud-torn skies to realms "sufficiently powerful to daunt the last few thousand years of thinking men."

ENCHANTER HANDLING

by L. RON HUBBARD

*E*NCHANTER, LIKE ANY LARGE sailing vessel, is sailed with attention only to (a) is the ship's helm balanced (always will on right sails up); (b) angle of a windward telltale to the booms; and (c) the speed of footing of the vessel; (d) is she making good toward her destination? It is not sailed by degree of heel or luffing as in little boats.

With sails up

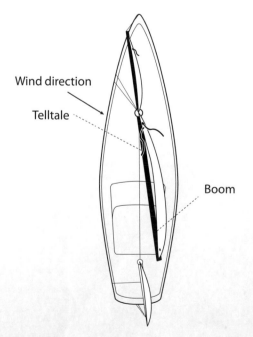

Wind direction

Telltale

Boom

Left Under sail off Tenerife in the Canary Islands, 1968

Courses

Enchanter behaves well in the ocean only when proceeding on courses which give her the minimum roll and pitch. When she begins to "knife sideways," cutting her bow into the sea sideways as she rolls, she is a bit too far toward the trough.

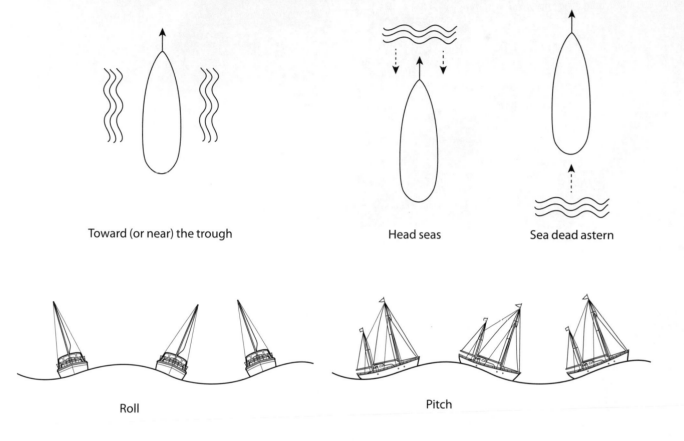

Toward (or near) the trough   Head seas   Sea dead astern

Roll   Pitch

There is no reason to beat her or her company up by savagely insisting on her going from Point A to Point B on the chart. She arrives at Point B as she can, not by a line on the chart.

She almost stops in head seas; she rolls her rigging loose when too near the trough. She doesn't steer with the sea dead astern.

The Formula is:

One tries to get her as close to her course as possible in keeping with her ability to make headway with maximum comfort. One makes good these divergences by steering as well to the other side of her course at times.

She will always foot well 90° port or starboard of where she *was* footing well. This can even be adjusted closer at times.

A sail vessel hull, even under power, is a sail vessel.

The *Diana* today, looking forward at her lovingly restored saloon

Her helm returned to original splendor

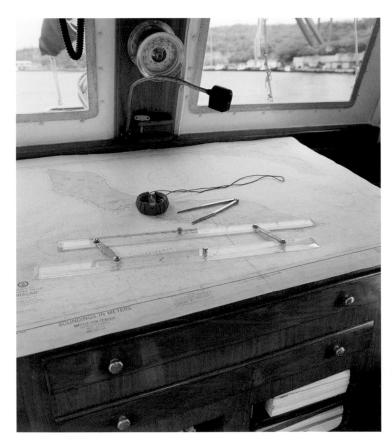

Chart table: *"Enchanter behaves well in the ocean only when proceeding on courses which give her the minimum roll and pitch"* —LRH

Saloon looking aft, replete with a bust of the Commodore

Right The lovingly restored *Diana* under sail in the Netherlands Antilles

The Sea Org Tradition

"Hereafter all general orders affecting the flotilla as a whole or issued by myself shall be termed 'FLAG ORDERS.'" —LRH, 1967

Thus he came to author a body of seafaring policy and thus came an enduring tradition of the Sea Organization. The designation is drawn from the fact vessels bearing a commodore traditionally hoist a Commodore's Flag: hence Flagship and hence Flag Orders. While some are specific to a particular time or place—a work order for *Apollo* decks or purchase order for diesel fuel—virtually all convey a lasting lesson in competence, efficiency, dedication and participation. In that respect, the Commodore's Flag Orders comprise a body of policy speaking to the spirit of the Sea Organization.

What follows is a case-in-point selection, replete with orders on nautical etiquette, seamanship drills and Old Man Sea himself. Also included are Flag Orders on specific sailing technologies, helmsmanship, navigation, "The Four Unprofitable Courses" and "Study of Seafaring." The latter, incidentally, further serves as the Commodore's introduction to the Ship's Org Book, authored within ten days of Sea Organization formation. That what amounted to his compendium of basic seafaring technology is a mainstay of Sea Organization vessels is to be expected. That it additionally serves as a mainstay manual within many another maritime organization underscores the veracity of all he discusses here.

STUDY OF SEAFARING

by L. Ron Hubbard

MOST BOOKS ON THE technology of the sea are written by men who do not do. And men who do seldom write.

Thus you can expect most standard texts on the sea to be a bit inadequate. If you looked to them for the whole story and then tried to do it, you would find some essential bits missing when you started to apply it. This, then, would give you a failure and you might conclude YOU were somehow wanting—which may be the reason for bad texts anyway.

Going to sea is basically common sense. Things that violate common sense (after your study and experience) are just simply incorrect.

Tradition of the sea in a large part is only compounded experience. Even etiquette. If you look, it makes sense.

But Man has two unfortunate things:

a. He tends to avoid confronting the real and so invents symbols as substitutes. This goes to the extent, in navigation, of making fun of direct-observation navigation, preferring calculation by symbols. Real navigation methodology by definition is "Navigate by direct observation or visual contact. In the absence of this seek to predict and establish position by a minimum of symbols and vias until visual contact can again occur." Man *prefers,* and in all his navigation courses insists, on navigation by symbols and calculations and even scoffs at and invalidates visual contact and direct observation! So Man in general *much* prefers to confront symbols rather than the real. And so 90 percent of your study of seafaring is in reality an effort to unearth the meaning of the symbols he uses and only 10 percent is devoted to understanding the subject itself.

b. The heyday of seamanship technology passed away with the last square-riggers and in these days of large ships the real technology is being lost. A feeble effort to keep real seamanship alive exists in small yachts but is very muddied by their text writers, who limit their seagoing to a cruise around the harbor in most cases. The real sailors of the planet for the most part dropped their technology when they dropped the sailing mock-up.

Man sought to solve the sea by building ships so big the sea could not affect them. And he is always surprised when even the biggest ships go down.

The real definition of proper ship construction is "A design capable of withstanding any sea or weather on the planet in complete safety and on schedule." You see, from that, that Man is far short of ideal ships. His ships are built to work in the average seas of specific areas and even the largest he builds avoid areas of storm or heavy seas.

Our own technology (Scientology) is so far in advance of general engineering, electronic and other current technology that we are always a bit amazed that Man's engines and electronic gear don't run without careful nursing and his ships don't sail well at all without extreme care. It behooves one to be pretty expert at sea to arrive at all.

The object of seafaring is to remain afloat, to have a useful home in harbor and at sea and to depart from and arrive at destinations with messages, people and cargo.

On the bridge wing of his Flagship, 1968

More than two decades after authoring "Courtesy" for his crew of the
PC-815, L. Ron Hubbard presented members of the Sea Organization with
"Etiquette." Although echoing formal traditions of shipboard conduct, with
"Etiquette" comes the vantage point from Scientology. Thus, for example,
the passing reference to valence—being a Scientology term denoting a
particular mechanism of the mind wherein a "synthetic personality" is
"borrowed" from another. And thus his remarks on a "pattern of agreement"
whereby a ship becomes a pleasant place and a world in which to savor what
he elsewhere describes as "the joy I take in the singing wind and sea."

ETIQUETTE

by L. Ron Hubbard

A SHIP IS A SMALL world. Courtesy and thoughtfulness make the elbows rub better and add certainty to conduct.

There are certain points of maritime courtesy which are observed on ships which should be followed.

Colors and flags are raised at 8 A.M. and struck at sunset, the national ensign raised first and struck last.

When aboard, on meeting an officer for the first time in the day, the junior says, "Good morning," "Good afternoon" or "Good evening" as the time of day applies. When aboard, one does not salute. The senior nods or replies.

Ashore, when meeting an officer or senior and one intends to address him, one salutes. The senior returns the salute. This applies, with us, in or out of uniform, cap on or cap off.

Before boarding a ship when not of its company, it is customary to obtain the Captain's or the OOW's permission to come aboard.

Obtain the Captain's (or senior officer's) permission to leave the ship.

Before changing course or speed or starting engines, obtain the Captain's permission.

When boarding or leaving a ship, always salute the quarterdeck, whether the flag is flying or not. The person on watch returns such salutes.

Work parties going on and off the ship do not salute.

When a senior officer comes aboard or leaves the ship, the Officer of the Watch "tends the rail" for him.

A Coxswain always offers the tiller to the most senior officer.

When a Coxswain is carrying an officer to a ship and is hailed, he calls "Aye, aye." When he is not carrying an officer, he says "No, no." When he is carrying a Captain, he says the name of the Captain's ship. When he is carrying the Commodore, he says "Flotilla." If he is not going to the ship and is hailed, the Coxswain says "Passing."

When the Captain comes aboard or leaves, the Chief Officer, or in his absence the Officer of the Watch, tends the rail for him.

When the Flag Officer or a senior Captain comes aboard or goes ashore, the ship's Captain tends the rail for him. But senior or junior, Captains usually tend the rail for visiting Captains when they arrive and depart.

One always tends the rail to greet or bid his guests goodbye.

Juniors always board a boat first and leave it last.

The senior officer of a party boards the boat last and leaves it first.

In our flotilla when a boat passes a boat carrying an officer, the Coxswain salutes.

When a Captain is not aboard his ship in our flotilla, we fly International Code flag N for "negative." (Not usually customary, but it is so in our flotilla.)

When the Commodore is aboard, the ship flies the Commodore's flag (blue with white stars).

When the officers or crew are at meals in harbor, we fly a red pennant to show usual services cannot be expected. (Usually reserved for the crew only but not in our flotilla.)

When walking with a senior, always let him go first.

When meeting a senior aboard, step aside to let him have the passageway or deck. However, when meeting a man with a burden, give him the right of way.

Inform the Captain of changes in wind and weather and new ships in sight.

At noon the OOW reports to the Captain, "12 o'clock, Sir. All's well (or not). The chronometers are wound. The glass (barometer) is (falling, steady, rising). (Add at sea) The course _____ and speed _____ and (no land) (land with name) is in sight (where relative to ship)."

Let seniors have the starboard side of the wheelhouse or deck.

When the Captain or the Commodore are in the wheelhouse, they have the starboard side.

Do not stand about on the bridge in the way of the OOD or Conning Officer when not on specific bridge (not watch) duties.

Do not use the possessions or quarters or chair or spaces or passageways reserved for the Commodore or Captain for any reason whatsoever and severely frown on anyone using them and turn in an Ethics Order.

Don't "borrow" another's possessions, toothpaste, towels, etc.

Never remove or use food or stores of the Cook's without specific permission. Stay out of food stores and iceboxes.

Wash your hands, face and comb your hair before sitting down to any meal served at table. Don't sit down at tables in greasy clothes or overalls or dirty up the seats. Don't linger over coffee, but let the table be cleaned up.

If your hands are dirty, don't grab rails where people with clean hands will get messed up.

Bathe and wash your clothes and bedding before somebody has to remind you. Ship spaces are very close.

The old-time sailor was notorious for being clean.

Help keep WCs and any shower spotless.

Do not put anything on anyone else's bunk or in his locker.

When you see a shipmate's bunk or gear are in danger, move them to safety or cover them to keep off dirt or water.

Give a shipmate or succored person dry clothes or a blanket and a drink when he is wet and chilled. Lend the clothes or blanket if he has none of his own.

At meals, stand and do not sit down until the senior officer or rating of the mess has been seated. Do not begin a meal until the senior officer of the mess is present or has sent word to begin unless he is of course ashore and won't be aboard for that meal.

Do not leave the table until the senior officer or rating of the mess leaves unless to go on watch and then by asking permission.

Don't "cadge" cigarettes or matches. Provide your own.

Do not smoke heavy tobacco in closed spaces where someone does not care for it.

Do not smoke on watch at sea or in the chartroom.

Do not occupy the chartroom at sea or in harbor.

Do not stand in doorways.

Do not sit on ladders.

Do not sleep or sit about in the salon or mess hall at sea and do not sleep in the salon unless quartered there by the Captain.

Do not use the personal binoculars or spyglass of an officer.

Reply to all officer's commands with "Aye, aye, Sir." Use "Sir" regardless of whether the officer is man or woman. Add "Sir" to Helmsman responses.

Remove your cap when entering the quarters of an officer or officers.

Don't ridicule or haze or pick on or do comic imitations of members of the company or seniors as the ship is their home and nothing should make them want to leave it and mutual confidence is all that keeps a ship afloat. And it is just bad manners. If you're short of valences, find yourself.

Don't issue orders to juniors at table. (Usually a mess fines anyone doing so two shillings, which goes into a teapot for party funds.)

Thank the Cook for a meal.

Thank anyone in the company for services rendered.

Thank assistance.

Thank a rescuer.

An officer pleased with a duty performed says, "Well done," indicating who he means.

Relieve the wheel or deck ten minutes before the watch is out.

Thank the Conning Officer of a cruise for a safe passage.

These are customs and courtesies. The main point is to be thoughtful and helpful to your shipmates (regardless of conduct to others) to make the ship a pleasant place regardless of the dangers of the sea and to form a pattern of agreement for right conduct.

THE FOUR UNPROFITABLE COURSES

by L. RON HUBBARD

IN ANY WAVES OF some size compared to the ship there are four unprofitable courses to steer and four most profitable courses.

The unprofitable courses are:

1. Head on into the sea.
2. In the trough to the right.
3. In the trough to the left.
4. Sea dead astern.

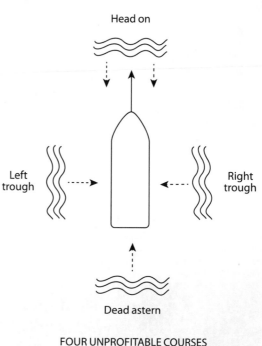

FOUR UNPROFITABLE COURSES

It is not wholly a question of strain on the ship and her company. It is a question of fuel and economy and the shortest time between two points.

Only a bad seaman thinks the shortest time between A and B (assumed points of departure, A, and arrival, B, on a chart) is a straight line from A to B. If this line is any one of the four unprofitable courses, IT WILL TAKE LONGER TO GO FROM A TO B than to choose a more profitable course.

(1) A head sea stops or checks a ship and pounds her so that she may use more than 50 percent more fuel than on an easier course and indeed may make no progress at all.

(2) and (3) In a trough a ship rolls so that the skin friction of passage through the water may be quadrupled and so absorb much time, fuel and speed.

Apollo, Eastern Atlantic, 1972

(4) A sea dead astern makes a ship hard to steer so she yaws all over the place, as much as 20° off course on the average, and so consumes time, fuel and speed. A sail vessel with fore-and-aft rig may also jibe with the wind dead aft. A square-rigger with the wind dead aft blankets four-fifths or more of her sail area. A steamer or motor vessel just yaws all over the place and goes a mile and a half or more through the water for every mile made good over the sea floor.

Besides all that, these courses are miserable for the company, imparting needless excess motion to the ship, and are hard on the ship's gear, hull and internal activities.

You only put a ship's head to the sea when lying to, stopped, with a sea anchor out or the aftermost sail only hoisted.

Thus the most profitable courses in any seaway at all are:

1. Sea on the port bow.
2. Sea on the starboard bow.
3. Sea on the port quarter.
4. Sea on the starboard quarter.

You can go further toward destination on these courses in less time and with less fuel. Also they are far easier on the ship and its company.

The "A to B direct" boys are often afraid to diverge from the A to B course because it is harder to keep track of navigation ded-reckoning (*ded*uced *reckoning*). They are in such a panic about getting lost that they beat up the ship and crew despite the fact that direct A to B may be an "unprofitable course."

FOUR PROFITABLE COURSES

Or they simply aren't seamen enough to know about this.

This applies not only to small vessels, but the very largest Man has and explains why even the old Queen Elizabeth was sometimes beat up and delayed in passage. It is all a matter of how much wave versus how big a ship.

The test is: Is the ship rolling or pitching excessively? If so, somebody is probably trying to do a direct A to B although the course is unprofitable. All ships Man can make roll or pitch somewhat. *Excessively* for the ship is the key. When it does, then modify the course and arrive sooner!

Helmsmanship

Helmsmen changing watch usually have a moment of juggling while the new Helmsman seeks to get her back on the course she left when the relieved Helmsman stepped aside.

This is commonly attended, amongst unskilled steersmen, with wild bucks and rolls as the ship moves off course and back on.

The tightness a profitable course is steered is the keynote. 5° or 10° to left and right of the profitable course can make the vessel careen and violently misbehave.

This is so true that the company often knows (a) when the steersmen change and (b) who is steering.

Helmsmen vary between overcontrol and undercontrol (too much and too little wheel). And in these days of cars most, when green, try to drive a car, find the ship won't stay on with that little wheel, then madly begin to shoot the ship all over the ocean with overcontrol. The thing to do is:

1. Find how much wheel exactly is needed to keep the course.
2. Exactly how much right or left rudder has to be left on (if any) to compensate for the effort of wind and sea to drive the ship off course.

In a sailing vessel, a good Steersman can make the vessel "foot" (go along) and a bad one makes her barely creep as steering is often done by the telltales, not the compass. I have found I can better use, with our people, degree compass courses to a Steersman in sailing a ship, although compass points (NNE, etc.) are traditional under sail, being wider and less precise.

The course of the ship is so vital that the offgoing Steersman reports it to the OOD (Officer of the Deck) or Conning Officer and the oncoming Steersman *also* reports it after he has taken over.

If a Steersman steers one course while the navigator thinks another is being steered, the ship can get wonderfully lost!

The Conning Officer (who is directing the ship's movements and is senior to the OOD) is the one who chooses the courses and eases the ship. But seas change and he must be apprised of it when there is any change of wind or sea so he can readjust the course *and* the navigation. It is a serious error for the OOD or Steersman not to advise the Conning Officer (usually the Captain) of a change in wind, sea or apparent *current*.

And it is a stupid Conning Officer who resents being disturbed or reported to and a stupid OOD who is *afraid* or unwilling to inform the Conning Officer or Captain, for any reason, of a change of wind, sea, current or ships in sight.

Fixed Bearings

When another vessel near or far assumes a fixed bearing (does not change right or left in relation to your own ship) and the distance is decreasing, action MUST be taken by the Conning Officer to make the fixed bearing shift so as to avoid collision.

Anything on a fixed bearing, with distance closing, *will hit you*. It is a peculiarity of geometry. And invariable.

Radar often detects a fixed bearing before it is seen by the direct eye (as at night). And radar is very accurate in distance indications, so you can tell by radar what you sometimes have trouble seeing by eye.

Rules of the Road

All the little landlubber clerks who drew up the rules of the road did not grasp two facts:

1. Ships don't know or don't follow them; and
2. Nothing requires special lights or signals to get you to avoid it—you just avoid ships whether towing, fishing or diving or just going along.

I have never seen another ship obey any rules of the road in putting ships of all sizes over 250,000 miles of sea. So it is a fool's dream that "right of way" and "privileged vessel" exist. They don't in actual practice.

In going to sea, most ships have a Steersman whose nose is in the compass, no Lookout and the OOD has HIS nose stuck in a coffee cup in the chartroom.

The reason more ships don't collide is that the ocean is big!

So you always take avoiding action early and never wait to have to take it in emergency.

A lot of modern "officers" are so afraid of losing their course they won't take avoiding action early and, when they do, they go in a big circle or do something silly.

Always log any course divergence in the Quartermaster's Notebook. But take avoiding action early.

The Rule of the Road *we* go on is "Avoid hitting ships."

On the *Apollo* flying bridge along the Moroccan coast, 1971

HELMSMANSHIP HOW TO STEER

by L. RON HUBBARD

SHIP IS *NOT* STEERED quickly like a car. Although the wheel turns in the same directions as a car, the response of the ship is much slower and requires a larger turning to keep a ship straight.

If you look at the wake of an expert Helmsman, you will see it is straight as a tape on the water. That of a poor Helmsman has ragged edges.

A ship travels in *two* things—*water* and *air*. The rudder at the stern guides the ship. The ship gets batted off course by waves and by tiny or great currents and by wind. Thus the rudder often has to be at an angle to guide the ship straight.

One *puts on* (turns the wheel) spokes to an exact number and takes off (turns the wheel back) an exact number when keeping a ship straight on course. By counting spokes "on" and then again "off," one knows where the "center" is exactly: i.e., he knows what exact position the rudder at the stern must be in to keep a straight course.

Green Helmsmen usually *over*control. And they don't know where "center" is for the course. They think they can watch the rudder indicator and find out. But center is where the rudder sits in order to overcome outside influences caused by wind and sea—and sometimes propeller imbalance as in twin screw ships. It is only center by the rudder indicator on a flat calm day. Otherwise "center" is to right or left of the rudder indicator.

You can only find "center" by actual test for any new condition of wind and sea. And you can only hold it by counting spokes on and off as you hold the course.

Ships answer differently to their helm. *Enchanter* is almost instant. *Avon* takes several seconds to respond. The *Royal Scotman* takes up to twenty seconds after a movement of the wheel to make the ship alter course slightly.

Helm of the *Apollo* bridge;
photograph by L. Ron Hubbard

The Helmsman pushes the "lubber line," the black mark *above* the compass. If he wants to go left, he pushes the lubber line left by making the wheel turn left. And so with right.

It is the compass card that is nailed to the earth. The ship moves around it. It *looks* like the compass moves and the lubber line is still, but this is not the case. The compass is still related to earth and the ship goes right and left.

So one *pushes* the lubber line. Always. It will then move to the compass course.

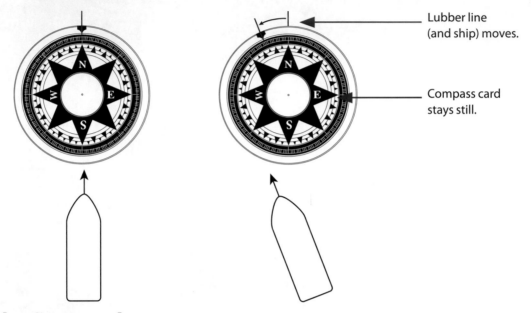

Lubber line
(and ship) moves.

Compass card
stays still.

Helm Commands

When a Conning Officer or Pilot is maneuvering the ship, he gives orders to the Helmsman. The Helmsman does not then steer by a compass course unless told to do so.

The commands most used are Right Rudder, Left Rudder, Ease her, Meet her, Steady as she goes, 5° Right Rudder, 5° Left Rudder, 10° Right Rudder, 10° Left Rudder, 20° Right Rudder, 20° Left Rudder, Hard Right Rudder and Hard Left Rudder. Sometimes you hear Right *Standard* Rudder and Left Standard Rudder: "Standard" is the optimum turning radius of a ship without strain or list, usually 25°.

"Ease her" means take some rudder off. "Meet her" means put on opposite rudder to stop the turn. "Steady as she goes" means to steer the direction she has just gotten to. One steers then by a landmark or a compass bearing the ship is at that moment on.

When the compass goes out, one steers by a landmark, the sun, stars or straightness of wake until a compass can be rigged.

Really good Helmsmen are rare. The degree one applies all the above makes one a good Helmsman.

DRILLS

by L. RON HUBBARD

FATALITIES AND ACCIDENTS AT sea are far more often personnel matters than weather or equipment.

It is lack of competence and lack of coordinated organization that causes accidents, fatalities, breakdowns and losses of ships and crews. It is not the sea. It is seldom the ship or its equipment.

Once one has learned this and accepts it and works with it, the sea becomes a safe, comfortable place. Until then it is all mystery and superstition and "luck."

One can have the most astonishing bad luck in the most rickety ship and still survive it *if* one has competence and coordinated organization.

This explains national differences of amounts of catastrophes at sea. Some nations regard the sea with awe and superstition and some with calm competence. The equipment is the same. The men and organization of them aren't.

Individual ships are incredibly different in performance and amount of untoward incident. Some are "lucky," some aren't. But the difference is *entirely* that of the competence and coordinated organization of the ship's officers and crew.

The difference is the difference between snap and lethargy.

A crew and its officers must be willing to work to a high standard of quick efficiency almost gone today on shore. When you see a ship's company drifting about, sloppy, rather ashamed of appearing quick and eager, you see a ship which may someday die. With all her people.

Old Man Sea is a worthy opponent. He is always waiting. He always has another trick, a taller wave, a mightier wind. He isn't looking for a weak ship. He is looking for a sloppy, slack, disorganized

On lookout watch;
photograph by L. Ron Hubbard

Drills   173

ship's company. And then he dines. Sometimes in the most surprisingly mild weather he dines very well indeed.

The whole point, then, is a competent ship's company, well organized, that can work quick and well as a group.

By competent we don't mean just well schooled. Somebody had to live long enough to learn. Well, he was competent before he learned. By competence we mean alert, clever and willing. Given those, one becomes experienced. Certain subjects like navigation are school subjects, but they also require practical learning.

The ship never takes anybody anywhere. It's the ship's company that takes the ship and its cargo and passengers somewhere. Equipment and hull don't do it. It's the ship's people from Captain on down who take the ship places.

Today people are used to driving cars. A car is controlled on a ribbon of road and the driver more or less is taken along on a narrow track, independent of the elements, guided by the road. A ship is not like that. When one tries to treat one so, at once casualty will occur. You don't just drive an ocean ship from port A to port B like a river ferryboat and if you do try to, then some day Old Man Sea will dine.

An oceangoing ship is subjected to continually varying conditions of operation, seasonal, climatic, meteorological. She is operating in a fluid medium. And she is a long way from any nearest AA box. And she operates in an additional dimension—right or left and yet another dimension—up and down. She also rolls.

It is the ship's company and their state of drill that foretell a long life or a short one. It is the interest and alertness of all on board that add up to easy, cheerful passages.

When officers and crew neglect something or fail to notice something at the dock, they often have to repair it at sea with no facilities. So their competence begins before the voyage. Not to notice rotten halliards, dirty fuel, rusty water, no charts and suchlike before casting off is pure suicide.

Drills in General

The essence in drills is knowing how many there are, what they are for and what one does personally in each.

Navy drills are all puppet, verbatim. Merchant drills are mostly not done at all or slopped.

What we are aiming for is adequate fast coverage of the required action with our few numbers so we know what we've each to do and what happens.

Therefore in practicing a drill, we really just name it and work it out as we go along. Then when we've got it worked out, we try for some speed.

When we get a new crew member taking somebody's place, we tell him what those duties were in the drill.

Beyond the purpose and scope, we don't write the drill down. What we study is the act of getting it done the best way and then our own parts in it.

Looked at this way, it is not very formidable.

The only formidable thing is on a dark night having to get one of these drills done in fact when we've never even heard of it in daylight. And that's formidable.

And men who go to sea *that* sloppy are dined upon. So our drills are not our peculiarity. They're our survival.

If we practice them, we will soon begin to work well together and life will get very easy and safe.

Other ships' companies wander in and out of these same actions. They do it usually by the dint of endless orders from an officer in a high temper against a high wind as he is the only one who knows the whole book.

In our "navy" we're all expected to know what we're doing and then to do it well. Our officers are busy enough already without making them put a hand on every hand that's on a line. ✍

SEA WATCH DRILLS
EXPERTS

by L. RON HUBBARD

SEA WATCH DRILLS ARE DRILLED BY THEIR CONS.

They are drilled on the bridge, with the equipment.

Each watch member is taught who the officers are and what they do, what the equipment is and 100 percent (not brush-off) operation of it with practice. (Such as identifying every building in a harbor on a chart, then on radar.)

Anytime there is a change in the watch lineup, the whole watch is again drilled by their CONNING OFFICER.

By this is meant the SEA Conning Officer.

Engine Room Drills

The engine room is drilled on their stations as a unit by the ENGINEER OF THE WATCH.

Every engineer is thoroughly briefed in the duties of every person on the watch.

Every engineer is thoroughly briefed in the operation of every piece of equipment that:

    a. He personally operates and (when that is done)
    b. Every piece of equipment that is operated in the engine room.

TEAMWORK IS BASED ON TOTAL AWARENESS OF THE DUTIES OF EVERYONE ON THE TEAM.

Sea Bridge work and Engine Room work and Org work are all *team* functions.

Her "imposing bow" emblazoned with
the symbol of the Sea Organization, 1971;
photograph by L. Ron Hubbard

The search for the stellar individual who can somehow do it all, for "only the best people" to block team spirit and TOTAL PARTICIPATION is suppressive.

Relying on "experts" to do it all because others can't understand is a fatal proceeding. The more suppressive a society becomes, the more specialists it has. The more specialists it has, the more it falls apart.

The basic error is considering, "Things are now too complex to be understood by any one man, so we have to have specialists."

What then happens is that the UNDERSTAND drops out on the part of the society as a whole, the ARC falls and you get a cruel, decaying society.

To raise ARC in a group, one has to raise the *Understand* which ARC adds up to.

You don't do this with specialists.

Also you can always detect the FRAUDULENT EXPERT by simply looking at the men under him. If they don't now understand how to handle things after serving under same man, then that one is NO EXPERT, but a fraud who uses the smoke screen of expertise to be important while he himself hasn't a clue.

It's great to be expert, but let's be expert on a lot of things. What we want is expert *teamwork*.

That's our target.

At watch in heavy weather, 1971;
photograph by L. Ron Hubbard

COMMUNICATION OF ORDERS

by L. RON HUBBARD

T HE MILITARY MAKE IT a *rule* to never explain an order! They believe a man is a puppet into whom can be trained a number of action patterns, any of which can be activated when the right button is pushed for that pattern.

Even if the think worked, we wouldn't do that. (It doesn't work.) We make stable terminals who handle their areas so as to carry out the agreed purpose for that post. So a basic operating principle is:

IF YOU DON'T TELL PEOPLE WHAT YOU'RE AT, YOU CREATE MYSTERY.

Say you issued three different military-type orders into the same area within a short timespan:

1. Lift that boat out of the water NOW.
2. Clean up the bridge AT ONCE.
3. Give me an immediate count of the fire extinguishers aboard.

You will achieve no more than:

The person in charge of the area will ignore them because he already has cycles to complete (there are rust spots all over the fo'c'sle, there are unsecured canvases on the boat deck, the lashings in the 'tween decks need tightening, decks have to be swept, the well deck has sprung a leak, etc., etc.) and he is fed up with interrupting them; or

He will be confused as to which one to do first; or

He will do them puppet fashion and, having done them, sit and wait for the next order, not knowing what your overall plan is (you didn't tell him) and he knows from experience it will probably not be the one that is desired. Your three orders above have put him out of ARC with his area of control and with you.

If you had bothered to let him know what you're at, he'd *know*.

1. That boat is leaking. It will *sink*. Get it out of the water!
2. The Admiral's coming this afternoon. The bridge better be spick and span.
3. There are some fire extinguishers missing from their stations. Where are they? Why are they removed?

He'd be able to judge relative importance *and* be able to give you a sensible answer *and* be able to maintain his position as stable terminal for his area.

He'd get the boat out of the water, he'd clean up the bridge and he'd tell you that the "missing" fire extinguishers are being charged and are already back in their stations, all accounted for and all correct.

If the junior is the type that goes into explanations, forbid them. If you know what the reality of the situation is and the pressure of the moment is high, you can add, "Regardless of any explanations, etc., get it done," having *given* him the R-factor.

If you are calling for information or materials for *inspection,* say *why* you are inspecting this area, what results you want to achieve and mention *who* is going to take care of it. You may find the whole scene is already taken care of or the guy at the other end is quite capable of handling it himself.

This operating principle holds good for both long *and* short comm lines.

We are in the business of *un*puppeting people. Puppets don't make stable terminals.

TELL PEOPLE WHAT YOU'RE AT. DON'T CREATE MYSTERY.

"Old Man Sea is the most amenable old fellow you ever met in your life. He hasn't got a kind bone in his body, but he does respect a ship which is well drilled." —LRH

"The ability of an individual depends upon his ability to communicate."
—LRH

Thus comes an axiomatic truth as drawn from fundamental Scientology and thus comes Scientology in application at sea. Dating from 1972, or when he regularly plied blue water between North Africa and Portugal, L. Ron Hubbard's "Con and Watch Officer Troubles" is a classic study of Scientology at work aboard his Flagship Apollo. That he further recommends a basic Scientology process—Reach and Withdraw—only serves to underscore the point: with central truths of Scientology in play comes a rare and penetrating understanding of wind, sea and ships. While if only to doubly underscore the point, we are told the Commodore himself possessed an uncanny knowledge of the deepest secrets in Old Man Sea.

CON AND WATCH OFFICER TROUBLES

by L. Ron Hubbard

A NY TROUBLE A Con or Watch Officer may be having in ship handling usually comes from: a lack of comm ability with the SHIP, SEA, WIND and FORCES.

This was established by actual observation as the real WHY of any trouble in handling a ship.

There can be too various case reasons such as having damaged ships or having forgotten what one once knew about ships.

The positive side, however, is the side to stress. Thus:

THE ABILITY TO HANDLE A SHIP OR BOAT DEPENDS UPON ONE'S ABILITY TO COMM WITH A SHIP, THE SEA, THE WIND AND FORCES.

This can be directly improved. Just like a pilot can reach and withdraw from an airplane and suddenly begin to fly better and without accidents, so can a Watch Officer reach and withdraw from a ship and so begin to handle it better.

Getting rid of any misunderstood words about any of these four items enormously assists.

Doing direct obnosis on these items is of great use.

Noting waves and what they do and how water moves in tidal streams as an exercise improves comm with the sea.

Tossing a bit of paper in the air to see what the wind is doing, feeling the wind with the hand, spotting directions of wind, all increase comm with air.

Doing the elementary arithmetic vector exercises with forces gives one an approach to understanding them.

Small objects to float in still and running water, small objects to blow around with the breath or a hand fan, all improve one's ideas of FORCE.

The hugeness of the forces involved in ships, sea and the wind can make for some tendency to flinch or withdraw. By overcoming this with reaching instead, one can actually work up one's ability to confront these forces. A considerable freedom can result quite in addition to ship handling.

If a Con or Watch Officer becomes familiar with these things, he can think in terms of force and can instantly find the Whys of any ship behavior and from this comes to be able to predict exactly where the ship will behave in any given situation and so can make accurate decisions based on real Whys.

It is a matter, basically, of improving comm.

A ship, like a plane, travels in three dimensions: up or down, forward or back, and sideways. Very unlike a plane, a ship travels in *two* elements: the sea and the wind.

A Bridge Officer, like a good flier, can handle his vessel smoothly and well or, like a student pilot, can wobble and bang all over the place.

The difference between a good Bridge Officer and a poor one is not the vague, incorrect Why "experience," but is the ability to comm with the ship, with the sea and with the wind and in terms of forces.

The answer is to improve that comm.

"The difference between a good Bridge Officer and a poor one is not the vague, incorrect Why 'experience,' but is the ability to comm with the ship, with the sea and with the wind and in terms of forces" —LRH

When relinquishing command of the Royal Scotman to pursue an archeological expedition aboard the Enchanter, the Commodore offered "The Hat of Master." It was so named for the fact he was indeed passing that hat to a first Royal Scotman officer. As such, it was a typical L. Ron Hubbard gesture and all the more so inasmuch as it bespeaks of a maritime tradition that is both beautiful and noble.

THE HAT OF MASTER

by L. RON HUBBARD

THE MASTER OF A vessel, in port or at sea, is responsible for the safety and activities of the ship, the cargo, the crew and any passengers, must be in control of these and must assure that the activities of the vessel are remunerative or not too costly and that they do not unnecessarily imperil her before the elements or authorities or forces on the shore.

The purposes of the vessel are laid down by her owners and are varied by the Master only to make the activities more profitable or successful, not to diminish them.

The Master makes certain that the vessel and all within her are in a state to carry out her purposes and that she maintains herself so as to continue carrying out her purpose.

The Master then assures that the vessel is carrying out her purposes and gives all orders and takes all actions to ensure that she does.

He enjoins upon his officers and crew that they carry out their specific or traditional tasks within the departments of the vessel and that cargo and passengers are cared for and comply with the ship's requirements.

It is the Master's task to bring about an atmosphere of confidence through the exhibition of personal competence and the requiring of officers and crew to display and raise their own competence. For in this exercise those within feel safe enough to do their duties and, in a truly confident vessel, seasickness is at a minimum and, with true competence and good judgment, the vessel and her goods and purposes are safe.

The sea and authorities of nations and ports are often difficult to handle, poor in comprehension and violent in action.

The Master must foresee and circumvent the consequences of violence from violent forces at sea or ashore and not be hopeful or supine that these will possibly pass him by.

LRH cap embossed with insignia designating
"Commodore of the Sea Organization Flotilla"

The essence of a Master's attitude for ship, cargo, crew and passengers is survival and the execution of the owner's purpose.

In activity, the good Master is not some aloof deity nor is he dedicated to some minor purpose in the ship like a hobbyist. He is everywhere about, omnipresent, helpful, comprehending and assisting, from his competence and authority, the ship's and company's needs.

No part of the vessel or its function should be unknown to him. And he should always be alert to incompetence on the part of his officers and crew and remedy it by instructions and discipline.

His ship must be clean yet useful and must present a sightly aspect to the beholder within and without and should discourage slovenly practices.

He should decry and discipline tendencies to be unsmart and alert to those who encourage slackness and protect his ship and crew from them by discipline or removal of the offender.

The officer who does not salute in greeting, the bosun who permits cowtailed lines are amongst a thousand signs of future disaster which will strike when all else is already in turmoil. The Master's discipline may be as slight as failing to recommend or as heavy as outright dismissal.

The Master who works to be liked will never be liked. The Master who works to be competent and to execute the ship's purposes and forward her survival and that of her company alone becomes favored by his men.

Useless work, engaged upon "to keep men busy," is the mark of a sadist, not of a competent officer. Men should be as busy as there is work to be done and as idle as they have worked well.

A Master has privileges: He cannot use these without guilt unless he has also measured up to his responsibilities.

"A Master has privileges: He cannot use these without guilt unless he has also measured up to his responsibilities" —LRH

As a supplemental word on the Commodore's ode to Old Man Sea, when remarking on "giving his bike some exercise," he is offering up a bit of wry humor. In fact, the bike was a 1973 Harley-Davidson 1200 and thus comprised an exercise in prowess to "open it up" along cliff-side roads above Setúbal harbor. Also of note: when referencing his work on "early discoverers and ships of five hundred years ago," he is alluding to a now famed LRH photographic shoot of the Lisbon Maritime Museum housing relics of Vasco da Gama.

OLD MAN SEA

by L. RON HUBBARD

I NOTICED TODAY WHILE I was giving my bike some exercise that the points and cliffs about eight miles to the west have very long reefs extending out from them. I had not noticed this before, but today waves were breaking over them and they looked quite dangerous. I recalled two or three years ago taking over the con when I felt the ship was too close to that coast and getting it well out to sea again. Today I observed from the beach that there had been ample reason to do so. Although such things are marked on charts, lines of ink are nowhere near as dramatic as the real thing.

As I am doing some work on early discoverers and ships of five hundred years ago, I am tremendously impressed by the courage and adventurousness of those fellows. Old Man Sea was many times more dangerous in those days than now, because of the lack of technical advances, the absence of charts and no real knowledge of winds or currents in the areas in which they were sailing. I have done some of this "off the chart" sailing in Alaskan waters, where the yellow of the land simply faded out into the blue of the sea and not even the coastline was known. That was hairy enough to suit most anyone.

When you realize that the old-timers did their great voyages of discovery in ships very little bigger than *Enchanter,* you will see that they had their nerve with them. But Old Man Sea is a playmate you have to respect in any age.

Cádiz, Spain, 1973; astride a classic
Harley-Davidson Electra Glide

I have a bargain with him: I respect him, know my tech and do it right; and he leaves me alone so far as sudden surprises.

This certainly is a beautiful coast and the moon shining over the fog banks seen from high in the mountains was a breath-catching sight. It was even more meaningful to a sailor seeing those threads of silver of breaking waves which mark the shoals on this coast. But even so, it added to the beauty of the scene.

What is life without challenge?

CHAPTER FIVE

A NAUTICAL LEGACY

A Nautical
Legacy

INDIVIDUAL SHIPS ARE INCREDIBLY DIFFERENT IN PERFORMANCE and amount of untoward incident. Some are 'lucky,' some aren't. But the difference is *entirely* that of the competence and coordinated organization." —LRH

To which we might add that competence and coordinated organization are indeed hallmarks of the Sea Org Motor Vessel *Freewinds.*

Her nautical profile and vital statistics read as follows: she measures 440 feet in length and weighs 7,000 tons. She was expressly appropriated to deliver the most advanced levels of the Scientology Bridge and so provide a distraction-free environment. Her maiden voyage dates from the 6th of June 1988 and launched from her home port at Willemstad on the island of Curaçao. She was subsequently refit and rechristened in 2008 and sails today as among the finest ships of her class and era. She is also the most regionally celebrated vessel in the Caribbean and, in fact, garnered well over a hundred proclamations/recognitions of gratitude for service to island governments. (Not to overstate it, but she is additionally the only Caribbean cruise ship honored with a commemorative stamp from the island of St. Kitts.)

Her fame largely follows from the fact she regularly delivers L. Ron Hubbard's nautical training regimen to island coast guards, navies and merchant marines. Indeed—and herein our story comes full circle—the *Freewinds* is the only Caribbean vessel authorized to train and certify seamen under international maritime authority. In consequence, her own complement of officers and specialists is altogether unparalleled. To cite but one example, she carries three times the number of licensed deck officers as even the largest commercial liners and no less than four qualified officers certified to captain any vessel of any tonnage on any ocean. Hence, the Maritime Institute of Training and Graduate Studies declaring: "If every ship ran like the *Freewinds,* international safety requirements would become unnecessary."

She has similarly seeded some forty Caribbean ports with specialists in the L. Ron Hubbard maritime tradition, including: the Curaçao Port Authority, Bonaire Harbor Master Authority, the Bonaire Shipping Line, tugboat companies for half a dozen islands and coast guards for a dozen more. Moreover, *Freewinds* specialist training spans the whole gamut of specialized skills—from basic firefighting and radar control to bridge control, crowd control and maritime disaster management. All such training is conducted under the auspices of the International Maritime Organization (IMO) in the name of "Safe, Secure and Efficient Shipping on Clean Oceans." In addition to routine nautical skills, *Freewinds* trainers direct specialized instructional programs for antiterrorist and antipiracy action. Of particular note are the regionally famed *Freewinds* firefighting drills—typically conducted below deck and replete with screaming sirens, jetting water and blindfolds to simulate electrical blackouts. The end result is indeed unshakable competence and, frankly, some of the finest maritime firefighting units on any ocean.

What the *Freewinds* brand of expertise spells in terms of lives saved and property preserved is, of course, difficult to gauge if only because one cannot measure the disaster that never was. Nevertheless, Caribbean maritime records tell of numerous incidents wherein *Freewinds* search and rescue teams plucked less prepared sailors from the sea. Included in the annals of Caribbean rescue is *Freewinds'* intervention to save a listing Bahamian ferry with an 800-degree conflagration in her engine room; the same again to save a hapless inter-island freighter left powerless in high seas and still another rescue of a crippled cruise liner. In consequence is an altogether legendary *Freewinds* that a United States Department of Homeland Security describes as perpetually sailing in "time-honored traditions of mariners assisting their own in peril at sea." Moreover, and in full, better than 90 percent of all regional emergency/security personnel are now *Freewinds* trained and certified, while L. Ron Hubbard maritime materials are now in force across entire Caribbean fleets. ■

Maritime Reporter: the veritable bible of maritime engineering, it enjoys the largest circulation within industry circles and is religiously read by the maritime restoration community. The *Reporter's* five-page coverage of the *Freewinds* renovation was among the most talked about issues of the year.

The World's Largest Circulation Marine Industry Publication • The Information Authority for the Global Marine Industry since 1939

MARITIME REPORTER AND ENGINEERING NEWS

www.marinelink.com

October 2009

Marine Design

The Renovation of M/V Freewinds

From Left: The new bridge; the restored original searchlight; and the telegraph.

Restored brass clearview screens.

"To put it bluntly, they don't build ships like they used to."
• Ludwig Alpers, Port Captain, M/V Freewinds

final sound powered phone.

June 2009 was done parallel to duled interior upgrades to the much more a mat-ship renovation are numerous. "The most challenging thing was the requirement to 'think outside the box. It ...... a lot of creation and new ideas

sight glasses and a new stainless steel base," said the M/V Freewinds Naval Architect. While the ship and plan were indeed unique, Tomas Tillberg of Tillberg Design U.S. said that the age of the ship

challenges are pretty similar to the refits that we do on the other ships. You plan the best that you can, but you will always have surprises. The challenge, really, is to get her to 'the expectation of the owner.' The expectation of the owner was

while also upgrading the looks. For example, the mooring bits take quite a bit of load and it was not wanted that they just replace them out with stainless steel piping and plate; that would not have the equivalent strength. So they clad the existing bits with stainless steel sheeting.

Wärtsilä Sulzer RD56-8 diesels, posed a dual challenge, first and foremost regarding the sheer size and surface areas (70,000 sq. ft.) of the spaces, but also the fact that it would remain in full operation. "There was no way we could just waterblast or sand all of the paint off of the equipment, bulkheads and piping," ..... gold. "In the end, we located an

use throughout the engine room spaces without creating dust or fire hazards ... this was really key to getting the machinery spaces into a pristine condition."
This included using 15 different sandpaper grits to help uncover and ultimately restore many of the brass highlights present but covered for decades by paint.
The renovations also included an envi-....mentally friendly hull treatment, a

no environmental impact. This provides a very hard coating which makes it difficult for marine growth to adhere.
Today the ship accommodates 340 passengers in 125 cabins and carries 256 crew. Renovations complete, the story of M/V Freewinds begins again.

MARINE DESIGN — M/V FREEWINDS

A magnificent ship renovation via

Elbow Grease, Heart & Soul

In today's "I need it yesterday" world, emphasis on quantity often overpowers quality, while the quick fix can supersede the correct one. Step back, take a deep breath and enjoy the fruits of a tremendous labor, a labor of love that resulted in the top-to-bottom renovation of storied ship with a unique owner.
• By Greg Trauthwein, Editor

A cruise ship earning a new lease on life via renovation is hardly a unique concept. Costing upwards of a half a billion dollars with a lifespan at 30 years or more, these specialty ships need to finetune décor and amenities to stay relevant to the cruising public's evolving taste.
But the cruise ship M/V Freewinds is no ordinary ship.
Born as the M/S Bohème and a founding member of the Caribbean cruise shipping industry operating out of Miami, M/V Freewinds has for more than 20 years been owned and operated as the cruise ship for the Church of Scientology, and was a recent recipient of a top to bottom, inside out renovation which qualifies it as one of the finest ship renovations ever.

M/V Freewinds to its crew and caretakers is much more than a ship: it is home, it is a refuge, a place of study and reflection. It was with this frame of mind that – when the decision was made to keep it as the Church of Scientology's aquatic platform for years to come – helped to plan and execute the job.
"This was a historic renovation, as this is one of the first ships to start the cruise shipping business in the Caribbean. To bring a ship like that back to better condition than when she first arrived is unheard of ... it is quite fantastic" said Tomas Tillberg, Tillberg Design U.S., who was responsible for taking the original plans of a land-based architect to their maritime con-

"The level of quality is incredible. Nobody can afford this level of quality anymore." • Jon Ruston, COO and VP Development, Ocean Development Group

"This was a historic renovation, as this is one of the first ships to start the cruise shipping business in the Caribbean. To bring a ship like that back to better condition than when she first arrived is unheard of ...it is quite fantastic" - Tomas Tillberg, Tillberg Design U.S.

Before

Before

Before

After

Starboard Main Engine

Original brass details in the engine room and around the ship were freed from 40 years of paint and restored to original quality by the Freewinds crew.

The engine control room was restored to whole new level, integrating traditional originality with modern graphics and lighting

(Photo Credit: Johny Riert)

34

Maritime Reporter & Engineering News

Maritime Reporter & Engineering News

....tians and overcome ll kinds as soon as the

jeppesen.com

Jeppesen is a Boeing Company

modern-day ..... offering year-round, seven-night cruises

A Nautical Legacy   201

Above Electronic Chart Display and Bridge Information Systems provide for continuous plotting of courses while accounting for all variables of wind, tide, current and potential hazards

The Bridge

"STEP BACK, TAKE A DEEP BREATH AND enjoy the fruits of a tremendous labor, a labor of love." —*Maritime Reporter* on the top-to-bottom renovation of MV *Freewinds*

In evidence thereof is the *Freewinds* bridge bearing all original equipment, but now reflective of an elegance and performance level surpassing even the day when she first set sail in 1988. Thus in addition to twenty-first-century bridge control systems, she also features a lovingly restored engine order telegraph

(inset) and brass Clear View Screens for exceptional clarity notwithstanding pelting rain. She further boasts a fully digitized Kelvin Hughes Radar System for a 96-mile wraparound view and an Auto Identification System providing speed, course and closest point of approach for all nearby vessels over 500 tons. The point: here is the perfect amalgamation to preserve the *Freewinds* heritage while simultaneously propelling well into the future. ▪

Left The resplendent *Freewinds* bridge, intrinsically reflecting the fact she sails with an entire complement of officers qualified to captain any ship of any tonnage on any ocean

MAIN ENGI
STARBOA

Above
Array of
color-coded
pipes
designating
fluid content:
blue for fresh
water, orange for
lubricants and
silver for steam

Right
An utterly classic
original engine
room telegraph
system for
dedicated
communication
with the bridge

Far right
Upon removal
of decades-old
encrusted paint
lay lustrous brass
relief valves and
fittings

Above The computerized central control room for the *Freewinds'* twin marine diesels, each generating 7,000 horsepower and weighing 6,500 tons

Engine Room and Control Room

"To put it simply, there is a passion surrounding this ship that is immeasurable." —*Maritime Reporter*

In fact, however, the passion is indeed measurable—as in 77,000 square feet of pipe and machinery stripped and refurbished to exceed even original luster. Likewise bespeaking of the passion is original brass freed from forty years of paint, 5,400 feet of deck plates replaced and the meticulous machining of new stainless steel.

The result is yet another integration of tradition with twenty-first-century technology. In this case, modern graphics, lighting and electrical equipment make for a *Freewinds* control room that monitors every vital sign at a glance: engine temperature and oil pressure, fuel, water and lubricant levels of all tanks as well as a closed-circuit viewing system. Or to phrase it as many a visiting seaman has phrased it: *"They don't build ships like they used to."* ∎

Decks and Lifeboats

I N THE WORDS OF ANOTHER MARITIME architect, "To bring a ship like that back to better condition than when she first arrived is unheard of...it is quite fantastic."

Witness the synthetic teak decks, cut and grooved to simulate planks but far more corrosion-resistant than original wood.

Witness, too, a *Freewinds* fleet of lifeboats and davits described by maritime safety inspectors as the finest ever seen. Moreover, while a typical cruise ship might dispatch three to four Survival Craftsmen per boat, the *Freewinds* maintains no less than ten sailors capable of treating any seaborne mishap. ∎

Epilogue

While many a decade has passed since L. Ron Hubbard last walked a "heavin' deck," the nautical legacy lives on. Most obviously, it lives in all he authored for seafaring competence and thus all who sail with the Sea Organization. Yet something of that legacy and a little of the legend would also seem reflected in sentiments such as this, a parting word on voyages to come from his final days at the helm:

Start bidding adieu to the loved ones on the beach
and begin to collect our kit and stores.
Button up the last cycles-of-action.
As the old poem says:

I'm curious where the
sun comes up
And think I'll go and see
I've heard the songs the folk
sing here
They sound all tame
to me.

I'm curious where the
sun comes up.
Let's us all go and
look
We've seen here all there
is to see
It's time we raised
the hook.

APPENDIX

GLOSSARY

A

AA box: a telephone box or booth for reaching the *Automobile Association,* a British organization providing help and information to motorists who are members of it. (A comparable organization in the United States is the *AAA,* the American Automobile Association.) Page 174.

abate: diminish or reduce in intensity, amount, etc. Page 9.

Aberdeen: a city in northeastern Scotland on the North Sea. It is an important seaport and the country's largest fishing port. Page 117.

achtung: a German word meaning, literally, *attention.* Used here as an instruction to engine room personnel to *stand by,* be ready to act. (Instructions on the telegraph are in German as it was German made.) Page 204.

across the wind: with the wind on the side of the boat. Sailboats can usually move faster when sailing across the wind than in any other direction. *See also* **run and reach.** Page 69.

adieu: goodbye; farewell. Page 209.

Admiralty: the governmental department or officials in charge of naval affairs, as in England. Page 124.

aerial: also called *antenna,* a metallic piece of equipment used in the sending and receiving of radio signals. Page 56.

aft(er): in, near or toward the back of a boat or ship. Page 33.

aftermost: nearest to the stern of a ship. Page 164.

Agadir: a seaport on the Atlantic Ocean in southwestern Morocco, a major fishing and commercial port despite its proximity to stormy weather of the Atlantic hurricane track. Page 135.

Agana Harbor: a harbor on the western coast of Guam in the northwestern Pacific. Page 7.

aggregation: a total or collection of various things added together. Page 71.

aground, ran: (of a boat or ship) became stuck with the bottom of the boat lodged in the ground or on the shore. Page 44.

air and sea lane(s): a path or course assigned to, or regularly followed by, aircraft (air lane) or ships (sea lane). Page 51.

air, for the: for the fresh air of the outdoors, as distinguished from the stale air in confined spaces. Page 17.

akin: having a similar quality or character. Page 12.

"Alaska Chief, The": a ballad composed by LRH for his Alaskan radio show the "Mail Buoy." "The Alaska Chief" tells of an all-too-typical disaster among the poorly maintained cannery fleets: an explosive mix of gasoline fumes and damp spark plugs. Page 53.

Alaskan Radio Experimental Expedition: a 1,500-mile (2,400-kilometer) voyage conducted under the Explorers Club to map coastlines between the northwestern shores of the continental US and southern Alaska. Page 25.

Alert Bay: a bay on the south side of Cormorant Island, a small island off the coast of British Columbia, Canada, about 200 miles (320 kilometers) northwest of Vancouver. Page 38.

Allied: having to do with the *Allies,* in World War II (1939–1945), the twenty-six nations that fought against the Axis (Germany, Italy and Japan, often with Bulgaria, Hungary and Romania) and, with subsequent additions, signed the charter of the United Nations. The term *Allies* especially applies to Great Britain, the United States and the former Soviet Union. Page 83.

amalgamation: a result of combining different things. Page 203.

amenable: willing to cooperate or accept suggestions; agreeable. Page 182.

American Fiction Guild: a national organization of magazine fiction writers and novelists in the United States. Page 101.

amidships: in the middle part of a boat, midway between the two ends. Page 36.

amphibious: designating a military operation involving the landing of assault troops on a shore by naval ships. Page 124.

anchorage: a place in or near a harbor where boats are *moored,* fixed to one place with cables, chains or an anchor. Page 29.

anchor, weigh: literally, raise the anchor (of a ship), as in preparation for moving. Used figuratively to mean prepare to start something. Page 3.

ancillary: that serves as an aid; assisting. Page 51.

and then some: and much more in addition. Page 8.

annals: historical records. Page 1.

antecedent: something that happens or exists before something else. Page 25.

antifouling paint: a paint used on the bottom of a boat, designed to prevent, reduce or eliminate *fouling,* an accumulation of seaweed, shellfish, etc. Page 54.

Arabian Night's dream: a fanciful hope or idea, similar to the descriptions found in *The Arabian Nights* (also called *A Thousand and One Nights*), a collection of approximately two hundred Persian-Indian-Arabian tales of magic, adventures and immense riches. Page 12.

ARC: Affinity, Reality and Communication (A-R-C) form a triangle that is the common denominator to all of life's activities. These three components are interdependent one upon the other. By way of example one has to have some degree of liking to be able to talk (communicate). Communication is possible only with an agreement (reality) of some kind. And agreement (reality) is possible only where there is Affinity of some kind or type. When one increases Communication, one raises Affinity and Reality. Affinity, Reality and Communication are the components of *Understanding.* Page 178.

arc(s): literally, a curve that forms part of the circumference of a circle or other curved figure. Also, figuratively, a motion that suggests such a curve. Page 51.

ardent: intensely devoted, eager or enthusiastic. Page 75.

a-reek: filled with a very strong and unpleasant smell. Page 44.

armada: a fleet of warships. *Armada* comes from Spanish, meaning a fleet or an army. Page 83.

armchair: with no direct experience or firsthand knowledge. Page 53.

Art Deco: a style of architecture and interior design, most popular in the 1930s, that used geometrical designs and bold colors and outlines. Page 130.

article(s): a section of a legal document that deals with a particular point. Page 19.

Asiatic: short for *Asiatic Station.* A *station* (in full, *naval station*) to which a naval ship or fleet is assigned for duty. *Asiatic Station* refers to any such place located in Asia, such as Guam, Hong Kong, Manila, etc. Page 101.

Asiatic Fleet: one of the three fleets of the United States Navy during the early and mid-twentieth century. The Asiatic Fleet was primarily stationed in the Philippines. Page 7.

askance, with: in a way that shows doubt or suspicion. Page 79.

askew: to one side; out of line; in a crooked position. Page 44.

assayed: tried or attempted. Page 45.

assuaged: satisfied or relieved. Page 62.

astern: in a position behind a specified vessel. Page 45.

asunder: into separate parts; in pieces. Page 12.

athwartship: from one side of a boat or ship to the other. Page 54.

Atlantis: the former name of a large yacht built in Greece at the Hellenic Shipyards by shipping billionaire Stavros Niarchos (1909–1996). Privately owned by the Saudi Arabian Royal Family, *Atlantis* has since been renovated and renamed *Issham Al Baher*. Page 125.

attack-transport: a naval ship for landing assault troops in an amphibious attack. Page 87.

augmented: made (something already developed) greater, as in size, extent or quantity. Page 10.

auspices of, under the: with the approval or support of. Page 200.

Author's League of America: a membership organization for authors and playwrights, founded in New York in 1912. Page 101.

Auto Identification System: an automated electronic tracking system used by ships. Once installed aboard a ship, the system automatically transmits data (such as name, position, course and speed) that can be picked up by ships and shore units within a certain range. The Auto Identification System is mainly used to avoid collisions and for search and rescue operations. Page 203.

auxiliary: a piece of equipment available as a backup or reserve. Page 9.

avidly: with intense eagerness; enthusiastically; dedicatedly. Page 52.

awash: level with or barely above the surface of the water so that waves break over the top. Page 41.

axiomatic: based on or having to do with *axioms,* statements of natural laws on the order of those of the physical sciences. Page 184.

aye, aye: in nautical language, a response to an order or command meaning, "I understand and will obey." *Aye* means yes. Page 94.

Azores: a group of nine Portuguese islands in the North Atlantic, approximately 800 miles (1,300 kilometers) west of Portugal. Page 122.

B

Bahamian: of or relating to the *Bahamas,* a nation consisting of hundreds of islands in the Atlantic Ocean southeast of Florida and north of Cuba. Page 200.

bailing: emptying water out of a boat, using a bucket or similar container. Page 55.

ballad(s): a story in poetic form, often of folk origin and intended to be sung. Page 102.

ballast: literally, a heavy substance placed in the lower part of a ship to ensure its stability. Used figuratively for something incorrect or misleading and which also happens to be heavy so that its only use would be as ballast. Page 31.

ballasted: provided with *ballast,* a heavy substance placed in the lower part of a ship to ensure its stability. Page 25.

bam: imitative of the sound of something hitting a surface with a hard, abrupt blow. Page 31.

bank: count or rely on with confidence. Page 41.

banshee scream: a long, loud, piercing cry, especially expressing extreme emotion or pain, such as from a *banshee,* a female spirit whose wailing, according to Irish legend, warns of an imminent death. Page 57.

bar: a long, raised area of sand below the surface of the water, especially at or near the mouth of a river or harbor entrance, usually formed by moving currents. Page 43.

Barbarossa: Barbarossa II, adopted name of Khair ed-Din (1466?–1546), a pirate who raided ships in the Mediterranean in the 1500s. The younger of two red-bearded brothers (*Barbarossa* means red beard), Khair ed-Din eventually became admiral of the navy of the Ottoman Empire, then centered in what is now Turkey. Page 93.

barometer, falling off of the: the reading on a barometer fell (went lower). A *barometer* is an instrument for measuring the pressure of the atmosphere. Such a reading shows the air pressure is dropping and signals worsening weather. Most storms occur in low-pressure areas. Page 9.

basin: a partially enclosed, sheltered area along a shore, often partly man-made, where boats may be moored. Page 29.

battened down: secured by covering with canvas so as to make a port or hatch watertight, in preparation for a storm. From the word *batten,* a thin, flat length of wood or metal used for various purposes such as to hold the canvas covering over a hatch in place. Page 9.

bay, kept at: prevented from approaching or having an effect. Page 84.

B.C.: an abbreviation for *British Columbia,* a province in western Canada. Page 32.

beacon(s): a radio transmitting station that emits special radio signals for use, such as on a ship, in determining direction or position. Page 51.

beam: the center of the side of a boat or ship at its widest point. Page 42.

beam-ends, on her: (of a boat or ship) rolled so far over on its side that it is in danger of overturning. *Beams* are the strong, horizontal timbers or metal bars that support the deck and hold the sides of a ship in place. When a ship is "on its beam-ends" or if it "beam-ends," it has turned so far over that it is lying on one of its sides. Page 98.

beard: confidently approach or confront a person, especially someone with an exceptional or remarkable reputation. Page 102.

bearing: the direction or position of something relative to a fixed point, normally measured in degrees. Page 51.

bearings: devices that support, guide and reduce the friction of motion between fixed and moving machine parts. Page 117.

becalmed: (of a sailing vessel) caused to stop moving because of lack of wind. Page 26.

before the elements: in the presence of, or when confronted by, the forces of the weather, such as wind, cold, rain or sunshine, especially when thought of as harsh and damaging. Page 189.

behooves: is right and proper or appropriate for somebody; necessary for. Page 156.

belaying pin: a short, removable wooden or metal pin fitted in a hole in the rail of a boat and used for securing a rope. Page 47.

beleaguered: threatened with difficulties. Page 65.

Belfast: the capital and largest city of Northern Ireland, in the eastern part of the country. Traditionally a chief area for shipbuilding, especially in the early 1900s. Page 125.

Bella Bella: a community on the east coast of Campbell Island, located in the Central Coast region of British Columbia, Canada, and home to the *Heiltsuk First Nation,* a Native North American people of the region. The town is also called *New Bella Bella* to distinguish it from *Old Bella Bella,* an earlier settlement, located to the southeast on Denny Island. Page 41.

belligerent: taking part in warfare. Page 3.

below: on, in or toward a lower level, such as a lower deck of a ship. Page 44.

bend on sail: fasten or extend the sail. Page 33.

benzine: a colorless, flammable, liquid mixture of various chemicals obtained from crude oil and often used as a solvent. Page 63.

Bering Strait: a narrow stretch of sea between Russia and Alaska that connects the northernmost part of the Pacific Ocean to the Arctic Ocean, named for Danish navigator and explorer Vitus Bering (1680?–1741). At its narrowest point, the strait is 51 miles (82 kilometers) wide. Page 9.

Bermuda ketch: a *Bermuda* is a tall triangular sail. A *Bermuda ketch* is a small sailing vessel rigged with Bermuda fore-and-aft sails, with a large mainmast toward the bow and a smaller mast toward the stern. Page 117.

beset: filled with or having many obstructions that can block or cause damage. Page 46.

bespeak: be a sign or indication of. Page 188.

better to, the: so as to do the specified thing more effectively. Used humorously. Page 29.

bidding: saying something as a farewell. Page 209.

bilge(s): the bottommost interior part of a boat or ship, where water collects. Page 63.

bilge water: water that collects in the bilge of a boat or ship through leakage or otherwise. *See also* **bilge(s).** Page 47.

bill: the list, usually placed on a board or chart, with the names of a ship's crew, showing each person's duties and position for various ship functions. Page 118.

binnacle: a fixed case that supports and protects a ship's magnetic compass. Page 105.

bitts: the strong posts firmly fastened in pairs in the deck of a ship, for fastening cables and ropes. Page 98.

Black Flag: also *Jolly Roger* or *Skull and Bones,* a flag used by a pirate ship, often with a white skull and two long, crossed bones on a black background. Such a flag was raised on approaching a merchant ship to cause an immediate surrender. Page 19.

blackjack(s): a short, leather-covered club, consisting of a heavy head on a flexible handle, used as a weapon. Page 71.

block: a system of two or more pulleys (wheels with a grooved rim around which a cord or rope passes) in a frame, with a hook, loop, etc., for attachment. Blocks with ropes running through them can be used on a boat to raise or move heavy objects, such as sails. Page 70.

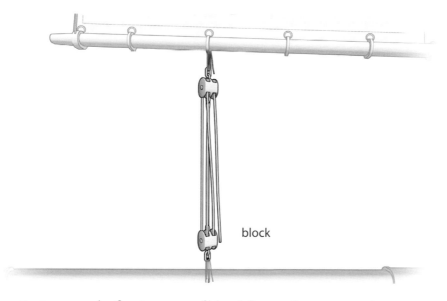

block

blood, draws first: causes the first instance of blood flow, as from a wound. Page 19.

blowie: the sound of something exploding. Page 63.

bludgeoned: forced to do, think or view something in a certain way as if hit with a *bludgeon,* a short club. Page 91.

boards, by the: over the side of the boat and into the sea. The term *boards* refers to the side of a boat or ship made of wooden boards. Page 47.

boat deck: the deck from which a ship's lifeboats are launched. Page 181.

Boats: a name used for the *bosun,* an officer on a ship whose job is to supervise maintenance of the ship and its equipment, including the boats, such as the lifeboats. Page 94.

boiler house: an enclosed structure on the upper deck of a ship, located above the boiler and engine room. A *boiler* is a large tank in which water is heated and stored, either as hot water or as steam, and used for heating or generating power. Page 117.

boiling along: cutting through the water, the motion of the boat creating swirls and bubbles, likened to the action of water as it boils. Page 27.

Bonaire: an island in the southern Caribbean Sea off the coast of Venezuela and part of the Netherlands. It is a popular tourist destination. Page 200.

book, the whole: the entire body of rules or procedures relevant to a situation. Page 175.

boom: a long pole extending from a mast to which the bottom edge of a sail is attached to hold the sail at an advantageous angle to the wind. Page 69.

booming: moving rapidly with a loud, deep sound. Page 105.

boot: a recruit undergoing basic training in the United States Navy. Page 92.

born of: brought into existence from; created or developed because of. Page 20.

bosom: the broad, expansive surface of the sea. Page 33.

bounded: having limits; limited (in knowledge, imagination, viewpoint, experience, etc.). Page 92.

bowling: moving smoothly and quickly. Page 44.

bow, on the: in a direction within 45 degrees of the point directly ahead, on either side of a vessel. The *bow* is the front part of a vessel. Page 164.

bow(s): a nautical term for the front (forward) part of a vessel. Page 9.

bracket: establish the limits of something that is varying, such as a signal, so as to locate its source. Page 57.

branding iron: a long-handled metal rod, one end of which is heated in a fire for treating wounds by cauterizing or for burning a distinctive mark (brand) on livestock to indicate ownership. *See also* **cauterize.** Page 17.

brawny: powerful and muscular. Page 15.

breaks out: (of an anchor) becomes dislodged from the bottom. Page 72.

breast: contend with or advance against; meet or oppose boldly; confront. Page 3.

breath-catching: astonishing or awe-inspiring, as if causing one to momentarily hold (catch) one's breath in surprise, wonder or the like. Page 135.

Bremerton: a city in western Washington, a state in the northwest United States, on the Pacific coast. The large US Naval Yard in Bremerton was established in 1891 and provides maintenance for every class of naval vessel. Page 8.

Bridge: in Scientology, the precise route to higher states of existence, also referred to as The Bridge to Total Freedom. Man, in his religious tradition, has long imagined a bridge across the chasm between where he is now and a higher plateau of existence. Today, Scientology has a bridge which spans the chasm and brings one to a higher plateau. It is an exact route with precise procedures providing uniformly predictable spiritual gains when correctly applied. The Bridge is complete and can be walked with certainty. Page 199.

bridge: 1. an elevated platform built crosswise above the upper deck of a ship, from which the ship is navigated and from where all activities of the ship are controlled by the Captain. Page 8.
2. any of several related card games played between four players who play in two teams. Thirteen cards are dealt face down, one at a time, to each player, in a clockwise fashion. In each round of play, the players lay down one card in turn and, of the four cards on the table, the highest card wins the round. Page 8.

bridge lamp: a small floor lamp, usually with an adjustable arm. Page 58.

bridge wing: a section at the side of a ship's bridge that contains a small shelter closed on three sides for protection against weather, used by lookouts on watch. Page 120.

brig: a military slang term for a jail. Originally referring to a jail on board a ship, the term came to be applied as slang for any military or naval prison. Page 83.

Bristol fashion: in good order, as in the expression *"all things shipshape and Bristol fashion,"* literally meaning that everything on board a ship is properly stowed (put away) and the ship is fully ready to go to sea. From the city of Bristol, in southwestern England, a major port with a reputation for efficiency and proper order of its shipping in the days of sail. Page 53.

Britannia: HMY (Her Majesty's Yacht) *Britannia,* the former royal yacht of the British monarch, Queen Elizabeth II. Built in Scotland, the ship was launched by the queen in 1953 and was used for hundreds of state visits until retirement in 1997. Since then *Britannia* has been an exhibition ship, moored in Edinburgh, Scotland. Page 125.

British Columbia: a province in western Canada on the Pacific coast. Page 44.

brute: involving physical force. Page 125.

B.S.: an abbreviation for the degree of *Bachelor of Science,* for studies in science and technology. Page 101.

buccaneer(s): any of the adventurers preying upon Spanish ships and settlements, especially in the West Indies in the seventeenth century. Page 11.

buck: a plunge or leap, likened to a horse that is bucking. Page 164.

Buckskin Brigades: a novel by L. Ron Hubbard, published (1937) by The Macaulay Publishing Company and hailed as a first-ever authentic description of Native North American people and way of life. Page 101.

bulkhead: any of various wall-like constructions inside a vessel, as for forming watertight compartments, subdividing space or strengthening the structure. Page 98.

bullhorn: a portable device that consists of a hand-held microphone with a cone-shaped speaker attached, used for amplifying the voice. Page 120.

buoy(s): an object floating in water but securely anchored to the bottom and acting as a navigational marker. Buoys are floating aids to navigation. They mark channels (passageways for boats or ships), safe waterways and dangerous areas such as rocks, shallow waters and wrecks. They come in different shapes, sizes and colors, have various colored and timed flashing lights, sometimes have a whistle, gong or bell (for foggy areas) and sometimes have numbers and letters on them. Buoys are marked on a navigation chart with their descriptions. A navigator can also confirm his location in the water by identifying a buoy and locating it on a chart. Page 31.

Burgess: Samuel Burgess, a pirate and slave trader of the late 1600s and early 1700s. In 1701 he was convicted of piracy but was later pardoned and was eventually killed in Madagascar, off the southeast coast of Africa. Page 105.

burst from a truck: (of a flag) suddenly raised to the top of a mast, just below the *truck,* a circular or square cap of wood fixed on the top of a mast, usually with small holes through which a rope can be run for raising a flag. Pirates would raise their flag on approaching a merchant ship to cause an immediate surrender. Page 19.

button up: complete (something). Page 209.

buzzard: a slang term for a person, especially one who is bad-tempered, mean or unpleasant. Page 103.

C

cabin boy: a boy acting as servant to the officers and cabin passengers of a ship. Page 89.

Cabin Cruiser: a power-driven boat having a cabin equipped for sleeping, cooking and the like. Page 107.

cable: a strong metal or wire rope used for lifting, pulling, towing or securing things. Page 117.

cable length: a nautical unit of length equivalent to 720 feet (219 meters) in the United States. Page 36.

cadge: obtain by imposing on another's generosity or friendship; beg. Page 161.

Cádiz: a seaport in southwestern Spain, on a bay of the Atlantic. Page 193.

calculating: marked by secret intentions to do something wrong. Page 120.

calking: material used to make a boat watertight by filling in its seams (small cracks where the edges of two pieces of wood touch each other). Page 33.

calling: one's job, profession or trade. Page 53.

campaign(s): a series of military operations in one area over a particular period, intended to achieve a specific objective. Page 125.

Campbell, Malcolm: (1885–1948) English journalist and racing enthusiast of automobiles, motorcycles and boats. Campbell held world speed records on land and on water during the 1920s and 1930s. Page 77.

canvas: a sail or sails of a sailing vessel. Page 10.

canvas, under all plain: with the normally used sails raised. *Plain canvas* or *plain sail* refers to the sails that a ship normally uses, as distinct from additional sails that are used only in light winds. Page 101.

Cape Cod Instrument Company: an instrument manufacturer that produced radio direction finders and other navigation equipment during the 1940s. The company was located on the southern coast of Cape Cod (off the coast of Massachusetts). Page 57.

Capital Ship: a ship that belongs to the largest class of warships, using the most powerful weapons and often including more than a thousand crew members and as many as one hundred officers. Page 42.

Capital Yacht Club: a private yacht club located at Washington Channel, a channel parallel to the Potomac River in the southwestern part of the city of Washington, DC. Page 106.

capsized: overturned on the surface of the water. Page 26.

carbon tetrachloride: a clear, nonflammable, highly toxic liquid that will not mix with water. It is used in fire extinguishers. Page 65.

carburetor: a device in an engine that mixes liquid fuel and air to give the correct explosive mixture for the engine to generate power. Page 69.

Cardena Bay: a bay located on the south coast of Kennedy Island, approximately 15 miles (24 kilometers) south of the city of Prince Rupert, British Columbia, Canada. Page 44.

careen: (of a ship) lean over on one side; tilt. Page 164.

Caribbean Motion Picture Expedition: a voyage organized in the early 1930s by L. Ron Hubbard aboard the sailing vessel *Doris Hamlin*. With roughly fifty students sailing with him, L. Ron Hubbard toured and captured on film a number of picturesque Caribbean ports. Page 1.

caroming off: striking and rebounding, as a ball when striking a wall and bouncing off. Page 47.

carrier: of an *aircraft carrier,* a warship equipped with a large open deck for the taking off and landing of warplanes and with facilities to carry, service and arm them. Page 123.

carvel-built: of a boat or ship, built with the planks meeting flush (level so as to form an even surface) at the seams instead of overlapping. Page 53.

case: the way a person responds to the world around him by reason of his aberrations (departures from rational thought or behavior). Page 185.

case-in-point: that is a relevant example or illustration of something. Page 154.

Castile and León: two early kingdoms—Castile (north and central Spain) and León (northwestern Spain)—that joined in the thirteenth century, forming a large part of the current country of Spain. The flag of Castile and León, which dates from 1230, incorporates the golden castles of Castile with the red lions of León. Page 12.

casting, one-piece: an object made by *casting,* pouring hot metal into a mold (shaped container) and allowing the metal to cool so that it keeps the shape of the mold. A *one-piece casting* is an object made using a single mold. Page 77.

cast off: untie the ropes securing a boat to its mooring so that it can move away. Page 55.

Catalina: also *Santa Catalina,* an island lying 20 miles (30 kilometers) off the coast of Southern California. Page 100.

cat-o-nine: short for *cat-o'-nine-tails (cat of nine tails),* a whip with nine knotted branches, or *tails,* used for whipping as a form of punishment. Until 1881, this was an authorized instrument of punishment in the British navy and army. Page 14.

cauterize: in treating a wound, burn with a hot *iron,* a long-handled metal rod, one end of which is heated in a fire. The hot iron can be placed against a wound whose edges are held together. Cauterizing (burning) the flesh closes up the cut and stops the bleeding. Page 17.

celestial navigation: the art and science of navigating by the stars, Sun, Moon and planets. It is one of the oldest of human arts. Page 8.

celluloid: a tough plastic that can be molded when subjected to heat, such as that used to make the frames of eyeglasses. Page 51.

Chacon: short for *Cape Chacon,* the southeastern point of Prince of Wales Island, Alaska. Ketchikan is further north, on an adjacent island. Page 68.

chafe: (of an object) rub abrasively against another. Page 64.

chain broadcast station: a local radio station linked by wire or radio relay to other stations, usually for simultaneous broadcasting of the same program, the entire group of stations often called a *network.* Page 56.

chain shot: a kind of ammunition fired from cannon and consisting of two balls or half balls connected by a short chain. After firing, the chain would extend to its full length as the shot swept through the target. Primarily designed to destroy the masts and sails of enemy ships. Page 17.

Charlotte: a reference to *Queen Charlotte Sound. See also* **Queen Charlotte Sound.** Page 45.

chart, off the: not shown on a chart, a reference to sailing in areas where no charts exist because no one has explored and drawn them. Page 135.

chart reckoning: the action of calculating the position of a ship on the sea with reference to a *chart,* a map showing coastlines, water depths or other information relevant to navigators. Page 120.

chart room: a room on board a ship for storing and working with charts, navigational instruments, etc. Page 128.

Chatham: Chatham Sound, a narrow body of water north of the city of Prince Rupert, British Columbia, Canada. A *sound* is a narrow body of water lying between the mainland and an island or connecting two larger bodies of water. *See also* **Prince Rupert.** Page 45.

Cherokee: a Native American people who originally occupied lands in southeastern parts of the United States and now live mainly in Oklahoma and North Carolina. Page 94.

Chief Officer: the officer of a ship, next in command beneath the Captain. Page 160.

choppy: of a sea characterized by waves that are breaking in short, abrupt movements due to a strong wind, a change of wind, etc. Page 43.

Chris-Craft: a brand of powerboats. Page 106.

Christie & Wilson: a firm that was located in Glasgow, Scotland, makers of nautical instruments, such as compasses, barometers and chronometers. Page 32.

chronometers: timepieces that meet certain strict standards of accuracy. The *chronometer* (*chrono-* means time and *-meter* means measure) was created to fulfill the need of navigators for a very accurate timepiece by which to determine their position while at sea. Page 98.

Chrysler: a large manufacturing company, organized in 1925 by US auto manufacturer Walter Percy Chrysler (1875–1940). From their automaking base, the company began making marine engines in the late 1920s and eventually grew to become one of the largest firms for marine engines. Page 107.

chunk of change: an informal way of saying "a large amount of money." Page 56.

Church of England: the established church in England, a Christian church formed in the early 1500s under the king of England, Henry VIII. The Church of England is ruled by bishops and has the reigning monarch as its head. Page 105.

Church of Scientology of California: an earlier nonprofit corporation of the Church of Scientology, founded in 1954, and a senior ecclesiastic body until the formation of the *Church of Scientology International,* mother church of the Scientology religion. Page 125.

circumnavigate: sail all the way around the Earth. Page 3.

circumvent: avoid by anticipating or outwitting; overcome or avoid the intent, effect or force of. Page 189.

cirrus clouds: clouds with a wispy, featherlike appearance. Cirrus clouds are composed of ice crystals and found at average levels of 5 miles (8 kilometers) above the Earth. Page 9.

cite(d): mention, especially as an example of what one is saying. Page 8.

civil engineering: the engineering field dealing with the design and construction of public structures, such as roads, bridges, canals, dams and harbors. Page 101.

Class I, II, III, etc.: a reference to a boat classification system based on the length of a vessel, ranging from Class I, less than 16 feet (4.9 meters), to Class IV, 40 feet (12.2 meters) and longer. Such classification affects the required number of fire extinguishers, lights and life vests. Page 63.

Clear View Screen: a glass disk mounted in a bridge window and equipped with a motor that spins the disk at high speed to disperse rain, spray and snow. It can also be heated to prevent formation of ice. Brass is used for the frame because it resists corrosion. Page 203.

clew: the lower corner of a sail. For a sail that extends lengthwise, the *clew* is the corner that is closer to the back of the boat. With a rope (called a *sheet*) attached to the clew, a sailor can hold the sail at an advantageous angle to the wind. Page 69.

closed-circuit: of or relating to a *closed-circuit television system,* in which the signals are transmitted from one or more cameras by cable to a restricted group of monitors (television receiving sets), usually to view some special event taking place remote from the viewers. Page 205.

clove: divided into two parts by a cutting blow; split. Page 12.

Coast Guard: the branch of the armed forces that is responsible for coastal defense, protection of life and property at sea, and enforcement of customs, immigration and navigation laws. Page 63.

Coast Pilot: an official government publication for sailors, providing descriptions of coastal waters, dangers, harbor facilities, etc. A *pilot* in nautical terms means something that serves as a guide through some unknown place or through a dangerous, difficult or unknown course. Page 32.

cockpit: an enclosure at the stern of a vessel where the tiller is located. Page 33.

coldcocking: striking so as to make unconscious. Page 71.

Collins transmitter: a radio broadcast transmitter produced by the *Collins Radio Company,* one of the United States' foremost designers and producers of high-quality radio equipment, founded in 1933. A *transmitter* is a device that generates radio waves carrying messages or signals and sends them out from an antenna. Page 56.

colonials: residents of a colony who come from the colonizing country. A *colony* is a country or area under the political control of another country and occupied by settlers from that country. Page 8.

colonization: also *colony,* a country or area under the political control of another country and occupied by settlers from that country. Page 13.

colors: a flag of a country, ship, organization, etc., often used for identification. Page 19.

Columbia: a ship that was part of the *Columbia Coast Mission,* a group of several such vessels, crewed by ministers and medical personnel and delivering medical and social services. The Columbia Coast Mission was formed in the early 1900s and, until the late 1960s, sent vessels out to regularly visit the remote settlements of British Columbia's coasts. Page 36.

Columbia River: a waterway more than 1,200 miles (1,900 kilometers) long that starts in southwestern Canada and flows through Washington and Oregon in the northwestern United States. Page 85.

combers: long, high waves that roll over or crash onto a beach. Page 100.

come what may: whatever happens. Page 74.

coming about: turning around. Page 47.

coming, had it: deserved what was experienced or suffered. Page 14.

comm: short for *communication.* Page 182.

commandante(s): a commanding officer, especially the military governor of a fortress, town or district. Often used as a title in French, Spanish or Portuguese. Page 12.

commemorative: honoring the memory of a person or an event. Page 1.

commensurately: in a manner that corresponds in size or degree to something else; proportionately. Page 25.

Commissioning Day: the day on which a ship of the United States Navy is officially accepted for service. Commissioning occurs after the ship has been equipped and manned, her officers appointed, and she is in readiness for active service. Page 81.

Commissioning pennant: in the United States Navy, a long, narrow flag that is blue at the wider end with seven white stars and then tapers into two long, horizontal stripes, one red and one white. The commissioning pennant is flown from a warship to signify that the vessel is officially a part of the US Navy. *See also* **Commissioning Day.** Page 88.

comm lines: short for *communication lines,* the routes along which communication travels from one person to another; the lines on which particles flow; any sequence through which a message of any character may go. *"Long and short comm lines"* refers to the distance of the comm line (long or short) that the communication travels to reach the other end. Page 182.

Commodore: a title for an officer ranking above a captain who commands several vessels. Page 1.

companionway: a staircase or ladder between decks on a ship or leading from a deck to the cabins or area below. Page 62.

company: also called *ship's company,* a ship's crew, including the officers. Page 18.

compass card: a freely turning circular disk to which the compass needle is fixed so the compass card always points north. It is mounted inside the compass and is marked with the points of direction (north, east, south, west) and the 360 degrees of the circle. Page 170.

compass course: a course steered by the line of direction indicated by a compass. Page 165.

compass, (magnetic): a device for finding direction, having a magnetic needle that is free to move and that always points toward the north. Page 36.

compass points: the points on a compass that show positions marked north, south, east and west plus the intermediate points, such as NE (*northeast,* the point between north and east), NNE (*north-northeast,* the point between north and northeast), etc. Page 165.

compendium: a collection of concise, but detailed, information that lays out the important features of a particular subject. Page 154.

compensatory: making up for (something undesirable) by exerting an opposite force or effect; offsetting errors or miscalculations. Page 51.

complement: a number or quantity that constitutes a complete group. Page 85.

Con: a shortened form of *Conning Officer. See also* **Conning Officer.** Page 184.

conflagration: a destructive fire, usually an extensive one. Page 200.

Conning Officer: the person in charge of directing the ship's movements, posted directly below the Captain of the ship. At sea the Conning Officer is totally responsible for the safety of the ship, the comfort and stability of the vessel and its economical progress toward its destination. Page 160.

connived: cooperated secretly in wrongdoing. Page 14.

Consolidated Edison: the company that provides electricity to New York City and surrounding areas. *Consolidated* refers to a number of businesses or business activities that combine into a single unit or entity. Page 59.

consternation: a feeling of alarm, confusion or dismay, often caused by something unexpected. Page 65.

constituency: the degree of firmness with which the particles of a substance hold or stick together. Page 38.

Constitution: a United States Navy sailing ship, originally launched (1797) from Boston, Massachusetts, where the ship is based. As a US Navy vessel, it is the world's oldest warship afloat. Page 15.

contrary: opposite in direction. For example, *contrary tides* are tides that flow in a direction opposite to the way a ship needs to travel. Page 107.

Cook, Captain: John Cook, or Cooke (?–1684), a buccaneer of the 1680s. After participating in raids in the Caribbean, he set out for the west coast of Africa, where he took a ship, the *Bachelor's Delight*. Sailing around the Horn and collecting other vessels along the way, he used his fleet to raid Spanish towns and ships on the west coast of South and Central America. *See also* **Horn.** Page 14.

cordage: ropes or cords, such as those used in a ship's rigging. Page 66.

Corfu: an island that is part of Greece; the northernmost of the *Ionian Islands,* a group of islands that lie off the northwestern coast of Greece and southwestern coast of Albania. Page 117.

corkscrews: moves in a twisting or winding course like a corkscrew. Page 46.

Cornish coast: the coast of *Cornwall,* the southwesternmost county of England, a peninsula bordered on three sides by the sea. The coast is lined with steep, rocky cliffs. Off the coast of the westernmost part of the county, Land's End, lie dangerous reefs. Page 120.

corvette(s): a lightly armed, fast ship used especially during World War II (1939–1945) to accompany a group of supply ships and protect them from attack by enemy submarines. Page 3.

coughed up the ghosts: stopped or quit doing some activity. Literally, died. Page 45.

counts: particular crimes that a person is accused of. Page 83.

coursing: moving or traveling swiftly on or as if on a certain path. Page 120.

covelet: a very small *cove,* a curved part of a coast that partly encloses a sheltered area of water. Page 31.

cowtailed: characteristic of a *cow's tail,* a nautical slang term for a frayed end of a rope where the strands have come apart. Page 190.

Coxswain: a person who is in charge of a boat and its crew. Page 159.

cracking on: energetically raising (a sail). Page 46.

Craig: a town and fishing port in the southern part of Alaska, approximately 56 miles (90 kilometers) northwest of Ketchikan. Page 68.

crankcase(s): the metal casing that encloses the crankshaft and other moving parts at the lower part of an engine. *See also* **crankshaft.** Page 45.

crankshaft: a rod within an engine that creates the motion needed to turn a boat's propellers. Page 70.

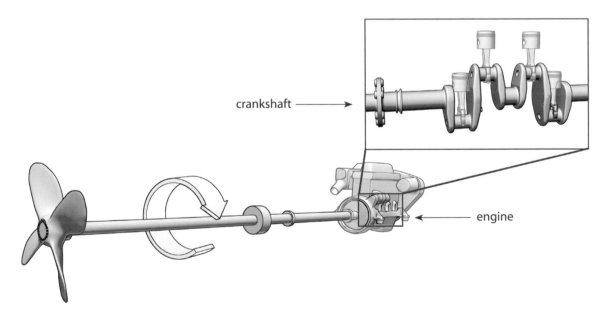

crankshaft

engine

cresting: reaching the top of something. Page 122.

crooning: singing in a soft, low voice. Page 56.

cropped up: appeared, especially suddenly or unexpectedly. Page 19.

crow's nest: a partly enclosed platform for a lookout on a ship, usually at the top of the foremast. Page 8.

cruiser: also called *cabin cruiser,* a power-driven boat having a cabin equipped for sleeping, cooking and the like. Page 31.

cruising range: the maximum distance that the fuel capacity of a vessel will allow it to travel at cruising speed. Page 26.

crystal set: a type of radio receiver built in the early 1900s that worked without batteries or any other source of power. Instead, it used a crystal that could receive radio waves transmitted from a radio station and convert them into audible sounds. Under good conditions a crystal receiver could pick up a radio signal from 1,000 miles (1,600 kilometers) away. Page 57.

Culebra: a small island belonging to Puerto Rico and lying about 18 miles (29 kilometers) east of the larger island, midway between Puerto Rico and St. Thomas. *Culebra* means snake in Spanish. The island served as a hideout for buccaneers and pirates, including such well-known characters as Henry Morgan. Page 18.

Curaçao: an island in the southern Caribbean Sea, lying off the coast of Venezuela. The island, an autonomous country within the Kingdom of the Netherlands, is a popular tourist destination. Page 135.

curators: persons in charge of a museum, art collection, etc. Page 1.

cutlass: a short sword with a slightly curved blade, formerly used by sailors. Page 11.

cut such a mark: attracted notice or created a great impression or effect. Page 103.

cutter: a sailboat with a single mast and one large triangular sail, often with one or more small triangular sails attached to or set forward of the mast. In regard to the *Magician,* the boat originally had two masts and was designated as a ketch. With the removal of the shorter rear mast, leaving only the one tall mast, the boat was referred to as a cutter. *See also* **ketch.** Page 29.

cycle(s)-of-action: the sequence that an action goes through, wherein the action is started, is continued for as long as is required and then is completed as planned. Page 209.

cylinder: a chamber in an engine where fuel is ignited, the explosion of which generates the power for moving. Page 31.

D

da Gama, Vasco: (1469?–1524) Portuguese explorer and navigator who discovered the sea route around Africa to India. Page 1.

daunt: lessen the courage of; dishearten. Page 148.

Davis, Edward: English buccaneer of the late 1600s and early 1700s, who was elected captain of the ship *Bachelor's Delight.* Davis raided Spanish towns of the west coast of Central and South America and captured Spanish ships. Davis is regarded as the first of many to have buried vast treasures on Cocos Island, an uninhabited island located 330 miles (523 kilometers) southwest of Costa Rica. Page 14.

davit: a crane that projects over the side of a ship and is used for raising and lowering the ship's lifeboats, cargo, etc. Page 207.

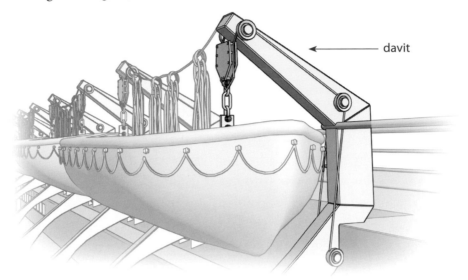

davit

Davy Jones's (locker): in sailors' folklore, *Davy Jones* is the personification of the sea and guardian of the deep. *Davy Jones's locker* means the bottom of the ocean, regarded as his storeroom and the grave of those drowned at sea or buried there. Page 11.

day was won: victory was gained. Page 105.

dead: directly, as in *"dead astern"* or *"dead aft."* Page 151.

dead run: a steady run at top speed. Page 119.

deckhand: a sailor on a boat or ship whose duties are performed mostly on the deck. Page 27.

deck officer(s): an officer responsible for tasks such as navigation, cargo handling, etc., that take place on a ship's main deck. Page 199.

decorated: given a medal or other honor or award to acknowledge bravery, dedication or achievement. Page 125.

decreed: commanded (something); ordered or assigned authoritatively. Page 31.

ded-reckoning: a simple method of determining the approximate position of a ship. It is done by charting its course and speed from a known fixed position (such as a shoreline or lighthouse, or from the last position calculated for the ship) and, from there, plotting a course based on speed and distance traveled, with as accurate allowance as possible being made for wind, currents, compass errors, etc. (*Ded* is short for *deduced,* arrived at by reasoning.) Page 51.

deep, the: the sea. Page 33.

deign: think it worthy of oneself (to do something); think fit. Page 33.

De Jure Maritimo et Navali: a work on maritime law, including discussion of privateers and piracy, translated as *Of Maritime and Naval Law: or, A Treatise of Maritime Affairs, and of Commerce.*

Written by Irish lawyer Charles Molloy (1640?–1690), the book was first published in 1676 with subsequent editions appearing during the next hundred years. Page 13.

Department of Commerce: a department of the United States Government established in 1903 with the purpose to promote the nation's economic development and technological advancement. During the early 1900s, one of the department's functions was issuing licenses to *masters,* those in command of nonnaval ships. This function was later assigned to the US Coast Guard. Page 3.

Department of Homeland Security: a department of the United States Government established in 2003 with the purpose to ensure the safety of the nation. The department oversees the security at the country's borders and transportation systems, ensures adequate preparations exist for terrorist attacks and natural disasters and also directs the US Coast Guard. Page 200.

deplore: condemn as wrong; disapprove of strongly. Page 11.

depth charge: a large can filled with explosive material designed to sink and explode at a certain depth, used to destroy submarines. Page 85.

dereliction: the fact of deliberately not doing what one ought to do, especially when it is part of one's job. Page 83.

despotic: unjustly cruel, harsh or severe. Page 18.

devil, raise the: make a commotion or disturbance. Page 59.

Dianetics: Dianetics is a forerunner and substudy of Scientology. Dianetics means "through the mind" or "through the soul" (from Greek *dia,* through, and *nous,* mind or soul). Dianetics is further defined as what the mind or soul is doing to the body. Page 90.

dinghy: any small boat, especially one that is towed behind or carried on a larger boat. Page 27.

dingle: a small, secluded, wooded valley. Page 43.

dingy: of a dark, dull or dirty color; lacking brightness. Page 36.

dint of, by the: by the force of. Page 175.

discharge: the action of being relieved from duty, as from the military; being granted permission to leave. Page 15.

distillation: something that has been refined by having essential elements discovered or brought to view. Page 118.

distress flare: a bright blaze of light or fire used as an emergency signal to indicate that a ship is in distress (in danger or in trouble, as from fire, taking on water or the like) and that help is needed. Page 120.

"Dive Bomber": the title of a story written by L. Ron Hubbard in the late 1930s and used by Warner Brothers (a major Hollywood film production company) in producing a movie of the same title, released in 1941. Page 102.

divination: the methods or practice of attempting to foretell the future or discover the unknown through omens or supernatural powers. Page 29.

division: a group of several ships of similar type, forming a unit under a single command in the United States Navy. Page 84.

Dixie Belle: a name for a boat, made up of *Dixie,* an informal name for the Southern states of the United States, and *belle,* a beautiful girl or woman. Page 107.

dogfish tired: a humorous variation and intensification of *dog-tired,* utterly exhausted and worn out. Page 44.

dogwatch: on a ship, either of two short evening watches (or the persons holding these watches). A watch is usually four hours long, but the dog watches are two hours, 4:00 to 6:00 and 6:00 to 8:00. This schedule permits sailors on these watches to have their dinner. Also used to refer to any night watch or night shift. Page 120.

doling out: distributing something. Page 18.

Dollar Steamship Line: a San Francisco–based shipping company founded in 1901 by the Scottish-born industrialist Robert Dollar (1844–1932). At its height in the 1920s, it was the largest and most successful steamship line in the United States and was known around the world. Page 7.

"Donald Duck" navy: after the attack on Pearl Harbor by the Japanese (7 December 1941), many Americans joined the US Navy and the Coast Guard Reserve. Often they were assigned to newly constructed submarine chasers, patrol craft, gunboats, tugboats, converted yachts and other small craft. During World War II (1939–1945), most of these craft never had names, only numbers, and the crew members of this fleet of small craft dubbed it the "Donald Duck" navy. Page 83.

Don(s): (in Spanish-speaking countries) a lord or gentleman. Page 13.

drag: the resistance experienced by a boat or ship moving through a fluid. Page 76.

Drake: Sir Francis Drake (ca. 1540–1596), an English navigator and admiral. He was the first English person to sail around the globe and famous for his adventures in the Caribbean, stealing a fortune in gold from the Spanish. Page 93.

draw: (of a boat or ship) sink to a specified depth in floating. Page 31.

drawl: a way of speaking in which the speaker draws out the vowel sounds and pronounces words slowly, characteristic of the speech of the southern part of the United States. Page 33.

draws first blood: causes the first instance of blood flow, as from a wound. Page 19.

drift: logs, sticks, boards, masses of wood, etc., that are floating on the water. Page 79.

drive (something) home: make a point strongly or firmly. *Drive,* in this case, means press or urge onward; bring about by urgency or pressure. *Home* here means to the vital center or seat; to the very heart or root of the matter. Page 17.

dry rot: a decay that causes wood to become brittle and crumble to powder. Page 55.

dubbed: given a name, often a descriptive nickname. Page 27.

dunno: a spelling of *don't know* representing an informal pronunciation. Page 29.

Dutchman: a ship of the Netherlands or run by people from the Netherlands. Page 105.

Dutch, war with the: the series of three wars between England and the Netherlands (1652–1654, 1665–1667, 1672–1674). Concerned over growing Dutch naval power, England hoped to seize the shipping and trading leadership from the Dutch. However, despite a number of key English victories, the attempt was unsuccessful. Page 105.

E

Ease her: a command given to the Helmsman on a ship instructing him to reduce the degrees of the turn of the ship slightly so as to cause a less abrupt movement. Page 170.

easy terms, on (such): in a friendly relationship that presents few difficulties and is free from worry or problems. Page 123.

eddy: a movement in a flowing stream, as of water, in which the current doubles back to form a small whirl. Page 36.

1812: a reference to the *War of 1812,* a conflict between the United States and Britain over the rights of the US at sea that lasted from 1812 to 1815. Page 85.

elbow grease: energetic labor, from the traditional idea that vigorous rubbing is the best thing to use when polishing furniture. Page 201.

elbows rub better, make the: associate more smoothly with others. Page 159.

Electronic Chart Display and Bridge Information Systems: also *Electronic Chart Display and Information System* (abbreviated *ECDIS*), a computer-based navigation information system that complies with regulations of the United Nations' agency for maritime affairs, the *International Maritime Organization.* An ECDIS not only displays information based on continuous plotting of the ship's motion, but also can integrate additional information, such as from the *Auto Identification System,* which shows information about the location and course of other ships. *See also* **Auto Identification System** and **International Maritime Organization (IMO).** Page 203.

elements, before the: in the presence of, or when confronted by, the forces of the weather, such as wind, cold, rain or sunshine, especially when thought of as harsh and damaging. Page 189.

Elliott Bay: the body of water on which Seattle, Washington, is located. Page 56.

Embarcadero: a waterfront section in San Francisco, from *embarcadero,* an American-Spanish term meaning a wharf or landing place. Page 7.

engineer, radio: a skilled technician in that branch of electrical engineering concerned with the construction, operation and maintenance of radio equipment. Page 56.

engine hatch: the covering (hatch) over the opening in the boat's deck that leads to the engine compartment. Page 36.

engine order telegraph: also called *engine room telegraph,* either of the devices, located on the bridge and in the engine room of a ship, used to communicate desired engine speed between the two locations. The engine order telegraph consists of a dial, pointer and bell, with a handle for moving the pointer. When bridge personnel wish to change speed, they move the handle on the bridge's telegraph to the desired speed. This in turn moves the pointer on the telegraph in the engine room to point to the speed desired on its dial, so that the engine room staff can make the change. Page 203.

engine room: the space in the ship where the engines and other machinery are located. Page 52.

enjoin: urge or impose with authority; enforce. Page 90.

ensign: 1. a low-ranking naval officer. Page 8.

2. a flag that shows the nationality of the ship it is flown on. Page 48.

"Ensign, Under the Black": an LRH story first published in *Five-Novels Monthly* magazine in August 1935, this pirate adventure is set in the Caribbean during the seventeenth century. An *ensign* is a flag that shows the nationality of the ship it is flown on. The *black ensign,* also called *black flag,* was traditionally flown by a pirate ship and often showed a white skull and two long, crossed bones on a black background. Page 10.

epitaph: a brief statement, such as a phrase or sentence, commemorating or summarizing a deceased person or something past. Page 63.

espies: suddenly sees and recognizes something at a distance. Page 120.

essayed: tried or attempted. Page 33.

essence, of the: of the highest importance for achieving something. Page 75.

ETA: an abbreviation for *Estimated Time of Arrival.* Page 109.

Ethics Order: an order issued under the authority of an executive of the organization giving details of any action done that is contrary to the best interests of the group and ordering a corrective action such as applying ethics conditions, cramming, amends, etc. An Ethics Order is usually issued by seniors on their juniors, but may be issued by any crew member on another crew member if authorized by an officer. Page 160.

eve of, the: the period leading up to an important event or special occasion. Page 34.

every man jack: every single person. *Jack* here means a common fellow or boy. Page 92.

evinced: revealed the presence of; indicated (a quality). Page 52.

evolution: an exercise or maneuver carried out according to a plan and for which various crew have a specific function—for example, tying the ship up at a dock. Page 118.

Execution Dock: a place for conducting hangings of pirates, from the original Execution Dock on the shore of the Thames River in London, where pirates and others guilty of murder at sea were hanged. Page 12.

exec(utive officer): the officer second in command of a naval ship. Page 8.

Explorers Club: an organization, headquartered in New York and founded in 1904, devoted exclusively to promoting the science of exploration. To further this aim, it provides grants for those who wish to participate in field research projects and expeditions. It has provided logistical support for some of the twentieth century's most daring expeditions. L. Ron Hubbard was a lifetime member of the Explorers Club. Page 25.

Explorers Club flag: a flag awarded to active members of the Explorers Club who are in command of, or serving with, expeditions that further the cause of exploration and field science. Since 1918 the Explorers Club flag has been carried on hundreds of expeditions, including those to both North and South Poles, the summit of Mount Everest and the surface of the Moon. Many famous persons in history have carried the Explorers Club flag, including L. Ron Hubbard. Page 25.

Express Cruiser: a type of cabin cruiser capable of traveling at very high speeds. *See also* **Cabin Cruiser.** Page 107.

F

fairway: the usual course taken by vessels through a harbor or coastal waters. Page 31.

fallen in with: joined in with; sided with. Page 12.

fathom(s): a unit of length equal to 6 feet (1.8 meters), used chiefly in nautical measurements. Page 31.

favored (by): had the advantage of. Page 41.

ferryboat: a boat used to transport passengers, vehicles or goods across water, such as one operating regularly across a river. Page 174.

Ferry Building: a well-known building in San Francisco with a famous clock tower. It is a terminal for ferryboats that carry passengers between the city of San Francisco and other points along San Francisco Bay. Page 7.

fertig mit motor: a German phrase meaning *finished with engine,* an instruction to engine room personnel to stop the engine, such as by stopping fuel pumps so that fuel is no longer flowing to the engine. (Instructions on the telegraph are in German as it was German made.) Page 204.

fiction, pulp: the adventure, science fiction, cowboy stories and the like published during the early 1900s. Produced in magazines printed on inexpensive, rough-surfaced paper, pulp fiction had a wide audience. Page 10.

fiend(s): an evil and cruel person. Page 18.

Fife: a reference to Alexander Selkirk (1676–1721), the buccaneer of Fife, a region in Scotland. As a crew member on a buccaneer voyage, Selkirk was put ashore on an island off the coast of Chile, where he lived alone from 1704 until rescued in 1709. Page 105.

fight, not yet begun to: an allusion to a famous line by American naval hero John Paul Jones (1747–1792) as he was fighting a British ship larger and better armed than his own. Jones maneuvered his vessel alongside the British one until the two ships were so close that their rigging became entangled and the muzzles of their guns touched each other. Jones's ship sustained heavy damages, but when the British commander asked if the Americans wanted to surrender, Jones is said to have replied, "I have not yet begun to fight!" After three hours of terrible hand-to-hand fighting, Jones and his crew captured the British ship, though their own was so badly damaged it sank the next day. Page 89.

fin: a fixed vertical surface, such as at the tail of an aircraft, for providing stability. Page 69.

fine point of business: work to be done that is handled in a precise form. Page 43.

fireroom: a compartment in a ship containing the boilers. A *boiler* is a large tank in which water is heated and stored, either as hot water or as steam, and used for generating power in the engine of the ship. Page 7.

first blood, draws: causes the first instance of blood flow, as from a wound. Page 19.

1st (First) Officer: the Captain's second-in-command on a merchant ship or any nonnaval vessel. Page 89.

Fisher Research Laboratories: a pioneering electronics and instrumentation research and design company founded in 1931 in Palo Alto, California, near San Francisco. The company was hired by the US Navy around 1933 to develop radio direction finders for one of its aircraft. The company went on to design and produce many sophisticated radio communication and detection products. Page 57.

fishpot: a reference to a fishing boat in poor condition. Literally, a *fishpot* is a basket that is sunk in the water with a float attached, used for catching crabs, lobsters, etc. Page 55.

fitting: a small, often standardized, part or piece of equipment that is used to join, adjust or adapt other parts. Page 64.

fix: the position (as of a ship) obtained by bearings of fixed objects, by observation of heavenly bodies or by radio means. Page 51.

fixed-pitched: a reference to a type of propeller, the blades of which are at a fixed and unchangeable angle as they rotate in the water. Propellers also exist with a variable pitch, allowing the angle of the propeller blades to be adjusted and providing greater and more immediate control of ship speed. *Pitch* here refers to the angle a propeller blade makes to the water. Page 122.

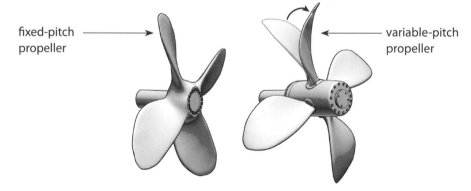

fixed-pitch propeller   variable-pitch propeller

flag bag: also called a *flag locker,* a trunklike container with numerous compartments, made for holding the various types of flags used aboard a ship. Page 98.

Flag Officer: an officer above the rank of Captain who is entitled to display a flag that indicates rank. Page 160.

Flags: a name used for the person on the ship whose job is to handle the flags, including signal flags (also called *code flags,* flags used to exchange messages between ships at sea, the distinctive pattern of each flag symbolizing a particular letter, word or phrase); national flags (flags designated as the distinctive flag of a nation), etc. Page 94.

Flagship: a ship carrying a *Flag Officer,* an officer in command of a group of ships, and which displays the officer's flag. During the 1960s and 1970s, with L. Ron Hubbard conducting research aboard the *Apollo,* this ship became the Flagship of the Sea Organization. *See also* **Sea Organization.** Page 1.

flat: stretched as to be tight, as in *"sails trimmed flat."* Page 25.

flight deck: the upper deck of an aircraft carrier, constructed and equipped for the landing and takeoff of aircraft. Page 123.

float(s): a platform that floats in the water and is anchored at or near the shore and used especially as a place for mooring boats. Page 32.

flog: beat with a whip as punishment. Page 15.

flood tiding: increasing as the water does during a *flood tide,* the increasing and inflowing water of the rising tide. Page 33.

flood, with the: with the rise or flowing in of the tide. Page 35.

flotilla: a group of vessels united under, and commanded by, one officer. Page 106.

flotsam: material or refuse floating on water. Page 98.

flounced: as if decorated with a *flounce,* a wide ornamental strip of material gathered into pleats and sewn to a garment. Page 39.

floundered: had become stuck or disabled on rocks, deep mud, etc., and was struggling awkwardly and ineffectively to move. Page 120.

flourishes: ornamental flowing curves used in decoration. Page 130.

fluke: a piece of good luck; something good that happens by chance. Page 13.

flying bridge: a small, open deck with a wide view, located above the bridge and containing a compass and other equipment for those on watch, for navigation or the like. Page 165.

flying jib: the outer or outermost of two or more jibs (triangular sails). Page 10.

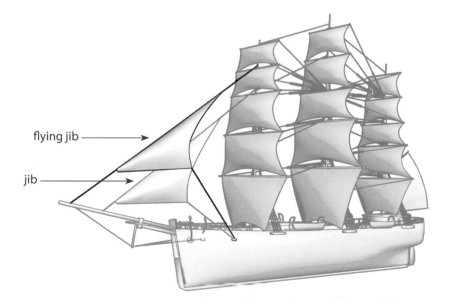

flying jib

jib

fo'c'sle: short for *forecastle,* a raised section of deck at the bow of a ship. From the name of a raised, castlelike deck on some early sailing vessels, built to overlook and control the enemy's deck. Page 181.

folklore: the traditional beliefs, legends, customs, etc., of a people. Page 102.

followed the sea: engaged in or practiced the career or occupation of being a sailor. Page 12.

following wind: a wind that is moving in the direction of the ship's course. Page 70.

foot: the bottom edge of a sail. Page 69.

fore and aft: lengthwise on a boat or ship. Page 54.

foredeck: the front part of the main deck of a ship. Page 83.

forefoot: the frontmost end of the ship's keel. Page 101.

foresail: a large sail that is the principal sail on a *foremast,* the mast nearest the front of the ship. Page 10.

42nd and Broadway: a major intersection of two well-known streets, Broadway and 42nd Street, in the heart of New York City, New York. This intersection forms *Times Square,* a busy entertainment center with crowds of pedestrians, bright lights, shops, restaurants and theaters. Page 18.

foundered: caused (a boat) to become filled with water and sink. Page 68.

Founding Church: the Founding Church of Scientology, Washington, DC, established in 1955. A *founding church* is one from which other churches have their origin or derive their authority. Page 106.

four-poster: a bed whose tall, often carved, corner posts were originally designed to support curtains or a canopy. Page 17.

foyer: an entrance hall, lobby or other open area. Page 130.

framat: a Swedish word meaning *ahead* or *forward.* (Instructions on the telegraph are in Swedish as it was Swedish made.) Page 129.

frazzled: worn to threads or shreds; frayed. Page 54.

freebooting: acting as a *freebooter,* an adventurer or one who goes about in search of plunder. Page 12.

free-roving: going or traveling about anywhere, especially over a wide area. Page 100.

freighter: a large ship for carrying cargo (goods transported for pay). Page 83.

freshen: (of the wind) increase in strength. Page 38.

fruitcake, nutty as a: crazy, eccentric or mentally abnormal. This American expression dates back to 1920. A *fruitcake* is a type of cake containing a lot of dried or candied fruits and nuts. *Nutty* here means crazy, so a person who is nutty as a fruitcake would be quite crazy. Page 59.

fruitless: producing no effect or result; useless. Page 13.

fruits: the benefits or advantages of an activity. Page 203.

fuel, dirty: unfiltered or incorrectly filtered engine fuel, containing impurities and particles that get into the engine, resulting in poor engine performance. Page 174.

full-rigged: literally, having all equipment. Used figuratively. Page 92.

full speed: (on a boat or ship) the speed normally maintained while sailing. Page 31.

G

gaff: a pole with a hook on the end, used to pull large fish out of the water. Page 31.

galleon(s): a large three-masted sailing ship used between the fifteenth and eighteenth centuries. Page 1.

galley: a kitchen or an area with kitchen facilities on a ship. Page 64.

game (at): play games of chance to try to win money; gamble. Page 19.

gamut: the entire scale or range of something. Page 200.

gangrene: decay of tissue in a part of the body when the blood supply is obstructed by injury, disease, etc. Page 20.

gangway: 1. a narrow, movable platform or ramp forming a bridge by which to board or leave a ship. Page 15.

2. used to indicate to people in a crowd that they should make way because somebody is coming through. Page 94.

ganz langsam: a German phrase meaning *dead slow,* the minimum possible speed, which is just enough to permit the ship to be steered. (Instructions on the telegraph are in German as it was German made.) Page 204.

garb: a style of clothing, especially official or other distinctive clothing. Page 105.

gave (one's) all: put a lot of effort into doing something. Page 15.

George Washington U.: George Washington University, a private university founded in 1821, in the city of Washington, DC. Named after the first president of the United States, George Washington (1732–1799), it maintains various schools of education, including the School of Engineering and Applied Science and the Columbian College of Arts and Sciences. Page 101.

Georgia, Straits of: also *Strait of Georgia,* a body of water between Vancouver Island and the mainland of southwestern British Columbia, Canada, approximately 150 miles (240 kilometers) long and up to 30 miles (50 kilometers) wide. Page 32.

ghosting: (of a boat or ship) sailing quietly with, or as if with, no apparent wind. Page 48.

ghosts, coughed up the: stopped or quit doing some activity. Literally, died. Page 45.

give out: come to an end. Page 46.

give way: help to make (a ship or boat) move through the water. Page 69.

glassy: (of water) having a smooth surface and looking like glass. Page 35.

gleaning: learning, discovering or finding out, usually little by little. Page 10.

glider: an aircraft without an engine that flies by riding air currents. Page 101.

godsend: an unexpected thing or event that is particularly welcome and timely, as if sent by God. Page 85.

going was tough: the progress of an activity was difficult or slow. Page 105.

gore: blood in the thickened state after having been shed from wounds. Used figuratively. Page 44.

gouts: masses or splashes of something gaseous or composed of fine particles; spurts. Page 62.

Government Cut: a man-made channel that connects the Miami, Florida, harbor with the ocean. The channel was dug in the early 1900s after approval from the US Government. Page 101.

Grand Banks: fishing grounds located in the North Atlantic, southeast of Newfoundland, an island off the east coast of Canada. Page 84.

Grand Canaries: the *Canary Islands,* a group of islands in the Atlantic Ocean near the northwest coast of Africa, forming a region of Spain. Page 117.

gray rollers: a reference to the waves (rollers) of a stormy (gray) sea. Page 9.

Great Depression: a drastic decline in the world economy starting in the United States, resulting in mass unemployment and widespread poverty that lasted from 1929 until 1939. Page 10.

green: lacking in experience, especially because of being new to something. Page 89.

green-scummed: covered with a layer of green freshwater algae on the surface of stagnant water. Page 11.

green water: also *green seas,* solid waves of water coming aboard a ship, so called from the green color of a mass or sheet of water that is too large to be broken up into small drops of spray. Page 33.

grind valves: a *valve* is a device with a spring that opens or closes to control the flow of gas into an engine. When the valve opens, the spring pulls it closed again. Valves are used to seal a container so that a liquid or gas can only enter it and not escape. *Grinding valves* is done to smooth the surfaces of the valve by removing surface defects, carbon deposits, etc., to create a tighter seal and thus better engine performance. Page 29.

grommet: a small, round hole, as in canvas, with its inner part reinforced to prevent wear, for a rope to run through. Reinforcing the inner part of the hole can consist of stitching with strong thread, sometimes with the addition of a piece of leather. Page 70.

gross ton: a measurement of the total internal capacity of a ship. Page 125.

ground: 1. smoothed the surface of something, such as a mechanical part, by rubbing against something rough to remove unwanted substances on the surface. *See also* **grind valves.** Page 29.
2. also *grounds,* an area in a body of water, such as an area with large groups of fish and where fishing is usually good (a fishing ground) or an area for some other activity, such as waiting (a waiting ground). Page 42.

grounded: ran a boat or ship onto the ground, especially a shore, rocks or the bottom of shallow water. Page 120.

Guam: an island in the northwestern Pacific Ocean, a territory of the United States and site of US air and naval bases. Page 7.

guild: an association of people for the pursuit of a common goal. Page 101.

guile: a cunning, deceitful and treacherous quality or type of behavior, or particular skill and cleverness in tricking or deceiving people. Page 63.

Gulf Stream: a warm ocean current of the North Atlantic Ocean about 50 miles (80 kilometers) wide, flowing from the Gulf of Mexico along the East Coast of the United States as far north as Canada, and then turning and continuing toward northwestern Europe. Page 101.

gulp, at a: all at once, in a single action. Literally, *gulp* means swallow something quickly or in large mouthfuls. Page 35.

gunboat: a small, armed warship, used in ports where the water is shallow. Page 35.

gun (type extinguisher): a type of fire extinguisher that uses cartridge-type refills containing a fire-retardant material that is discharged at a fire to put it out. Such an extinguisher resembles a gun in that it shoots a single round and must then be reloaded. Page 63.

gunwale: the top edge of a ship's sides that forms a ledge around the whole ship above the deck. Page 43.

gunwales under: with the gunwales submerged in the water. *See also* **gunwale.** Page 45.

gusting: suddenly blowing very hard. Page 33.

guts: the inner or central parts (of something). Page 43.

H

hair's width, to a: within a very small margin or width. Page 56.

hairy: dangerous and causing anxiety or fright. Page 193.

halb: a German word meaning *half* (speed). (Instructions on the telegraph are in German as it was German made.) Page 204.

half-caste: of mixed European and Asian descent. Page 9.

halliard(s): also *halyard,* a rope used for raising and lowering something on a ship, such as a sail, flag or the like. Page 174.

hallowed: regarded with great respect or reverence. Page 25.

halyard(s): also *halliard,* a rope used for raising and lowering something on a ship, such as a sail, flag or the like. Page 101.

hand, nasty: a hand, a single round in a card game, that is difficult to deal with or worrying (to one's opponents). Page 8.

hand(s): a sailor belonging to the crew of a boat or ship. The phrase *all hands* means the whole crew. Page 36.

hapless: unlucky or unfortunate. Page 200.

Harbor Island: an island in Elliott Bay, the body of water on which Seattle, Washington, is located. It is used for commercial and industrial activities. Page 56.

harbor master: an official who supervises and administers the general activities of a harbor or port and enforces its regulations. Page 200.

hard on our starboard beam: in a direction that is on the right side of a vessel (as one faces forward). Page 44.

hard-won: achieved only after much effort and difficulty. Page 10.

Harland and Wolff: a company founded in the 1860s in Belfast, Northern Ireland. Expanding with shipyards in Scotland and England, the company built hundreds of ships for commercial and military purposes. Beginning in the late 1900s, Harland and Wolff branched into the design and construction of other types of large projects, such as bridges, offshore oil platforms and wind generating stations. Page 125.

Harley-Davidson 1200: a type of large motorcycle made for highway touring, manufactured by *Harley-Davidson Motorcycles.* The numeral *1200* (for 1200 cubic centimeters) refers to the size of the engine and indicates a large, powerful engine. Page 192.

harlot: a disreputable woman; a prostitute. Used figuratively in reference to the difficult sailing conditions of the Queen Charlotte Sound. *See also* **Queen Charlotte Sound.** Page 45.

hat: slang for the title and work of a job or position; taken from the fact that in many professions, such as railroading, the type of hat worn is the badge of the job. Page 188.

haughty: unpleasantly proud and behaving in a superior way, as if emphasizing (one's) importance and making less of others. Page 12.

hauled wake: moved rapidly, as if pulling the wake along behind. The *wake* is the visible trail (of agitated and disturbed water) left by something, such as a boat or a ship, moving through water. Page 39.

haunts: places frequently visited. Page 10.

Havana: the capital, port and largest city of *Cuba,* an independent country in the Caribbean, made up of the island of Cuba and more than one thousand smaller islands. Page 100.

hawser: a large rope for mooring or towing a ship or securing it at a dock. Page 71.

haze: harass or try to embarrass. Page 161.

head: the closed, detachable end of a cylinder in an engine. *See also* **cylinder.** Page 29.

headland(s): a high point of land or rock reaching out into the water beyond the line of coast, especially one that is strikingly visible, as from a distance. Page 35.

head sea: waves coming from directly ahead. Page 163.

head to the sea, put a ship's: position the bow (head) of a ship so as to directly face or point toward the oncoming waves (sea). Page 164.

head wind: a wind blowing from directly in front. Page 43.

heard tell: learned of or been informed about something. Page 1.

heart in the throat: characterized by anxious or fearful feelings, used in reference to the violent beating and apparent leaping of the heart due to a sudden startle or frightening situation. Page 39.

heavin': a shortening of *heaving,* rising and falling rhythmically. Page 3.

heel: lean over to one side, as a boat or ship in a high wind. Page 26.

heels would have swung, (one's): a reference to a person being executed by hanging. Page 12.

Helena: city and capital of Montana, a state in the northwestern United States bordering on Canada. Page 8.

hellion(s): a loud, disorderly troublemaker. Page 17.

helm: guide or steer with, or as if with, a *helm,* the wheel or other mechanism by which a ship is steered. Page 1.

helm balanced: the *helm* is the wheel or other mechanism by which a ship is steered. Having the *helm balanced* means that the helm is positioned to direct the vessel efficiently in relation to the direction of the wind. For example, balancing the helm would mean not steering the vessel so close to the direction of the wind that the vessel tends to lean over to the side. Page 149.

Helmsman: the person in charge of steering a ship. The Helmsman is stationed at the *helm,* the wheel by which the ship is steered. Also called *Steersman.* Page 123.

Herreshoff: a traditional anchor designed for better penetration of hard sea floors. Page 72.

herring rake: a device used to catch *herring,* a small, silvery food fish of northern seas. The rake is shaped like a long oar, having sharpened nails on the wider end. This end is swished through the water and the herring are caught on the nails. Page 71.

hied: made (one's) way; progressed. Page 38.

high-compression: a type of engine using intense pressure to compress a mixture of air and fuel to create more power than regular engines. Page 106.

high-water marks: figuratively, the highest points reached of intensity, excellence or the like; literally, the marks showing the greatest height to which water has risen, as that made by the tide. Page 7.

Hispaniola: also called *Santo Domingo,* an island in the Caribbean Sea, lying between Cuba and Puerto Rico. Christopher Columbus landed there in 1492 and named it *La Isla Española,* the Spanish Island. Page 12.

Ho!: an exclamation used on boats and ships to call attention to the place for which the vessel is heading; hence, generally, with a sense of destination. Page 46.

hold: the interior of a ship below decks, especially the cargo compartment of a ship. Page 17.

holding out: withholding something expected or due. Page 18.

hold (one's) own: maintain (one's) position against an opposing force of any kind. Page 18.

holds good: proves to be, or continues to be, valid; proves true or applicable over time. *Holds* means maintains (a condition, situation, course of action, etc.) over time. Page 182.

Hollander: a ship of the Netherlands. Page 105.

home port: the port from which a ship normally operates and where it is docked between trips. Page 7.

honey chile: characteristic of the slow, pleasant speech of states in the southern United States, such as Georgia, where the phrase *honey chile (honey child)* is commonly used to express affection. *See also* **Georgia, Straits of.** Page 33.

honorably discharged: having been discharged (granted permission to leave) from the armed forces with a commendable record. Page 83.

hoodwinking: tricking or deceiving by false appearance. A *hood* is a loose covering over the head that sometimes blocks vision and the term *hoodwink* originally meant to blindfold. Page 71.

hook(s): another term for an anchor. Page 38.

hoops: figuratively, sounds with a regular, repeated pattern, as of rising and falling volume. Page 38.

Horn: *Cape Horn,* the southernmost tip of South America, at the southern end of a small island (Horn Island). Storms, strong currents and icebergs make passage around Cape Horn extremely hazardous. A *cape* is a point of land that projects out into water. Page 14.

Hornigold: Benjamin Hornigold (?–1719), an English pirate of the early 1700s. Hornigold avoided robbing English ships. He eventually commanded five pirate vessels before accepting a pardon in 1717. He hunted pirates until he disappeared during a hurricane in 1719. Page 105.

hot: that has not had time to lose its freshness. Used in reference to waves created in the wake of large steamers. Page 31.

housebreaker: a person who breaks into and enters a house to commit robbery. Page 18.

Howard Bond yacht basin: a yacht basin that was located in the harbor of Miami, Florida. A *basin* is a partially enclosed, sheltered area along a shore, often partly man-made, where boats may be moored. Page 101.

hulking: of great size or powerful build. Page 117.

hull: the hollow, lowermost portion of a ship, floating partially submerged and supporting the remainder of the ship. Page 25.

Hurricane Ten: the name given to the last of ten hurricanes and tropical storms recorded during the 1970 Atlantic hurricane season. Hurricane Ten formed on 20 October 1970 west of the *Azores,* a group of islands in the North Atlantic that are located about 800 miles (1,300 kilometers) west of Portugal. By 27 October the storm became a hurricane, with winds greater than 75 miles (120 kilometers) per hour. Page 122.

husbandry: management of affairs in any activity, especially involving careful management and conservation of resources. Page 3.

hydroelectric engineer: a person trained in generating electricity by using the force of flowing water. For example, water falling from a height, such as from a reservoir held behind a dam, is used to drive equipment that in turn creates electricity. Page 77.

Hydrographic Office: a section of the Department of the Navy charged with making hydrographic surveys and publishing charts and other information for naval and commercial vessels, information key to national defense. *Hydrographic* means of or relating to the scientific charting, description and analysis of the physical conditions, boundaries and flow of oceans, lakes, rivers, etc. Page 25.

I

idled: moved slowly, with the engine operating at a low speed. Page 33.

ignominiously: in a humiliating or degrading manner. Page 45.

imbibe: take in or receive with the senses or mind. Page 92.

imperial: having to do with *imperialism,* the policy or action by which one country controls another country or territory, using military means to gain economic and political advantages. Page 11.

imperialists: people who support and follow a policy of imperialism. *See also* **imperial.** Page 19.

impressed: forced to serve in a navy or army. Page 17.

inaugural: of or relating to a ceremony to open or mark the beginning of something. Page 83.

incontrovertible: not open to question or dispute; undeniable. Page 148.

incumbent upon: resting upon as a duty or obligation. Page 106.

Indies: a shortened form of *West Indies,* a large group of islands between North America and South America in the North Atlantic. Page 103.

inextricably: so closely linked to a person, place or thing that it cannot be considered separately. Page 3.

ink, in the: figuratively, in the darkness. From the literal meaning of *ink.* Page 48.

inlet: a narrow strip of water extending into a body of land from a sea, ocean, river, lake, etc.; small bay. Page 43.

innocent of: completely lacking (in something, such as a particular substance, quality or the like). Page 10.

inside passage: a natural protected waterway in northwestern North America, 950 miles (1,500 kilometers) long. It extends along the coast from Seattle, Washington, past British Columbia, Canada, to southern Alaska. The passage is comprised of a series of channels running between the mainland and a string of islands. Page 3.

International Code: an international communications system used at sea by means of flags, the distinctive pattern of each flag symbolizing a particular letter, word or phrase. Page 160.

International Maritime Organization (IMO): an agency of the United Nations created (1948) to develop international standards and treaties covering such areas as maritime safety, security of shipping and prevention of marine pollution by ships. Page 199.

in tow: figuratively, under discussion, as if being pulled out for examination. From the literal meaning of *tow,* use a vehicle or boat to pull (another vehicle or boat). Page 68.

Intracoastal Waterway: a system of protected waterways, including rivers, bays and canals, in the southeastern and eastern United States. It consists of natural and artificial channels along the coast of western Florida. Using the Intracoastal Waterway enables smaller vessels to sail in protected areas along the coast of the Gulf of Mexico and the Atlantic coast. The system is about 2,500 to 3,000 miles (4,023 to 4,828 kilometers) long. Page 109.

inversely proportional: of or concerning a relationship between two quantities in which one increases in the exact proportion as the other decreases. Page 33.

Irish Sea: an arm of the Atlantic Ocean, between Ireland on the west and Great Britain on the east. It connects to the Atlantic Ocean through channels on the north and on the south. With a distance of about 140 miles (225 kilometers) at its widest point, the Irish Sea is crossed by numerous vessels traveling between ports on both coasts. Page 125.

iron Mike: a slang term for *auto(matic) pilot,* a control in the steering system of a boat or ship that can be set to keep the vessel on a steady course. Page 109.

iron shot: a solid iron ball for firing from a cannon. Page 17.

issue rhum: a distribution of a ration of rhum. Page 20.

J

jack, every man: every single person. *Jack* here means a common fellow or boy. Page 92.

jar: an act of knocking against something with a sudden blow. Page 64.

Java: the main island of Indonesia, northwest of Australia. Page 3.

jib: a triangular sail set at the bow (front end) of a sailing vessel. *See* **flying jib** for illustration. Page 32.

jib boom: an extended pole that projects from the front of a sailing vessel to support the *jib,* a triangular sail set at the bow (front end) of a sailing vessel. Page 101.

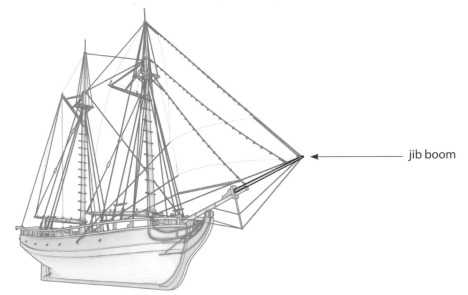

jib boom

jibe: (of a fore-and-aft sail) shift suddenly and with force from one side to the other. This can occur when the wind is behind a sailboat and the direction in which the boat is traveling is changed, causing the sail to swing violently from one side of the boat to the other. The sudden shift of the sail could cause the boat to overturn. Page 164.

jib, flying: the outer or outermost of two or more jibs (triangular sails). *See* **flying jib** for illustration. Page 10.

jib sheet: a rope (sheet) attached to a *jib,* a triangular sail set at the bow (front end) of a sailing vessel. Page 46.

Jolly Roger: also *Skull and Bones* or *Black Flag,* a flag used by a pirate ship, often with a white skull and two long, crossed bones on a black background. Such a flag was raised on approaching a merchant ship to cause an immediate surrender. Page 11.

Jones, John Paul: (1747–1792) Scottish-born American naval officer in the American Revolution, who destroyed or captured numerous British ships. In 1779, while in command of the American ship *Bonhomme Richard,* he defeated the British warship *Serapis* off the English coast in a famous battle. Page 93.

Juan de Fuca, Strait of: a body of water approximately 100 miles (160 kilometers) long and 15–20 miles (24–32 kilometers) wide that stretches east from the Pacific Ocean between northwestern Washington State and southern Vancouver Island, British Columbia, Canada. The strait is noted for having strong winds and a complex system of tides and currents. It is named for a Greek who sailed in the service of Spain and may have visited the passage in 1592. Page 29.

juice: an informal term for electricity or electric power. Page 59.

jump-off: the place where something begins. From the military usage, meaning the place where a planned military attack is to start. Page 41.

K

kedge: an anchor of a traditional design, often of a lighter weight. A traditional anchor has curved arms at one end either one of which dig into the sea bottom when the anchor is lowered. Page 72.

keel: 1. the long piece of wood or steel along the bottom of a boat that forms the major part of its structure and helps to keep the boat balanced in the water. Page 9.
2. a ship or vessel. Page 53.

kelleting: the practice of putting a small, light anchor on the same line that is being used for a heavy anchor, with the lighter one closer to the boat. The weight of the small anchor absorbs sudden pulls on the heavy anchor, preventing the latter from pulling out and dragging on the sea bottom. Page 72.

kelp: a mass or growth of large, cold-water seaweeds, especially *giant kelp* of the Pacific coast of America, which may have hundreds of branches and measure up to 200 feet (60 meters) long. When many kelp grow together, they form underwater forests. Large pieces of kelp sometimes break off and become caught on the bows of passing boats and ships, which greatly increases the drag as the vessel moves through the water. Page 78.

Kelsey Bay, Salmon River: *Kelsey Bay* is a small community located at the mouth of the Salmon River on the northeastern coast of Vancouver Island, British Columbia. Page 36.

Kelvin Hughes: a British company that is a leading designer and supplier of radar and other devices for marine navigation. The firm is known for its technologically advanced equipment and systems. Page 203.

Kennedy: Walter Kennedy (?–1721), an Irish pirate in the Caribbean. After stealing the ship of another pirate, Kennedy sailed for Ireland but, due to his poor navigation, he landed in Scotland. After escaping to London, he was eventually captured and hung for piracy at Execution Dock. Page 18.

ketch: a two-masted sailing boat with sails set lengthwise (fore and aft) and with the mast closer to the front taller than the mast behind. Page 1.

Ketchikan: a seaport in southeastern Alaska, one of the chief ports on Alaska's Pacific coast. Ketchikan is a transportation and communications center. Page 25.

KGBU: the group of letters (termed *call letters*) that identify a radio transmitting station, in this case the public radio station located in Ketchikan, Alaska. Radio KGBU operated from the late 1920s until the early 1940s. It was the second radio station in Alaska. Page 52.

K-gun launcher(s): a mechanism resembling a "K" in shape, mounted on a ship's deck, that launched a single depth charge (canister of explosives) for use against submarines. Page 85.

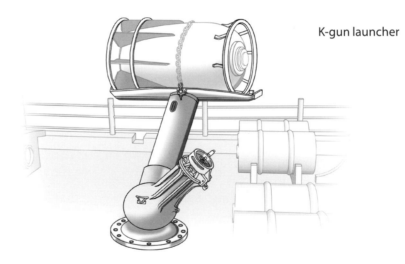

K-gun launcher

Kingston, Jamaica: the capital and chief port of *Jamaica,* an island in the Caribbean Sea, southeast of Cuba. Founded in 1693, Kingston is located on the southeastern coast of the island. Early in his career as a British naval officer, Horatio Nelson was stationed in Jamaica during the late 1770s. *See also* **Nelson.** Page 135.

kissing the cow, old lady said: a variation of the phrase "everyone to his own taste, said the old woman as she kissed the cow," emphasizing the differences in people's personal tastes and opinions.

The phrase was used and popularized by English author Charles Dickens (1812–1870) in his story *The Pickwick Papers* (1836–1837). Page 38.

klar: a Swedish word meaning, literally, *clear,* keep the engine running but not transmitting motion. Used here as an instruction to engine room personnel to stand by, be ready to act. (Instructions on the telegraph are in Swedish as it was Swedish made.) Page 129.

knavish: like or characteristic of a *knave,* a man who is considered dishonest and untrustworthy. Page 19.

knife: progress or move as if with the action of a knife cutting or passing through. Page 151.

knot(s): a unit of speed, one nautical mile per hour, approximately 1.15 land miles (1.85 kilometers) per hour. Page 8.

KOL: one of the first radio stations to broadcast in Seattle, Washington. The station was founded in 1929 and had studios until the mid-1970s. Page 56.

kraft: a Swedish word meaning *power* or *speed.* Hence *half kraft* (half speed); and *full kraft* (full speed), the speed normally maintained while sailing. (Instructions on the telegraph are in Swedish as it was Swedish made.) Page 129.

L

laboring: (of an engine or machine) having difficulty in running or functioning smoothly because of being overloaded, defective or the like. Page 76.

lacing: literally, a beating. Used figuratively to mean severe criticism or disapproval. Page 11.

landfall: an arrival at land on a sea journey. Page 52.

landlocked: confined to land as if by some barrier. Page 10.

landlubber: an informal term for a person who has had little experience at sea or who is unfamiliar with the sea or sailing. Page 118.

land's end: the extreme point of a country or region. Used here in reference to the town of Ketchikan, Alaska, which is located very close to the southern tip of the state. Page 25.

lane(s), air and sea: a path or course assigned to, or regularly followed by, aircraft (air lane) or ships (sea lane). Page 51.

langsam: a German word meaning *slow* (speed). (Instructions on the telegraph are in German as it was German made.) Page 204.

lapping: flowing or moving in small waves against a surface, with a light slapping or splashing sound. Page 117.

larder(s): a large cupboard for storing food. Page 18.

Las Palmas: a city and seaport in the *Canary Islands,* a group of islands in the Atlantic Ocean near the northwest coast of Africa, forming a region of Spain. Page 117.

latitude: the distance measured in degrees of angle of a point on the Earth's surface north or south of the equator. The North Pole is 90 degrees north; the South Pole is 90 degrees south. Latitude along with longitude is used to determine location. Page 51.

Lawley & Son's shipyard: a shipbuilding company in Boston, Massachusetts, that built hundreds of yachts and ships throughout the nineteenth and early twentieth centuries. The company was started in 1866 by George Lawley (1823–1915) and ceased business in 1945. Page 84.

lay-up: a period of time when a ship is not in active use, such as when under repair. Page 79.

lead pellet: a small ball of lead, as for use in a gun. Page 14.

league: a measure of distance, usually about 3 miles (4.8 kilometers). Also used figuratively in reference to any sort of distance, degree, etc. Page 4.

leave, by your: the asking of permission. *Leave* here means permission asked or granted to do something or for some specific course of action or conduct. Page 94.

led: (of electricity) conducted or channeled. Page 60.

lee: the side (as of a ship, island, mountain, etc.) or place that is away from the source of the wind. Page 46.

Lesser Antilles: islands of the West Indies that extend in an arc from Puerto Rico to the northeastern coast of South America. Page 10.

liberty: a period, usually short, during which a sailor is authorized to go ashore. Page 97.

lieutenant-governor: one who substitutes for a *governor,* an appointed official who is in charge of a colony or the like; deputy governor. Page 14.

light: a light to warn ships at sea, such as a *lighthouse,* a tower or other structure containing a light, or a buoy. *See also* **buoy(s).** Page 29.

light globe: another name for a light bulb. Page 65.

light plant(s): any of the large stationary engines produced in the early half of the 1900s as a means of bringing electrical power to rural communities across the United States. In World War II (1939–1945) many electric companies produced light plants to meet military specifications for use on navy vessels. Page 60.

line pluggers: objects that will plug (close up or block) a line (piping for conveying a fluid such as gas, steam, oil, etc., from one location to another). Page 64.

line(s): 1. a cord with a hook or hooks, used in fishing. Page 31.
2. rope, such as a rope used to tie a boat to a dock or a rope tied to an anchor. Page 33.

line, white: rope (line) that is not coated, in contrast to line that is black due to being coated with tar. (Tar is used to preserve lines that are constantly soaked in water.) Page 36.

lint: a soft material for use in treating wounds, made of loosely woven cloth fibers. Page 15.

list, by name and: according to the *prize list,* a list of persons entitled to receive a share of a *prize,* an enemy ship, cargo or property taken or captured by force, such as during wartime. Page 18.

list(ing): (of a boat or ship) an instance of leaning to one side. Page 170.

l'Olonnais: Jean-David Nau (1635?–1668), French pirate active in the Caribbean during the 1660s who used the name François l'Olonnais, from his birthplace in *Les Sables-d'Olonne* (meaning the *Sands of Olonne*), a town on the Atlantic Ocean coast of western France. He led hundreds of pirates in raids against Spanish ships and towns, becoming known as one of the cruelest pirates of the period. Page 11.

longitude: the distance measured in degrees of angle of a point on the Earth's surface east or west of a line that runs from the North Pole to the South Pole through Greenwich, England. A circle (the Earth) is 360 degrees—lines of longitude run from 0 (line through Greenwich) to 180 degrees east (E) and from 0 (line through Greenwich) to 180 degrees west (W). Longitude along with latitude is used to determine location. Page 51.

Long Range Navigation (LORAN): a system by which the position of a ship or aircraft can be determined by the time interval between radio signals received from two or more known stations. A *signal* is a series of energy waves that are modified to carry information. Such a signal can be picked up by a receiver. Page 25.

lookout(s): (on a ship) the crew member with the duty of spotting and reporting on any hazard or danger to the ship. This includes other ships or boats, rocks or any objects in the environment of the ship, conditions of the sea or weather and the like. Page 8.

lore: accumulated facts, traditions or beliefs about a particular subject. Page 100.

low water mark: the level reached by the sea at low tide. Page 54.

Lt.: an abbreviation for *lieutenant,* an officer of middle rank in the United States Navy. Page 8.

lubber line: a fixed mark on a ship's compass that indicates the direction toward which a vessel is, or should be, moving. Page 170.

luffing: (of a sail) flapping when a boat is in a position too close to the direction of the wind. Page 149.

lusting: having an intense desire or need for something. Also, exhibiting intensity and ferocity. Used figuratively. Page 33.

lustrous: having *luster,* the state or quality of shining softly by reflecting light. Page 204.

lying to: staying as nearly stationary as feasible, with the bow directed toward the oncoming wind. Page 164.

M

MacArthur Causeway: a roadway built to connect the city of Miami, located on the mainland of Florida, with islands to the east of the city. Where the causeway crosses a channel, it originally included a drawbridge that permitted parts of the roadway to be raised, allowing boats and ships to pass through. The causeway was later increased in height, eliminating the need for a drawbridge. Page 101.

Madeira: the chief island of the *Madeira Islands,* a group of eight islands that belong to Portugal. They are located off the northwest coast of Africa. The capital of the islands is *Funchal,* a seaport located on the island of Madeira. Page 1.

mail buoy: a *buoy* is an anchored float serving as a navigation mark, to show hazards or for mooring. A "mail buoy" is a prank used on naval ships in which new recruits are told to stand watch at the bow of the ship for a buoy that passing ships supposedly attach mail to. Used humorously as the name of LRH's radio program in Ketchikan, Alaska, a program in which listeners' questions were taken up and answered. Page 52.

Main: short for the *Spanish Main,* the Caribbean Sea or that part of it adjacent to the northern coast of South America, traveled during the sixteenth through eighteenth centuries by Spanish merchant ships that were often harassed by pirates. Page 11.

mainsail: also called *main,* the principal sail of a ship. On a ship with sails set lengthwise (fore and aft), the mainsail is the largest sail. Page 25.

mainstay: a thing that acts as a chief support or part. Page 154.

make: (in traveling) arrive at (a place), which can also include the meaning of arriving when the tide is at a certain point, as in *"make slack water." See also* **slack (water).** Page 33.

make good: carry out or accomplish successfully. Page 149.

make provision: make previous arrangement or preparation for; provide for. Page 70.

Manassas, Va.: a town in northeastern Virginia (abbreviated *Va.*), a state in the eastern United States. Page 101.

manifest: readily perceived by the eye or the understanding; evident; obvious. Page 110.

manner of, all: all sorts or kinds of. Page 13.

man, to a: with no one as an exception; everyone. Page 12.

marauding: roaming about and making sudden small-scale attacks or raids. Page 85.

maritime: relating to the sea, shipping, sailing in ships or living and working at sea. Page 1.

maritime law book: a reference to *De Jure Maritimo et Navali,* a work on maritime law, including discussion of privateers and piracy, translated as *Of Maritime and Naval Law: or, A Treatise of Maritime Affairs, and of Commerce.* Written by Irish lawyer Charles Molloy (1640?–1690), the book was first published in 1676 with subsequent editions appearing during the next hundred years. Page 13.

Maritime Museum, Portuguese: also *Lisbon Maritime Museum,* a museum founded in the mid-1800s, it is one of the premier maritime museums of Europe, with artifacts and models covering the nautical history of Portugal. Page 1.

Maritime Reporter: *Maritime Reporter and Engineering News,* a monthly magazine published in the US and covering the maritime industry. Page 201.

mark, cut such a: attracted notice or created a great impression or effect. Page 103.

marooning: putting ashore and abandoning on a desolate island or coast, a form of punishment used by buccaneers and pirates. Page 18.

Martel: John Martel, Jamaican pirate captain of the early 1700s who plundered vessels off Jamaica. He eventually associated with pirate Walter Kennedy, but was last heard of in 1717 after an attack by an English naval vessel. Page 105.

Martinique: an island in the West Indies, noted for its many volcanic mountains, the highest and most famous being Mount Pelée, which erupted in 1902 (killing about 38,000 people) and again during the late 1920s and early 1930s. During his Caribbean Motion Picture Expedition, one of the islands L. Ron Hubbard visited was Martinique, where he climbed Pelée, his inspection of the peak leading to an encounter with an actual volcanic eruption. Page 102.

mate: as used on ships, an assistant to someone, such as an officer, who can take over the functions of the higher-ranking person. Page 38.

materially: to a great extent; considerably. Page 69.

Maynard: Robert Maynard (1684–1751), lieutenant, later captain, in the Royal Navy. In November 1718 Maynard sailed to Edward Teach's pirate base, located off the coast of North Carolina. In the ensuing battle, Maynard and his men defeated and killed the infamous English pirate. Page 14.

Meet her: a command given to the Helmsman to stop a ship from turning any further. The command is most often used to stop the swing of the vessel's head (forward end) in a turn, as when the vessel is maneuvering in close quarters. When the command is given, the Helmsman turns the wheel in the opposite direction to compensate for the momentum of the original turn. Page 170.

men-o-war: short for *men-of-war*, plural of *man-of-war*, an armed ship belonging to the recognized navy of a country; warship. When *man* is used in combination with another word or words, such as in the term *man-of-war*, it means a ship. Page 13.

merchantman: 1. a sailor on a *merchant ship*, a seagoing ship designed to carry goods, especially for international trade. Page 15.
2. a seagoing ship designed to carry goods, especially for international trade. Page 17.

merchant marines: the officers and crews of the privately or publicly owned commercial vessels of a nation, as distinguished from its navy. Page 14.

mess: a place where a group of people have meals together; also, the group of people who have meals together. Page 94.

meteoric: developing very fast and attracting a lot of attention. Page 106.

meteorological: of or having to do with *meteorology*, the study of the Earth's atmosphere and its phenomena, such as heat, moisture and winds, especially for purposes of forecasting the weather. Page 174.

Metlakatla: a village about 10 miles (16 kilometers) northwest of the city of Prince Rupert, British Columbia, Canada. Page 46.

midshipman: formerly, one of the boys or young men who formed the group from which naval officers were chosen. Page 15.

"Mike," metal: also called *iron Mike*, a slang term for *auto(matic) pilot*, a control in the steering system of a boat or ship that can be set to keep the vessel on a steady course. Page 7.

mill: another term for a typewriter. Page 32.

millrace: a strong current of water flowing in a narrow channel. Literally, a *millrace* is the current of water that drives a mill wheel. The water of the millrace falls against the paddles attached to the mill wheel, pushing the mill wheel around and around. This, in turn, drives machinery, such as large stone wheels used for grinding grain to make flour. Page 43.

millraced: poured or flowed down like a millrace. Page 45.

missionaries: persons sent to another country by a church to spread its faith or to do social and medical work. Page 9.

Mission into Time: the LRH expedition to locales in the Mediterranean, where his memories of former lifetimes led to the uncovering of a number of sites from past civilizations. Page 148.

missive: a letter or written communication. Page 87.

misunderstood word: a word that is not understood or is wrongly understood. Misunderstood words can lead to an inability to perform in the area of the misunderstoods. Clearing up these misunderstood words restores understanding and ability. Page 185.

mock-up: (military) small scale models or objects such as tanks, airplanes, etc., made in order to create an illusion of the real thing, used in planning attacks. A *sailing mock-up* would include the various attributes and activities of a sailor, such as procedures, attitude, know-how and other characteristics associated with old-time sailing ships and their crews. Page 156.

moltenly: in a way that appears to be giving off the great heat of melted metals; so as to glow with great heat. Page 44.

mooched: moved or proceeded along in a slow, quiet way. Page 31.

mooring: a place where a boat or ship is secured with cables, chains, ropes or an anchor. Page 38.

morale: the mental and emotional attitude of an individual or a group; sense of well-being; willingness to get on with it; a sense of common purpose. Page 87.

Morgan, Henry: (1635–1688) Welsh buccaneer who raided Spanish ships and towns of the Caribbean Sea. In 1671, he defeated Spanish troops for control of Panama City, Panama, then the largest Spanish city in Central America. In 1674 he was knighted by English king Charles II and was made lieutenant-governor of Jamaica. Page 10.

Morocco: a kingdom on the northwest coast of Africa, bordering the Mediterranean Sea on the north and the Atlantic Ocean on the west. Page 135.

motive power (force): the mechanical energy, such as force of wind on sails, combustion of fuel in an engine, steam power, electricity, etc., that acts on (something) to move it. Page 68.

motor vessel: also *MV*, a designation for a ship that is driven by an engine. Page 101.

mounted: put into operation or started something, such as a voyage, expedition, campaign or the like. Page 25.

much as, so: used to suggest that something mentioned as a possibility is an extreme case or an unlikely instance. Page 18.

Mutual Broadcast(ing) System: an American radio programing and news network formed in 1934 by a group of independent stations. At its peak, the network had some 950 affiliated radio stations. Page 56.

MV: an abbreviation for *motor vessel,* a designation for a ship that is driven by an engine. Page 203.

myriad: of an indefinitely great number; innumerable. Page 102.

N

name and list, by: according to the *prize list,* a list of persons entitled to receive a share of a *prize,* an enemy ship, cargo or property taken or captured by force, such as during wartime. Page 18.

Nanaimo: a city located on the southeast coast of Vancouver Island, in the province of British Columbia, Canada. Page 32.

narrative: a story or account of events, experiences or the like. Page 27.

nautical mile: a unit of distance used chiefly in navigation, equal to 6,080.20 feet (1,853.25 meters) in the US, now replaced by the international nautical mile, which is 6,076 feet (1,852 meters). Page 78.

Naval Examination vessel: a Canadian naval ship whose function was to meet every ship entering a port; inspect papers, cargo and crew to make sure the ship was doing what she claimed to be doing; and investigate anything suspicious. Page 45.

naval yard: also *navy yard,* a navy-owned *shipyard,* a place where warships are built and repaired. Page 83.

navigation(al): the science of locating the position of ships or aircraft and plotting and directing their course (the route along which a vessel or aircraft proceeds); directing a ship by determining its position, course and distance traveled. Navigation is concerned with finding the way, avoiding collision, meeting schedules, etc. Navigation uses various tools (such as charts; observation of the Sun, Moon and stars; and various electronic and mechanical instruments) and methods to determine a ship's direction and verify its position. Derived from the Latin *navis,* ship, and *agere,* to drive (literally, ship driving). Page 3.

Nelson: Horatio Nelson (1758–1805), England's greatest admiral and naval hero. His victory over the French at the Battle of the Nile (1798) forced Napoleon to withdraw from the Middle East, while his 1805 victory over the combined French and Spanish fleets broke France's naval power and established England's rule of the seas for the rest of the 1800s. Page 93.

Neptune: in Roman mythology, Neptune was the god of the sea, with power over the sea and seafaring. Page 47.

Netherlands Antilles: islands in the Caribbean that are a part of the Kingdom of the Netherlands, having formerly been colonies. Page 135.

Netherlands ketch: a reference to the ketch *Enchanter* (later named *Diana*), which was built in the Netherlands. Page 148.

New Bella Bella: also called *Bella Bella,* a community on the east coast of Campbell Island, located in the Central Coast region of British Columbia, Canada, and home to the *Heiltsuk First Nation,* a Native North American people of the region. There is also an earlier Bella Bella, or *Old Bella Bella,* a community located to the southeast on Denny Island. Page 41.

Nimitz, Chester: (1885–1966) American naval officer who served in the navy during both World War I (1914–1918) and World War II (1939–1945). In December 1941, Nimitz was appointed commander in chief of the US Pacific Fleet and, in 1944, he was promoted to fleet admiral (highest rank of naval officers). Page 51.

nipple, pipe: a short piece of pipe with threads at both ends, used for joining other pipes. *Thread* means the raised line that runs around the end of a pipe or around a screw that allows them to be fixed in place by twisting. Page 36.

NNE: an abbreviation for *north-northeast,* as used with a compass. *See also* **compass points.** Page 165.

North African landings: the combined landings of three groups of Allied troops in western areas of North Africa (Morocco and Algeria), on 8 November 1942. These landings involved hundreds of ships bringing some 65,000 Allied soldiers from the United States and the United Kingdom, the start of the military campaign to take control of North Africa. Page 125.

North Sea: the arm of the Atlantic Ocean lying between the eastern coast of Great Britain and the continent of Europe. Page 117.

nor'wester: a strong wind blowing from the northwest. Page 41.

notion, took a: figuratively, had a sudden impulse or idea. Page 31.

notoriety: famous for some undesirable feature, quality or act. Page 13.

nutty as a fruitcake: crazy, eccentric or mentally abnormal. This American expression dates back to 1920. A *fruitcake* is a type of cake containing a lot of dried or candied fruits and nuts. *Nutty* here means crazy, so a person who is nutty as a fruitcake would be quite crazy. Page 59.

O

obnosis: *obnosis* is a coined term meaning observing the obvious. *Ob-* means toward; *-nosis* means know. It is the action of a person looking at another person or an object and seeing exactly what is there, not a deduction of what might be there from what he does see. Drills developed by LRH are designed to improve a person's ability to observe the obvious. Page 185.

obviate: make unnecessary. Page 39.

octant: an early instrument used by navigators for measuring the angle between a celestial body and the horizon. An octant is operated similarly to a sextant but is a smaller instrument, having an arc that is an eighth of a circle. *See also* **sextant.** Page 102.

ode: a poem, especially one that is written in praise of a particular person, place or event. Page 27.

officer and a gentleman, an: a reference to the commissioning procedure for officers in the United States. A *commission* is a formal government document that empowers someone to serve in a command position, making the individual a commissioned officer. *Commissioned officers* are traditionally defined as officers who have been designated as *officers and gentlemen* by the US Congress on the advice of the president. A gentleman is considered to be civilized, educated, sensitive or well-mannered and US officers are expected to conduct themselves as such. Page 89.

Officer of the Deck (OOD): a ship's officer who is in charge of the safe and proper operation of the ship for an assigned period (as a four-hour watch) while it is in port. At sea he keeps the ship located on the chart at all times and assists the Conning Officer in the product of a safe, comfortable voyage. As the direct representative of the Captain, the OOD is stationed on the bridge while at sea or on the quarterdeck while in port. Page 94.

Officer of the Watch (OOW): the officer primarily responsible for the navigation of a ship, in the absence of the Captain, during a certain watch (a period of time during which one part of a ship's crew is on duty). Page 159.

oil turbines: ship engines that derive power from the burning of oil, which in turn heats water and creates steam that rotates one or more turbines, turning the ship's propellers. Page 8.

Old Man Fire: a personification of fire. The phrase *old man* is often used to show the largeness or significance of the thing specified. Page 62.

Old Man Sea: a personification of the ocean. The phrase *old man* is often used to show the largeness or significance of the thing specified. Page 3.

Old Nick: an informal name for the devil. Page 62.

Old Providence: an island in the western Caribbean Sea, an early English colony (1629) whose original settlers named it *providence,* meaning God's wisdom and guidance. Page 13.

old-time standard: the type, model or example that has been used or practiced over a long period of time. Page 76.

Old World: the part of the world that was known to Europeans before Columbus's first voyage to the Americas (1492), comprising Europe, Asia and Africa. Page 13.

Olympic Mountains: a mountain range in northwestern Washington State. The highest peak is Mount Olympus, which is 7,965 feet (2,428 meters) tall. The lower slopes of the range are heavily forested, while the peaks contain many small glaciers. Page 38.

one-lung: having only one cylinder and therefore low in power. A *cylinder* is a chamber in an engine where fuel is ignited, the explosion of which generates the power that makes the engine run. Page 122.

one-piece casting: an object made by *casting,* pouring hot metal into a mold (shaped container) and allowing the metal to cool so that it keeps the shape of the mold. A *one-piece casting* is an object made using a single mold. Page 77.

OOD: abbreviation for *Officer of the Deck,* a ship's officer who is in charge of the safe and proper operation of the ship for an assigned period (as a four-hour watch) while it is in port. At sea he keeps the ship located on the chart at all times and assists the Conning Officer in the product of a safe, comfortable voyage. As the direct representative of the Captain, the OOD is stationed on the bridge while at sea or on the quarterdeck while in port. Page 160.

OOW: abbreviation for *Officer of the Watch,* the officer primarily responsible for the navigation of a ship, in the absence of the Captain, during a certain watch (a period of time during which one part of a ship's crew is on duty). Page 159.

open-bridge signal: the signal designated by local regulations for boats or ships that require the opening of a bridge to permit passage. Page 101.

"open it up": increase the speed of the engine, a reference to opening the throttle to allow more fuel to enter the engine. Page 192.

Operation and Transport Service: a company of the 1960s and '70s that was involved in ship chartering. Page 125.

Operation Anvil: the code name used for the Allied landings of August 1944 in Southern France. These landings involved more than eight hundred warships, with hundreds of additional ships landing troops ashore. This was the start of a second invasion to win control of France, in support of the June 1944 invasion of Normandy, in the north of France. Page 125.

operations (vessel): a ship used for planning and directing an *operation,* a naval action, mission or maneuver, including its planning and execution; often used in combination with a designating code word. Page 120.

Org: short for *organization,* a group of people that has a more or less constant membership, a body of officers, a purpose and usually a set of regulations. Page 118.

Org Board: short for *Organizing Board,* a board that displays the functions, duties, communication routes, sequences of action and authorities of an organization. It shows the pattern of organizing to obtain a product. Page 118.

orgies: instances of unrestrained indulgence in a particular activity, such as killing. Page 19.

outboard (motor): a portable, detachable, gasoline engine fastened to the back (stern) of a boat and used to propel it forward. Page 53.

outcrop: the part of a rock formation that has emerged through the surface of the ground and is visible. Page 120.

outhaul: a mechanism for *hauling,* pulling a vessel. Page 54.

outside: beyond the boundaries of. Used here in reference to the more open waters outside of, or beyond, the harbor. Page 33.

overarching: embracive and all-encompassing, likened to a curved structure (arch) that spans or extends across the entire width or space of something. Page 106.

oyster, the world's his: the world is the place to gain opportunity or success, as a pearl can be taken from an oyster, an often-quoted phrase first recorded in the play *The Merry Wives of Windsor* (1600) by English poet and playwright William Shakespeare (1564–1616). A character in the play asks an associate for a loan and when refused replies, "Why then, the world's mine [my] oyster, Which I with sword will open." Page 101.

P

pack rat: a reference to the actions of a *pack rat,* a large rat noted for taking small articles to store in its nest and always leaving something in place of what was taken (such as a piece of wood, pine cone, etc.). Used here in reference to a sound (howl) being left in place of a station signal. Page 57.

pall: something that covers or overspreads, especially with darkness or gloom. Page 35.

palm: also called *sailmaker's palm,* a piece of heavy leather that fits over the palm of the hand, worn for protection in sewing the heavy canvas of a sail. At the base of the thumb, the palm is equipped with a metal disk for pushing the needle through the material. Page 70.

panhandle: a narrow section of land shaped like the handle of a cooking pan, that extends away from the body of the landmass it belongs to. Page 3.

parish: also *parish house,* the residence of a clergyman. Page 9.

passage, inside: a natural protected waterway in northwestern North America, 950 miles (1,500 kilometers) long. It extends along the coast from Seattle, Washington, past British Columbia, Canada, to southern Alaska. The passage is comprised of a series of channels running between the mainland and a string of islands. Page 3.

patent (anchor): any of several types of anchor that improved on the traditional anchor and that were protected by a *patent,* a government license giving an inventor a right to make, use or sell an invention. Patent anchors rely on a variety of designs to permit the anchor to dig into the sea bottom. Some of these designs omit the stock or use a stock that folds up to lie parallel to the main part of the anchor. The *stock* is the crosspiece at the top of the main part of the anchor and at right angles to the arms (the part of the anchor that digs into the sea bottom). *See also* **kedge** and **stockless.** Page 71.

PC: an abbreviation for *Patrol, Coastal,* a designation for a class of naval patrol vessels also referred to as *submarine chasers.* Between 1942 and 1944, several hundred of the 173-foot (53-meter) ships were constructed. Page 81.

peaking: attaching a *halyard,* a rope used for raising and lowering something on a ship, such as a sail, flag or the like, to the *peak,* the top rear corner of a fore-and-aft sail, so that the sail can be raised. Page 101.

Pelée, Mt.: *Mount Pelée,* a volcano on the island of Martinique, in the West Indies. Pelée erupted violently in 1902, destroying the city of Saint-Pierre and killing about 38,000 people. Milder eruptions occurred during the late 1920s and early 1930s. *See also* **Martinique.** Page 102.

pellet, lead: a small ball of lead, as for use in a gun. Page 14.

pelting: (of rain, hail or snow) continuing to beat with force or violence; driving. Page 203.

pennant: a long, narrow triangular flag, used on ships for signaling or identification. Page 160.

Peruvian: of Peru, a country in western South America. Peru was colonized during the sixteenth century after the Spanish conquest of the Incas, the rulers of a rich empire that extended more than 2,500 miles (4,020 kilometers) along the western coast of South America. During the succeeding centuries, the wealth of Peru's mines was shipped to Spain. Page 13.

petcock: a small, manually operated valve or faucet used to drain off waste material or excess fluid, as from an engine. Page 64.

Philco: a shortened form of *Philadelphia Storage Battery Company,* a United States corporation that originated in the late 1800s and was a pioneer in early battery, radio and television production. Page 58.

Phi Theta Xi: also *Theta Xi,* an engineering society begun in the mid-1800s, later becoming a general membership organization. Page 101.

pickup (station): a device that receives radio waves. Page 56.

picture film: also called *photographic film,* a thin, flexible strip of plastic coated with a light-sensitive covering for use in a camera. Photographic film, until 1951, was made with an explosive chemical and was therefore extremely inflammable. Page 65.

piece: a weapon for shooting, such as a *musket,* a gun used in the seventeenth and eighteenth centuries. A musket had a long barrel that fired ball-shaped bullets and was loaded from the front end of the barrel. Page 19.

Pier 2: a large pier that extended from downtown Miami into the northwestern part of *Biscayne Bay,* an inlet of the Atlantic Ocean that separates the cities of Miami and Miami Beach. Pier 2 included the facilities that were designated as the Sub Chaser Training Center (SCTC). Page 84.

pike(s): a weapon consisting of a long wooden shaft with a pointed metal head. On ships, pikes were usually 6 to 7 feet (1.8 to 2.1 meters) long, while those used by army infantry (foot solders) were twice that length. Page 17.

pile (something) over: move, push or force something over. Page 98.

pillow block: a part that encloses and supports the shaft, as of a propeller. Page 79.

Pilot: also called *Coast Pilot,* a manual published by a government for sailors, containing descriptions of coastal waters, dangers, harbor facilities, etc., for a specific area. A *pilot* in nautical terms means something that serves as a guide through some unknown place or through a dangerous, difficult or unknown course. Page 39.

pilothouse: also called *wheelhouse,* an enclosed place in the forward part of a vessel, containing the steering wheel, compass, charts, navigating equipment and, in larger vessels, communication systems to the engine room and other parts of the vessel. Page 69.

pipe nipple: a short piece of pipe with threads at both ends, used for joining other pipes. *Thread* means the raised line that runs around the end of a pipe or around a screw that allows them to be fixed in place by twisting. Page 36.

pirate islands: a nickname for islands in the *West Indies,* the islands between North and South America, that were used as havens by the pirates that sailed in the region, especially during the 1600s and 1700s. Page 101.

pitch: 1. the distance a propeller drives a boat for every revolution, less the amount lost by slippage. Page 75.

2. an alternating dip and rise of the bow and stern of a ship. Page 123.

pitched: thrown with great force or vigor. Page 15.

pitched, fixed-: a reference to a type of propeller, the blades of which are at a fixed and unchangeable angle as they rotate in the water. Propellers also exist with a variable pitch, allowing the angle of the propeller blades to be adjusted and providing greater and more immediate control of ship speed. *Pitch* here refers to the angle a propeller blade makes to the water. *See* **fixed-pitched** for illustration. Page 122.

pitting: setting in opposition or combat, as one against another. Page 92.

plain canvas, under all: with the normally used sails raised. *Plain canvas* or *plain sail* refers to the sails that a ship normally uses, as distinct from additional sails that are used only in light winds. Page 101.

plane: a hand tool for smoothing or shaping wood, consisting of a wooden or metal body with a flat base in which an adjustable metal blade is held at an angle. Page 54.

plank(ing): long, narrow, flat pieces of wood, such as those used in forming the decks, outer shell and inner lining of a vessel. Page 15.

plant, power: an engine supplying power to move a boat, automobile, aircraft or other self-propelled object. Page 33.

plate(s): in ship construction, steel sheets that form the sides and decks of the ship. Also, in the ship's fireroom, the steel sheets inside the enclosure for the fire of the boiler. Page 7.

playing out: letting out or releasing something gradually, little by little. Page 122.

plot: mark a route or position on a *chart,* a map showing a certain area of a coastline, water depths or other information of use to navigators. Page 14.

ploughed: an alternate spelling of *plowed. See also* **plow.** Page 103.

plow: (of a ship or boat) to part the surface of the water; to follow a course in this manner. Page 9.

plug, damp: a spark plug that is damp from having had gasoline spilled on it while the fuel tank was being filled. When the engine starts up, a spark from the damp spark plug could ignite gasoline that has spilled on the outside of the engine, leading to a explosion and fire. A *spark plug* is a part in an engine that produces an electric spark, exploding the fuel to provide the force that drives the engine. Page 63.

plugged: moved along steadily and persistently. Page 43.

plug wire: a wire leading to a spark plug in an engine. *See also* **spark plug.** Page 29.

ply: run or travel between certain places, said of ships. Page 3.

p/m., revs.: an abbreviation for *revolutions per minute,* a phrase that indicates how many times per minute something (such as a mechanical part) will go around in a circle. Page 8.

Point No Point: a small, sandy piece of land extending from northwestern Washington State into the west side of Puget Sound. Point No Point was named in the 1840s by a United States exploring team when they found it to be a relatively small point of land. Page 29.

point of business, fine: work to be done that is handled in a precise form. Page 43.

point(s): a piece of land that projects out into a body of water. Page 29.

Polynesian(s): someone from *Polynesia,* a group of islands in the central and southern Pacific Ocean, extending from the Hawaiian Islands to New Zealand. Page 31.

Ponta Delgada: a seaport on the southwestern coast of the island of São Miguel and the largest city in the Azores. Many ships anchor in the port while en route to and from Europe and the Americas. *See also* **Azores.** Page 122.

port: 1. the shutter or cover for a *porthole,* an opening (as a window) in the side of a ship. Page 9. 2. the left-hand side of a ship as one faces forward. Page 42.

port authority: that organization or group of individuals entrusted by local government to construct, improve, manage and maintain a harbor. Also called a *harbor authority* or *harbor board.* Page 200.

Port Orchard: a resort and fishing community located in western Washington State on *Puget Sound,* a long, narrow bay of the Pacific Ocean on the northwestern coast of the United States. Page 22.

ports of call: harbor towns or cities where a ship stops during the course of a voyage. Page 135.

Portuguese Maritime Museum: also *Lisbon Maritime Museum,* a museum founded in the mid-1800s, it is one of the premier maritime museums of Europe, with artifacts and models covering the nautical history of Portugal. Page 1.

Position Nomograph: a navigational instrument by which an unknown position may be discovered in terms of latitude and longitude, given the latitudes and longitudes of two known positions. Page 51.

post: a position, job or duty to which a person is assigned or appointed. Page 119.

postscript: an addition or supplement to something already said or written so as to supply further information. Page 26.

Potomac: a river that runs 287 miles (462 kilometers) in a southeast course from inland mountain areas to the *Chesapeake Bay,* a long, narrow arm of the Atlantic Ocean. Washington, DC, is located on the east bank of the river, approximately 115 miles (185 kilometers) from its mouth. Oceangoing ships can travel up the river as far as Washington. Page 106.

powder: *gunpowder,* an explosive mixture of substances in the form of a powder, formerly used to fire bullets from firearms. Page 19.

power plant: an engine supplying power to move a boat, automobile, aircraft or other self-propelled object. Page 33.

powers that were: those who were in command. Page 15.

precipitously: in a sudden and dramatic manner; hastily. Page 8.

predicated: based on (a given fact or facts). Page 119.

President Madison: a ship built in 1921, named after American president James Madison (1751–1836), on which LRH and his mother crossed the Pacific in 1927, visiting Hawaii, Japan, China and the Philippines. The final leg of their journey took them to the naval station in Guam. Page 7.

press agent: a person employed to promote the interests of an individual, organization, etc., by obtaining favorable publicity through advertisements, mentions in columns and the like. Used humorously. Page 39.

press gang(s): a group of men under the command of an officer, who round up other men and force (press) them into service in the army or navy. Page 17.

Prince Rupert: a city in western British Columbia that has one of the world's largest natural ice-free harbors. Prince Rupert is 470 miles (750 kilometers) northwest of Vancouver. The city is named for Prince Rupert (1619–1682), one of the founders of the *Hudson's Bay Company,* a Canadian company noted for having helped explore and settle the western parts of Canada. Page 44.

privateer: a sailor on an armed ship that is privately owned and manned, authorized by a government to fight enemy ships. Page 12.

prize: an enemy ship, cargo or property taken or captured by force, such as during wartime. Page 18.

process(es): in Scientology, a precise set of questions asked or directions given to help a person find out things about himself or life and to improve his condition. Page 184.

prodigal: unrestrained in spending (one's) money; carelessly extravagant. Page 19.

Promenade Deck: *promenade* means a walk or stroll. The Promenade Deck of a passenger ship is an upper deck where passengers can walk outside in the open air. Page 127.

prop.: an abbreviation for *propeller.* Page 8.

propeller: a device with a revolving shaft and angled blades for propelling a ship or aircraft. Page 44.

propeller shaft: a shaft for transmitting power from an engine to a propeller. Page 44.

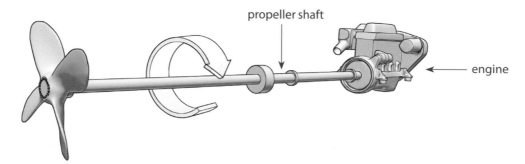

provocation: reason for attacking somebody. Page 15.

prowess: exceptional or superior skill, strength, bravery, etc. Page 52.

public stocks: property held by and for the entire crew. Page 19.

public-utility: of or relating to an organization supplying the community with electricity, gas, water, etc. Page 59.

Puget Sound: a long, narrow bay of the Pacific Ocean on the coast of Washington, a state in the northwestern United States. Page 7.

pulp: flesh so severely injured as to resemble *pulp,* a soft, wet mass. Page 15.

pulp fiction: the adventure, science fiction, cowboy stories and the like published during the early 1900s. Produced in magazines printed on inexpensive, rough-surfaced paper, pulp fiction had a wide audience. Page 10.

punt: a long narrow flat-bottomed boat with square ends, usually propelled with a pole. Page 8.

puppet: characteristic of or being like a *puppet,* a person whose actions are prompted and controlled by another or others. Literally, a *puppet* is a small figure of a human, often made with jointed limbs and moved by strings or wires from above. Page 181.

put out: leave a port, harbor or the shore and start sailing in a boat or ship. Page 118.

putrid: foul and smelly; filled with, or as if filled with, decaying matter. Page 15.

putting: proceeding or traveling in a boat that makes *putt-putts,* the flat, regularly repeated explosive sounds of a small gasoline engine. Page 38.

put to sea: set out in a boat or ship; sailed out to sea. Page 83.

put up: taken up lodging (at a hotel, inn, etc.). Page 11.

Q

quarterdeck: the rear part of the upper deck of a ship, usually reserved for officers. Page 95.

quartermaster: 1. on a pirate ship, the officer second to the captain. The quartermaster was elected to the position by the crew. Besides leading the charge when boarding another ship, the quartermaster also oversaw the division of captured treasure and kept an accounting of it. He maintained the peace and determined punishments for any pirates who broke their laws. Page 19. 2. in the navy, a junior-level officer who assists the navigator and serves as helmsman, also in charge of training other crew members who also function as helmsmen or as lookouts. The quartermaster is also in charge of signals, navigating apparatus, charts, etc. Page 42.

Quartermaster's Notebook: (on a ship) a notebook for entering data about all noticeable matters and all or any comments. For example, at sea this would include all sightings of ships and landmarks, changes of course and speed, data on the sea, wind and weather and the like. The *quartermaster* is a junior officer having charge of signals, navigating apparatus, steering and the like. Page 166.

quarter, on the: in a direction within 45 degrees of the point directly astern (behind), on either side of a vessel. The *quarter* is the part of a vessel's side near the stern. Page 164.

Queen Charlotte Sound: a large body of water off the west coast of British Columbia, Canada, north of Vancouver Island. Because the Sound is open to the Pacific Ocean, it frequently experiences the powerful waves of the open ocean. The Sound was named in 1786 for Queen Charlotte, wife of King George III of England. Page 39.

Queen Elizabeth: one of the largest luxury passenger liners of the twentieth century. Constructed in England and launched in 1938, she weighed over 83,600 tons, measured 1,031 feet (314 meters) in length and 118.5 feet (36 meters) in width. She traveled the Atlantic Ocean with her sister ship, the *Queen Mary,* until the 1960s when she was retired. Page 164.

Quién sabe?: a Spanish phrase meaning *who knows?* Page 101.

R

rabble: those regarded as the common, low, disorderly part of the populace. Page 12.

radar: an electronic device on a ship, plane, etc., used to detect the location of remote objects. *Radar* comes from the words *ra*dio, *d*etection *a*nd *r*anging. A radar detects objects by emitting radio waves from a continuously rotating antenna. The waves bounce off objects and return to the antenna, and the objects so detected are displayed as pictures on a screen. Radar is used by ships in bad weather so they can steer clear of nearby vessels or dangerous objects. Page 90.

radical: favoring or making economic, political or social changes of a sweeping or extreme nature. Used ironically. Page 12.

radio direction finder: a device for finding out the direction from which radio waves or signals are coming, as an antenna that can be rotated freely on a vertical axis. It is usually used to assist in determining a ship's position. Page 52.

ragtag: made up of a wide-ranging mix of people or things, often ones that are of questionable quality. Page 83.

rail: a structure of wood or metal serving as a guard at the outer edge of a deck. Page 46.

rail, tends the: waits at the ship's rail by the top of the gangway to greet a senior officer as he comes aboard or see him off as he leaves. Page 159.

Rangers: highly trained troops in the United States Army, formed for special operations, including surprise raids and attacks in small groups. In November 1942 the Rangers arrived at the coast of North Africa where, after a secret nighttime landing, they successfully conducted a surprise raid on enemy targets, clearing the way for a larger assault group. Page 125.

rate(s): the rank of an enlisted man (as in the United States Navy). Page 94.

rating: a classification of a ship's personnel according to specialized skills and training. Page 94.

RCA: an abbreviation for *Radio Corporation of America,* an electronics corporation established in 1919. Page 26.

reach: a single stretch or spell of movement or travel, as in *"a nightlong reach."* Page 101.

Reach and Withdraw: in Scientology, a procedure used to get a person familiar and in communication with things in the environment so that he can be more at cause over and in control of them. This involves reaching for and withdrawing from objects, people, spaces, etc. Page 185.

reach(ed): sail *across the wind,* with the wind on the side of the boat. Sailboats can usually move faster when sailing across the wind than in any other direction. Page 43.

reaches: continuous extents of water. Page 25.

reach, run and: the way a boat moves using wind direction to arrive at its destination. *Run* means sail *before the wind,* with the wind coming from astern. *Reach* means sail *across the wind,* with the wind on the side of the boat. Page 69.

ready, at the: in a position or state of being prepared for immediate action. Page 119.

rear admiral: a high naval rank. *Admiral* is the title of the commander of a fleet or of a subdivision of it. The four ranks of admiral that are found in most navies are fleet admiral, admiral, vice admiral and rear admiral, in descending order. Page 51.

reason, out of: not in accordance with reason; going beyond what is reasonable, proper or manageable. Page 76.

receiver: a device that picks up incoming radio signals and converts them to sound. A *signal* is a series of energy waves that are modified to carry information. Page 26.

reef fever: a humorous reference to a state of intense nervous excitement or agitation concerning *reefs,* ridges of rocks, sand or the like that lie at or near the surface of the water. Page 41.

reef(s): a ridge of rocks, sand or the like that lies at or near the surface of the water. Page 18.

reeking: 1. becoming piled up or heaped, as with large numbers or amounts of (something). Page 75. 2. having or giving off a very strong and unpleasant smell. Page 117.

reeve: (of a rope) pass through a pulley or similar device. Page 54.

refit: a thorough overhaul of something, especially a ship, in which it is repaired and reequipped. Page 119.

regenerative receiver: an early type of radio receiver that redirected power from one circuit so that it would feed back into and reinforce another circuit, the final result being that the signal would be stronger. Page 57.

relief valve: also called *safety valve,* an automatic valve for a steam boiler that opens if the pressure becomes excessive. Page 204.

religious warfare: the wars in parts of Europe during the sixteenth and seventeenth centuries that resulted from conflicts between Catholics and Protestants, members of two branches of Christianity. Where a government, such as France, approved of Catholicism, it fought to suppress Protestant churches. Conversely, where a government, such as in the Netherlands, favored Protestantism, it fought to throw off rule by the Catholics of Spain. Page 13.

remark (something): notice or observe (something). Page 93.

remote reception (line) station: a complete assembly of radio or television equipment, including antenna, transmitting or receiving set and signal-making or reproducing device, located at a distance from the main station. Page 56.

Rennes: a reference to René Duguay-Trouin (1673–1736), French sea captain and admiral, from the famous pirate region of Brittany, the capital city of which is Rennes. His fame rests on his numerous conquests of English and Dutch ships and the capture (1711) of the Brazilian city of Rio de Janeiro. Page 105.

replete (with): including or having something. Page 120.

reprobate: lost to all sense of religious or moral obligation; unprincipled. Page 8.

respite: a short period of rest or relief from something difficult or unpleasant. Page 7.

resplendent: having a dazzlingly impressive appearance; magnificent; splendid. Page 203.

revs. p/m.: an abbreviation for *revolutions per minute,* a phrase that indicates how many times per minute something (such as a mechanical part) will go around in a circle. Page 8.

R-factor: a shortened form of *reality factor,* a statement of purpose and what one is going to do at each new step. Page 182.

rhum: the French term for a type of alcoholic liquor traditionally made in the West Indies and in parts of Central and South America. It is made from the juice of fresh sugar cane. During the seventeenth and eighteenth centuries, the drink was used as a beverage and a medicine and, in some cases, as a form of currency. Page 20.

ribbon: a narrow strip of land, as of a path or road. From the literal meaning of *ribbon,* a long, narrow strip of material used to tie things together or as a decoration. Page 174.

rig: (on a sailboat) the sails, masts, ropes, etc., and the way they are arranged. Page 70.

rigging: 1. the system of ropes, chains, etc., used to support and control the masts and sails of a sailing vessel. Page 9.

2. assembling and adjusting (the sails and equipment of a sailing vessel) in readiness for operation. Page 52.

Ringrose: Basil Ringrose (1653?–1686), English buccaneer and surgeon. He published the story of his adventures in the West Indies during the early 1680s and included in the publication his own charts and descriptions of daily activities of buccaneers. Page 103.

Ripple Rock: a dangerous rock in the Straits of Georgia over which the water was relatively shallow resulting in damage and loss of ships. It was removed in 1958. Page 33.

Riverside Drive: a famous street in New York City, overlooking the Hudson River. The street is known for its impressive buildings, monuments and fine parks, as well as being a fashionable residential area. Page 59.

rocks, off the: (of a boat or ship) away from a projecting mass of rock or boulders in the sea. Page 91.

rode: the *anchor line,* usually consisting of the line (rope) and chain that are attached to an anchor. Page 72.

rogue(s): a dishonest or immoral man. Page 19.

roller(s): one of a series of long, swelling waves that move with a steady sweep or roll. Page 3.

rolling: (of a ship) rocking from side to side. Page 9.

romance: a spirit or feeling of adventure, excitement and the potential for heroic achievement. Page 10.

Romantic Isles: a nickname for the *West Indies,* the islands between North and South America, because of their tradition of *romance,* a spirit or feeling of adventure, excitement and the potential for heroic achievement. Page 102.

ropes, master the: become thoroughly familiar and expert with a particular field or activity, from sailors learning how to handle the ropes and rigging on a ship. Page 8.

Royal Navy: the naval warships, personnel and armaments of Great Britain. First organized in the 1500s, the naval forces of England became the primary defense of the country during the 1600s. Eventually the Royal Navy became the means by which the British built an empire of colonies around the globe. Page 14.

Royal Victoria Yacht Club: the yacht club of Victoria, a city and seaport on the southern end of Vancouver Island in the province of British Columbia, Canada. The yacht club was founded in 1892 and is the oldest sailing association in western Canada. Page 29.

rpm: an abbreviation for *revolutions per minute,* a phrase which indicates how many times per minute something (such as a mechanical part) will go around in a circle. Page 75.

rudder: a vertical blade usually at the rear of a ship that is turned from side to side to change the ship's course. *See* **tiller** for illustration. Page 117.

Rudder, Hard Right (Left): a command given to the Helmsman to rotate the wheel of a ship all the way (hard) to the right (or left) to change the direction of the ship's travel. Page 170.

rudder indicator: also called *rudder position indicator,* a device that displays the *rudder angle,* the angle between the rudder and the fore-and-aft line of a boat or ship. *Fore-and-aft* means lengthwise from the front to the back of the vessel. Page 169.

Rudder, Right (Left): a command given to the Helmsman to turn the wheel of a ship to the right (or left) to change the direction of the ship's travel. The command is usually preceded by a specific number of degrees to turn the rudder, as in *"5° Right Rudder"* or *"20° Left Rudder,"* etc. Page 170.

Rudder, Right (Left) Standard: a command given to the Helmsman to turn the wheel of a ship to the right (or left). *Standard* indicates the optimum turning radius of a ship, usually 25 degrees. Page 170.

rules of the road: the regulations concerning the safe handling of vessels under way with respect to one another, imposed by a government on ships. These rules cover general requirements (such as keeping a lookout and maintaining a safe speed), signals that are to be used by ships (including the lights that a ship must display and the sound signals it must use), as well as regulations concerning how ships must steer when approaching one another (such as which direction each of two ships should move to pass one another and avoid collision). Page 166.

runabout: a light motorboat. Page 62.

run and reach: the way a boat moves using wind direction to arrive at its destination. *Run* means sail *before the wind,* with the wind coming from astern. *Reach* means sail *across the wind,* with the wind on the side of the boat. Page 69.

running: of the sea or a body of water, flowing along strongly. Page 8.

running, fish are: referring to a time when fish are migrating and moving in large groups. Hence periods when fish are running are productive for fishermen because they can catch large numbers most easily. Page 79.

S

saga: a long story or series of incidents, often one of adventures, heroic events or the like. Page 11.

sail, set: depart(ed) in a boat or ship. Page 33.

sail, under full: with all sails raised. Page 34.

Salerno landings: the landings of British and American forces in the Gulf of Salerno in southwestern Italy in September 1943, following the surrender of Italy, which had been fighting on the side of the Germans. The Salerno landings involved over six hundred transport ships and warships and marked the start of the military campaign to take control of Italy. Page 125.

salient: that stands out as important; particularly relevant. Page 122.

sallied: set out on a journey. Page 46.

Salmon River (Kelsey Bay): Salmon River is a small river on the northeastern coast of Vancouver Island, British Columbia. The community of Kelsey Bay, located at the mouth of the river, was settled in the late 1800s and developed with the addition of a wharf and post office during the 1920s. Page 36.

salon: on a boat or ship, same as a *saloon.* Page 161.

saloon: also *salon,* a large public cabin for use as a lounge on a ship. Page 152.

salt horse: a slang term for salted meat (such as beef or pork). Salting was the only form of preserving meat until the nineteenth century. The term *salt horse* derives from an alleged incident on an old sailing ship where the salted beef was particularly tough and a horseshoe was found at the bottom of the beef barrel, whereupon one of the sailors made up the following rhyme:

> *"Old horse, old horse, what brought you here?*
> *From Saccarrappa to Portland pier, I was dragging lumber for many a year*
> *I was kicked and cuffed with sore abuse*
> *and salted down for sailors' use."*

(Saccarrappa is a former town in the state of Maine, near Portland pier.) Page 11.

Samaritan: helpful to a person in distress. From the story in the Bible of the *good Samaritan,* a man who stopped to help someone who had been beaten by robbers. A *Samaritan* is someone from

Samaria, an ancient region located north of Jerusalem, at the eastern end of the Mediterranean Sea. Page 120.

Santo Domingo: 1. another name for the island of *Hispaniola. See also* **Hispaniola.** Page 13. 2. capital and largest city of the Dominican Republic, a country founded by Spain in the 1500s and occupying the eastern part of the island of Hispaniola in the Caribbean Sea. Page 135.

sap: a weapon such as a *blackjack,* a short, leather-covered club, consisting of a heavy head on a flexible handle. Page 71.

sardonic: characterized by a grim sense of humor; mocking. Page 33.

Sargasso Sea: an area of the Atlantic Ocean, northeast of the Bahamas, covered with a dense mat of a brown seaweed called *sargassum.* Known for its weak winds, the Sargasso Sea is traditionally an area of difficult travel for vessels propelled only by sails. Page 10.

sashay: a trip or journey, often one having a specific purpose; expedition. Page 102.

satellite navigation: the use of multiple satellites to locate the position of ships, aircraft or automobiles that are equipped with special receivers. The satellites transmit signals that can be picked up by these receivers. The receivers then compute position information by comparing the time it takes for signals from three or four different satellites to reach the receiver. Page 25.

Sayward: a small community located in northeastern Vancouver Island, British Columbia. Founded in the late 1800s, the town is approximately 1 mile (1.6 kilometers) from the community of Kelsey Bay. Page 36.

scarp(s): a steep slope or cliff. Page 43.

schooner: a sailing ship with sails set lengthwise (fore and aft) and having from two to as many as seven masts. Page 1.

Scientology: the term Scientology is taken from the Latin *scio,* which means "knowing in the fullest sense of the word," and the Greek word *logos,* meaning "study of." In itself the word means literally "knowing how to know." Scientology is further defined as the study and handling of the spirit in relationship to itself, universes and other life. Page 106.

screw: another name for a *propeller,* a device with a revolving shaft and angled blades for propelling a ship or aircraft. Page 69.

scudded: moved quickly and easily due to being driven forward by the wind. Page 9.

scuppers: openings in the sides of a ship that allow water on the deck to drain overboard. Page 9.

scurvy: a disease marked by swollen and bleeding gums, bluish spots on the skin, physical weakness, etc., due to deficiency in vitamin C. Page 15.

scuttle: sink a ship by making or opening holes in the bottom. Page 11.

sea anchor: a large, canvas-covered frame, usually conical, that is thrown overboard as a drag or float to reduce drifting or to keep the ship heading into the wind. Page 164.

seaboard: a region bordering on or close to the sea. Page 83.

seafaring: of or having to do with life at sea, or the profession of a sailor. Page 1.

sea legs: the ability to adjust one's sense of balance to the motion of a ship at sea. Page 89.

seaman second class: the rank given to a seaman in the navy upon successful completion of basic training or indoctrination at a recruit school. Page 87.

seams: (of a ship) joints between steel plates or the joints between wooden planks. Page 98.

Sea Organization: the religious order of the Scientology religion, consisting of Scientologists who have pledged themselves to eternal service. The Sea Organization derives its name from its beginnings in 1967 when Sea Org members lived and worked aboard a flotilla of ships. Page 1.

seaplane anchor: an anchor developed during the 1930s for use by a *seaplane,* an airplane designed to land on and take off from water. Such anchors use lightweight materials, fold into a compact size when not in use and feature large, tapered arms that dig securely into the sea bottom. Page 72.

sea rover: a pirate. Page 18.

seas, short: an area of water with short, choppy waves. Page 43.

seat: a residence, especially a large house associated with a specific family. Page 8.

seawall: a strong wall or embankment made to break the force of the waves and protect the shore from erosion. Page 1.

seaward: in a direction toward the sea. Page 31.

Sea Watch Picture Book: a book containing basic data on key duties aboard a ship. The *Sea Watch Picture Book* gives a ship's crew general training, after which they become trained as specialists. Page 118.

seaway: a rough sea in which to sail. Page 63.

seaworthy: (of a boat) in a condition good enough to sail on the sea. Page 83.

seconded: supported. From the definition of a *second,* an assistant to a contestant, as in a duel. Page 14.

second engineer: the lower of two engineers or the next to the highest of several engineers. Page 7.

seeded: filled or furnished with something that grows or stimulates growth or development. Page 200.

seed, went to: lost vitality or effectiveness; decayed; deteriorated. Page 9.

seine boats: also called *seiners,* a general term for fishing boats that use a *seine net,* a large commercial fishing net that is weighted so that it hangs vertically in the water. Such boats are common on the Pacific coast of the US and usually measure 55 to 85 feet (16 to 25 meters) in length. Page 44.

service record: the record of a person's employment in a branch of military service. For example, a naval service record contains documents such as birth certificate, school certificates, letters of commendation, enlistment contract, history of assignments, performance record, medical record, rank, etc. Page 83.

service(s): same as *military service,* any one of a nation's organized fighting forces (as the army, navy or air force). Page 19.

service surgeon: a doctor in the naval service. Page 20.

serving: binding a rope by tightly winding it with string or lighter rope so it is covered completely, for protection or strengthening. Page 104.

set(s): a device that receives radio signals. Also called a *radio set*. Page 57.

set sail: depart(ed) in a boat or ship. Page 33.

Setúbal: a seaport in southwestern Portugal. Page 135.

seven seas: a reference to all the seas and oceans of the world or a great expanse of water in general. Throughout the centuries, the term has been used for the various seas and oceans known to people at the time. Page 1.

sextant: a hand-held instrument for measuring angles. Sextants are used by navigators to find a ship's position in relation to a heavenly body, such as the Sun, a star, etc. From the Latin *sextant,* sixth part, so called because the instrument's arc is a sixth of a circle. Page 48.

sextant shot: (in navigation) a measurement taken by a sextant to determine the altitude of a heavenly body. *See also* **sextant.** Page 51.

shaft: the long connecting piece that connects the engine with the propeller. Page 41.

shakedown cruise: a cruise for the purpose of testing a ship under operating conditions to locate and handle problems and to familiarize the crew with the ship's features and peculiarities as well as their duties. Page 97.

shallows: a shallow place in a body of water. Page 120.

Shanghai: a seaport and the largest city in China, located on the eastern coast of the country. Shanghai is a center of industry, trade and finance. Page 9.

sharp: (of an attack or battle) carried on fiercely; violent. Page 14.

sheet: a rope attached to the lower corner of a sail. *See also* **clew.** Page 27.

sheet, jib: a rope (sheet) attached to a *jib,* a triangular sail set at the bow (front end) of a sailing vessel. Page 46.

shelves: ledges or platforms of earth formed on the bottom of a bay or harbor. Page 38.

shied: flung or thrown at a target. Page 65.

shilling: a coin used in the United Kingdom prior to 1971. One shilling was equal in value to twelve pennies and twenty shillings was equal to a pound. Page 161.

ship: also *ship out,* take a job aboard a vessel. Page 17.

shipshape: arranged in a manner as would be found on a ship; tidy and orderly. Page 53.

Ship's Org Book: a text by L. Ron Hubbard for instruction of those on ships and containing some of the vital technology needed in sailing and in working on ships that is often not found in other manuals. Page 118.

shipyard: a place where ships are built and repaired. Page 31.

shoal(s): a sandbar or piece of rising ground forming a shallow place in water that is a danger to ships. Page 31.

shoot: succeed in sailing through (a dangerous strait, passage, etc.). Page 36.

shore leave: time spent ashore by a sailor off duty. Page 15.

short seas: an area of water with short, choppy waves. Page 43.

shortwave: employing *shortwaves,* radio waves used for long-distance reception or transmission, so called as their wavelength (between about 30 and 300 feet, or 10 and 100 meters) is shorter than those used in commercial broadcasting. Page 59.

shot, (iron): a solid iron ball for firing from a cannon. Page 15.

shot out from under: had one's ship sunk by enemy fire, requiring the crew to abandon ship. Page 84.

shot, sextant: (in navigation) a measurement taken by a sextant to determine the altitude of a heavenly body. *See also* **sextant.** Page 51.

Siberia: a vast, thinly populated region of eastern Russia, extending from the Pacific Ocean on the east and the Arctic Ocean in the north to cover most of northern Asia. It is the closest landmass west of Alaska, only 50 miles (80 kilometers) away at its closest point. Page 41.

Sicilian: of or pertaining to *Sicily,* the largest island in the Mediterranean Sea. Sicily is a region of Italy located off the southwestern tip of the mainland. Page 120.

sidelight: a piece of incidental information that helps to clarify a subject, lend more interest, etc. Page 19.

sight(s): an observation taken with a surveying, navigating or other instrument to ascertain an exact position or direction. Page 51.

singularly: extraordinarily; remarkably; to an unusual degree or extent. Page 11.

sinking into: investing (money) into something with the hope of making a profit or gaining some other return. Page 10.

sisal: a fiber made from a Mexican plant that has large, sword-shaped leaves. The sisal fibers are used especially for ropes or matting. Page 104.

skeleton crew: a crew consisting of the smallest number of persons who can care for the ship and do essential work. Page 120.

skipper: the Captain of a ship. Page 68.

skippered: commanded a ship as the Captain. Page 1.

skirmish: a brief fight between small groups. Page 14.

Skull and Bones: also *Jolly Roger* or *Black Flag,* a flag used by a pirate ship, often with a white skull and two long, crossed bones on a black background. Such a flag was raised on approaching a merchant ship to cause an immediate surrender. Page 20.

slack off: loosen or reduce the amount of tension on a line. Page 46.

slack (water): the time when the tide is not flowing visibly in either direction; water that is free of currents and therefore calm (slack). Page 32.

slate colored: having a dark gray or bluish-gray color. Page 46.

slide(s): a downhill displacement of rock, mud or earth, often caused by rainfall or erosion. Page 43.

slip: also *slippage,* a calculation of how far the propeller should make the boat move and how far the boat actually moves. Page 76.

sloshing: (said of a liquid) moving about actively within a container. Page 69.

small craft: a vessel that is of relatively small size. Page 8.

smoke screen: something intended to disguise, conceal or deceive. Page 178.

smothering: extinguishing or deadening a fire by covering so as to exclude air. Page 64.

snap: vigorous in spirit, mind or body; alert and energetic. Page 173.

sniggers: laughs disrespectfully. Page 35.

snugged down: properly prepared and made comfortable, tidy and in order. Page 101.

soda: *baking soda,* a white, powdery chemical that, when mixed with an acid, creates a foam that can smother a fire and extinguish it. Page 64.

solace: a source of relief or comfort. Page 41.

some little time: an unspecified, but possibly considerable, length of time. Page 58.

sonar: an abbreviation for *so*und *na*vigation and *r*anging, a system using underwater sound waves that are transmitted and reflected off objects (such as ships, submarines, rocks, etc.) to detect and locate them. Page 84.

song and dance: a detailed description or explanation of something. Page 58.

sou'easter: a storm or wind that blows from the southeast. Page 71.

sound: a narrow body of water lying between the mainland and an island or connecting two larger bodies of water. Page 7.

sounded: measured the depth of water—for example, by a weight attached to the end of a rope, the weighted end being dropped overboard. The rope is marked to show distances so one can see how deep the water is, depending on what mark is showing above the water. Page 31.

Southampton: a city in southern England. It is one of England's principal ports. Page 120.

South Carolina: one of the original thirteen states that formed the United States of America. South Carolina is located on the Atlantic Ocean. Page 14.

Southern France: the Allied landings code-named *Operation Anvil,* which took place in August 1944 in Southern France. These landings involved more than eight hundred warships, with hundreds of additional ships landing troops ashore. This was the start of a second invasion to win control of France, in support of the June 1944 invasion of Normandy, in the north of France. Page 124.

sou'wester: a storm or wind that blows from the southwest. Page 39.

Spanish Main: the Caribbean Sea or that part of it adjacent to the northern coast of South America, traveled during the sixteenth through eighteenth centuries by Spanish merchant ships that were often harassed by pirates. Page 10.

spark plug: a part in an engine that produces an electric spark, exploding the fuel to provide the force to drive the engine. Page 79.

Sparks: a name used for the *radioman,* the radio operator on a ship whose job is to transmit and receive messages via radio. Page 94.

spars: strong poles of wood or metal mounted crosswise on the mast of a ship. On nonsailing ships, these are used to hold lights, flags, etc. Page 120.

speed by ear method: the method of determining the approximate speed of a running engine by listening to it. An engine makes a certain sound or series of sounds for each revolution, so as the engine speed increases, the sound becomes higher. With experience one can estimate how fast an engine is running by the sound it makes, but this method of determining engine speed is not usually very accurate. Page 76.

Speed, Sam: Samuel Speed (1631–1682), English buccaneer and chaplain. Speed graduated from Oxford but, due to his conflicts with the government, had to escape to the West Indies, where he became a buccaneer. He eventually returned to England, becoming a pastor and then chaplain on a ship that fought the Dutch (June 1665), a deed that won him fame as one who "prayed like a Christian and fought like a Turk." Page 105.

spherical trigonometry: an application of trigonometry (a branch of mathematics dealing with properties of triangles and their application) used principally in navigation and astronomy. *Spherical* here refers to spherical triangles (triangles consisting of curved lines as opposed to straight lines) that are formed when dealing with three positions on the surface of a sphere, i.e., Earth. By knowing some of the values of a spherical triangle, one can determine the remaining values. Page 51.

spick and span: spotlessly clean and neat. Page 182.

spinning: fishing with a rod, line and reel, constantly drawing a revolving (spinning) bait or lure (a device attached to a fishing line to attract fish) through the water. Page 36.

spitting distance: a very short distance, from the relatively short distance over which a person's spit will carry. Page 45.

splicing: joining (ropes or rope ends) by weaving the end strands of each into the other. Page 104.

splutter: 1. rain scattered in small splashes. Page 32.

2. figuratively, a short, explosive, popping sound, such as made by an engine that is not running well. Page 44.

spluttery: suggestive of *spluttering,* the action of rain when it scatters in small splashes. Page 32.

spokes: projecting handles fixed along the rim of a ship's steering wheel. The Helmsman holds a spoke in each hand and turns the wheel as needed to steer the ship. Page 169.

spotting: the action of locating enemy positions and directing where to aim the ship's guns for firing on the enemy, including observing the results of gunfire for the purpose of correcting aim. Page 84.

spume: froth or foam, especially that found on waves. Page 33.

spyglass: a small telescope. Page 161.

square, by the: multiplying a number by itself. For example, in the statement 10 × 10 = 100, 100 is the square of 10. A speedboat increasing its speed needs only a steady increase in power to continue to make the boat go faster. However, at a certain speed (depending on the type of boat, shape of hull, etc.), the drag suddenly shoots up (increases "by the square"). At that point, using more power increases the speed very little. Page 76.

square-rigger: a vessel whose principal sails are square in shape and are arranged across the width of the ship. Page 156.

stable terminal: a *terminal* is any person who receives, relays or sends communication. A *stable terminal* is a person who deals with the actions that belong to his area and handles or suppresses the confusions of that area. Page 181.

standard, old-time: the type, model or example that has been used or practiced over a long period of time. Page 76.

starboard: the right-hand side of a boat or ship as one faces forward. Page 44.

starboard beam, hard on our: in a direction that is on the right side of a vessel (as one faces forward). Page 44.

starboard tack, on the: so as to move the boat forward with the wind on the *starboard,* the right-hand side of a boat or ship as one faces forward. *Tack* means direction of movement of a sailing vessel in relation to the side from which the wind is blowing. Page 101.

static: electrical interference in a radio or television broadcast, causing a random crackling noise or disruption of a program. Page 59.

station, chain broadcast: a local radio station linked by wire or radio relay to other stations, usually for simultaneous broadcasting of the same program, the entire group of stations often called a *network.* Page 56.

stationmaster: the person in charge of the operation of a radio station. Page 52.

station, remote reception (line): a complete assembly of radio or television equipment, including antenna, transmitting or receiving set and signal-making or reproducing device, located at a distance from the main station. Page 56.

Steady as she goes: a command given to the Helmsman to keep the ship heading in the exact direction it is heading. Page 170.

steam condenser: a device for heating water until it changes to steam and then cooling the steam so that it changes back (condenses) into a liquid. As an example of turning seawater to fresh water, the condensed liquid is allowed to run off into a container, leaving the salt behind and resulting in fresh drinking water. Page 15.

steamer chair: also *deck chair,* a folding chair, usually with arms and a full-length leg rest, commonly used for lounging on the decks of passenger ships. Page 31.

steamer(s): a large vessel propelled by one or more steam engines; steamship. Page 7.

steam navy(ies): a nation's warships, especially of the early 1900s, that were powered by steam engines, as opposed to the sailing vessels formerly used. Page 11.

steam-turbine: describing a type of ship that derives power from steam that rotates one or more turbines. The resultant rotation turns the ship's propellers and drives the ship through the water. *See also* **turbine(s).** Page 7.

Steersman: the person in charge of steering the ship. The Steersman is stationed at the *helm,* the wheel by which the ship is steered. Also called *Helmsman.* Page 164.

stem: the main upright timber or metal piece at the bow of a boat or ship. Page 44.

stern: the rear part of a ship or boat. Page 27.

sternpost: the central, upright beam (long, thick piece of wood or metal) at the stern of a vessel. The sternpost extends from the bottom of the vessel to the deck and usually supports the rudder. Page 79.

Stevenson: Robert Louis Stevenson (1850–1894), Scottish novelist and poet. In his adventure novel *Treasure Island* (1883), about the search for buried pirate treasure, Stevenson includes rhum as the favored pirate drink. Page 20.

St. Kitts: also *Saint Kitts* or *Saint Christopher* (*Kitts* is short for *Christopher*), an island in the eastern Caribbean Sea. In 1493 when Christopher Columbus reached the island, he named it for his patron saint. The island was settled by the British and French during the 1600s, becoming a British colony in the early 1700s. Independent since 1983, St. Kitts and the neighboring island of Nevis form the country called *St. Kitts and Nevis.* Page 13.

stock: the crosspiece fitted at the top of an anchor at the opposite end from the curved arm. When the anchor hits the sea bottom, the strain on the cable causes the stock to move the anchor at an angle, enabling it to bite into the sea floor. Page 73.

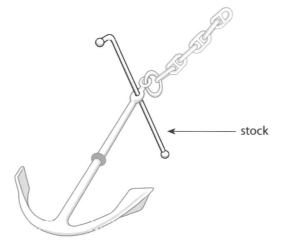

stock

stockless: having no *stock,* the crosspiece fitted at the top of the main part of an anchor at the opposite end from the part of the anchor that digs into the sea floor. In traditional anchors the stock causes the anchor to dig into the sea floor. Stockless anchors use other methods to do this and are also convenient because they take up less room when stowed aboard. Page 72.

stocks, public: property held by and for the entire crew. Page 19.

stokehold: figuratively, a term used for Hell. Literally, a compartment (hold) in a ship, containing the boilers. Page 63.

Stooge: literally, an assistant or a subordinate, often one performing routine tasks. Used here for the small boat, named *Three Sheets,* that was towed behind the *Magician. See also* **Three Sheets**. Page 27.

stores: quantities of food, clothing, supplies, etc., needed for something, such as a ship or an expedition. Page 18.

Stormalong: a sea captain and hero of seafaring songs and tales dating back centuries. His legendary adventures traditionally include such things as encounters with huge sea monsters. Page 102.

stormed: rushed or attacked with the violence of a storm. Page 102.

storm warnings: visual and radio warnings given of approaching gales and storms. The visual signals vary from country to country. In the US, for example, pennants and flags are hoisted to indicate dangerous sea conditions. Page 33.

stout: brave and determined. Page 11.

stove tanks: compartments in a ship for holding fuel for the ship's stove. Page 64.

Strait of Juan de Fuca: a body of water approximately 100 miles (160 kilometers) long and 15–20 miles (24–32 kilometers) wide that stretches east from the Pacific Ocean between northwestern Washington State and southern Vancouver Island, British Columbia, Canada. The strait is noted for having strong winds and a complex system of tides and currents. It is named for a Greek who sailed in the service of Spain and may have visited the passage in 1592. Page 29.

Straits of Georgia: also *Strait of Georgia,* a body of water between Vancouver Island and the mainland of southwestern British Columbia, Canada, approximately 150 miles (240 kilometers) long and up to 30 miles (50 kilometers) wide. Page 32.

strake: each of the continuous lines of planking in the side of a vessel, extending from the front (bow) to the back (stern). Page 71.

strangling: choking or suffocating. Here used to mean unable to breathe because of the carbon tetrachloride fumes. Page 65.

stream, in the: away from the shore in a body of water, a channel, river, etc., so that boats have to be used to get back and forth between the ship and the shore. Page 94.

strokes, broader: literally, a wide mark of a pen or pencil when writing or a brush when painting. Hence, *broader strokes,* a more general view or picture of a topic or subject. Page 1.

strove: worked vigorously or tried hard to do something. Page 90.

struck: lowered (a flag) as a sign of surrender. Page 19.

strung up: put to death by hanging. Page 19.

St. Thomas: one of a group of islands in the northeastern Caribbean Sea, now the Virgin Islands of the United States. In the late 1600s the island was settled by Danes and formed part of a colony owned by Denmark. Its governors allowed a pirate base to be established, deciding that the sale of pirate goods would help the economy. Page 18.

studded: set or scattered at intervals over the expanse of something. Page 31.

stuffing box: a device containing compressed packing that is used to prevent leakage of fluid around a moving shaft. The stuffing box on a boat is used around the propeller shaft at the point where it exits the hull underwater. It prevents water from entering the boat while still allowing the propeller shaft to turn. Page 79.

subchaser: a shortening of *submarine chaser,* a small patrol vessel, usually 100–200 feet (30–60 meters) long, designed for military operations against submarines. Page 84.

subjugated: brought under complete control; conquered. Page 14.

succored: helped or aided. Page 161.

suchlike: others of the same kind as those just mentioned. Page 174.

sunfished: bucked and twisted, similar to a horse that is *sunfishing,* bringing the shoulders alternately nearly to the ground and raising them. While bucking this way, sunlight hits the horse's belly and such a horse was said to be sunning his belly (or sides). *Sunfish* is a name for various fishes that swim close to the surface of the water, sunning themselves. Page 9.

Supercargo: an officer who is in charge of the cargo and commercial matters aboard a merchant ship. Page 8.

Super-Pro receiver: a radio receiver of the 1930s and '40s that was used extensively by US and British Government agencies in World War II (1939–1945) and by many American amateur radio enthusiasts. Page 56.

superstructure: all those cabins and structures built above the level of the main or upper deck of a vessel, including the deckhouse and bridge. Page 98.

supine: failing to act; inactive. From the original meaning, lying on one's back with the face or front upward. Page 189.

suppressive: relating to or of the nature of suppression. To *suppress* is to squash, sit on, make smaller, to refuse to let one reach, to make uncertain about his reaching, to render or lessen in any way possible by any means possible to the harm of the individual and for the fancied protection of the suppressor. Page 178.

surety: the state of being firm or steady. Page 26.

Survival Craftsman: a person who has completed a course of training that covers such things as launching and operating lifeboats; the safety, survival and first-aid equipment of a lifeboat;

and survival techniques. The Survival Craftsman Course is one of several courses that all crew members on ships are required to do. Page 207.

swamped: caused a boat to fill with water and sink. Page 47.

swamper: the lowest deckhand on a ship, literally, one who cleans up, usually a designation for new recruits prior to receiving further training. Page 118.

Swan, Captain: Charles Swan (?–1690), an English buccaneer who participated in the raid conducted by Henry Morgan against Panama (1671) and later, with his ship the *Cygnet,* in raids with Edward Davis along the west coast of South and Central America. Page 14.

swashbuckling: of or characteristic of a *swashbuckler,* a bold swordsman, soldier or adventurer. Page 10.

swathed: wrapped or covered in something. Page 31.

Swavely Prep School: a preparatory school that was located in *Manassas,* a city in northeastern *Virginia,* a state in the eastern United States. A *preparatory school* is a private school at which students live while attending classes that provide a college-preparatory education. Page 101.

swell(s): the rising and falling movement of a large area of the sea as a long wave travels through it without breaking. Page 31.

swig: a large amount of drink taken in one swallow. Page 20.

swilling: drinking heavily or excessively. Page 18.

swing: 1. a reference to tossing overboard the weighted end of a rope that is marked to show distances. In this way one can see how deep the water is, depending on what mark is showing above the water. Page 31.

2. achieve a desired change or result; succeed in bringing something about. Page 44.

3. (of a boat at anchor) move in alternate directions or around a fixed point, such as when the wind causes a vessel to swing around and point in different directions, even to the degree of rotating around the anchor. Page 45.

4. cause to turn on an axis; make rotate or pivot. Page 75.

swing, room to: figuratively, space to move about freely. Page 91.

swung, (one's) heels would have: a reference to a person being executed by hanging. Page 12.

T

tabulation: a category of something, likened to a section within an arrangement of information in a table or in columns and rows. Page 33.

tachometer: an instrument for measuring the speed of an engine in revolutions per minute. Page 70.

tack: a course of action or conduct, especially one differing from some earlier or different course. Page 92.

tack, on the starboard: so as to move the boat forward with the wind on the *starboard,* the right-hand side of a boat or ship as one faces forward. *Tack* means direction of movement of a sailing vessel in relation to the side from which the wind is blowing. Page 101.

tag, playing: literally, playing the children's game in which one player chases others until he touches one of them, who in turn becomes the pursuer. Used figuratively to indicate the action of moving this way and that to avoid running into rocks. Page 44.

take it away: used as a cue or signal, as in beginning a radio broadcast, and equivalent to saying "you're on the air." Page 56.

take up: 1. occupy oneself with the practice of; come to use. Page 29.

2. pull (the lines) up or in, so as to tighten or shorten. Page 46.

tapping: opening up and reaching into for the purpose of using (something). Page 148.

Teach, Edward: Edward "Blackbeard" Teach (?–1718), English pirate. During 1717 and 1718, he terrorized parts of the Caribbean and the coasts of what is now the southeastern United States. He captured ships in the harbor of Charleston, South Carolina, and held citizens until ransom was paid. Sailing north, he set up a pirate base off the coast of North Carolina, where he was eventually killed in a battle with British naval vessels sent to catch him. Page 10.

teak: a valuable wood from a tree native to parts of Asia. Teak has been used extensively in shipbuilding because of its strength and durability. Page 120.

tech: an abbreviation for *technology,* the methods of application of an art or science as opposed to mere knowledge of the science or art itself. Page 194.

Telegraph Passage: one of several channels near Kennedy Island, located in the area at the mouth of the Skeena River, a large river of British Columbia, Canada. Page 73.

telegraph (relay): a reference to the engine order telegraph, which relays (sends) information between the bridge and the engine room. *See also* **engine order telegraph.** Page 128.

telltale(s): a wind-direction indicator, such as a ribbon, feather, string or similar device, attached to the rigging or to a sail to indicate the direction of the wind relative to the course of the ship. Telltales on a sail are placed one on either side of the sail. The windward telltale is the one on the side of the sail that the wind is blowing on. A telltale streaming back indicates that air is flowing over that side of the sail. A telltale hanging limp means no airflow on that side. Ideally, both telltales would indicate airflow, because that shows that the sail is positioned for efficient use of the wind. Page 149.

temper, high: a state of anger. Page 175.

tender: a small boat used to go to and from a larger one. Page 41.

tends the rail: waits at the ship's rail by the top of the gangway to greet a senior officer as he comes aboard or see him off as he leaves. Page 159.

Tenerife: the largest island of the *Canary Islands,* a group of islands in the Atlantic Ocean near the northwest coast of Africa, forming a region of Spain. Page 149.

ten moves ahead of the game: a reference to someone having extremely accurate prediction of future events, likened to a game such as chess and being able to predict an opponent's next ten moves and thereby avoid defeat. Page 122.

teredo(s): a long worm called a *shipworm* that drills into wood and feeds on it, thus damaging structures and vessels that are made of wood. Page 54.

theater: an area of land, sea and air that is, or may become, involved directly in war operations. Also called *theater of war*. Page 83.

therefrom: from that thing; from that. Page 31.

Theta Tau: a society for engineering students and engineers, founded in the early 1900s. Page 101.

Thomas Basin: a boat harbor located at the southern end of Ketchikan, Alaska. A *basin* is a partially enclosed, sheltered area along a shore, often partly man-made, where boats may be moored. Page 47.

thong: a narrow strip of leather or other material, used as a lash of a whip. Page 14.

Three Sheets: the name of the small boat that was towed behind the *Magician*. A humorous use of *three sheets to the wind*, a slang term meaning very drunk, in reference to a drunken person being as disorganized and helpless as a sailboat with its sheets flying in the wind. A *sheet* is a rope attached to the lower corner of a sail. A slack sheet is said to be "in the wind" or "to the wind" and results in an uncontrolled and ineffective sail. With several sheets to the wind, a boat will move erratically, as a drunken person does. Page 27.

thresh: also *thrash,* move violently; beat. Page 69.

throat, had (one) by the: had (someone or something) in (one's) power; controlled. Page 12.

throbbing: beating with a strong, regular rhythm; pulsating. Page 56.

throes of, in the: in the act of dealing with the disorder or confusion that is characteristic of starting a new activity. Page 102.

throttle down: reduce speed by decreasing or turning down the throttle. Page 76.

throttle, under a full: at maximum power or speed. The *throttle* is a control that regulates the power output of an engine. Page 44.

Through Hell and High Water: the anthology (collection of selected writings by various authors) of the *Explorers Club,* an organization, headquartered in New York and founded in 1904, devoted exclusively to promoting the science of exploration. The article "It Bears Telling" by L. Ron Hubbard appeared in *Through Hell and High Water* in 1941, recounting an incident from his 1940 Alaskan Radio Experimental Expedition, a voyage during which he carried the famed Explorers Club flag. *See also* **Explorers Club flag.** Page 101.

tidal current (stream): a current, stream or the like that is caused by the periodic rise and fall or flowing in and out of the tides. Page 33.

tidal wave: a large, destructive ocean wave, not produced by tides but by an underwater earthquake, hurricane or strong wind. Page 74.

tide book(s): a book containing tables that predict the times and heights of tides for specific dates and places. Tide books, also called *tide tables,* are used in navigation. Page 35.

tide rip(s): an area of rough water typically caused by opposing tides or by a rapid current passing over an uneven bottom. Page 42.

tideway: a rush of tidal water through a channel or stream. Page 46.

Tilden, Neb.: a town in the northeastern part of Nebraska (abbreviated *Neb.*), a state in the central part of the United States. Page 101.

tiller: a wooden or metal lever on a boat, connected to the rudder and used for turning the rudder from side to side as required for steering. (The *rudder* is the flat board fitted at the rear of the boat which sits in the water.) Page 31.

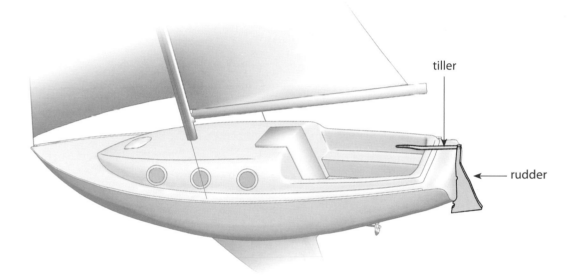

tip: fasten or secure at the end of. Page 74.

Titusville: a city located in central Florida on the Atlantic coast. Page 108.

took a notion: figuratively, had a sudden impulse or idea. Page 31.

topographical: having to do with *topography,* a detailed description or representation on a map of the arrangement of the natural and man-made physical features of an area. Page 42.

topside: on or to the upper parts of a boat or ship; on deck. Page 26.

Tork Clock: a timer that applies a rotation or twisting motion to switch on an appliance at a specified time. Page 56.

torpedoed: attacked with *torpedoes.* A *torpedo* is a self-propelled underwater naval weapon with an explosive charge, equipped with an internal-guidance system that controls its direction, speed and depth. Page 83.

torpedo, war-headed: a reference to a *torpedo,* a self-propelled underwater naval weapon with an explosive charge, equipped with an internal-guidance system that controls its direction, speed and depth. *War-headed* refers to the portion of the torpedo filled with explosives, called the *warhead*. Page 64.

torrents: rushing streams of water, as from an extremely heavy rainfall. Page 9.

Tortuga Island: a small island off the north coast of Hispaniola (the island also called *Santo Domingo*). It was named *Tortuga* (the Spanish word for *turtle*) because of its shape, which rises to a rounded mountain peak like the back of a turtle. Tortuga was a buccaneer settlement during the seventeenth century. It is now part of the country of Haiti. *See also* **Hispaniola.** Page 13.

tortured: twisted, as from the extreme pressure of the wind. Page 9.

torturous: having many turns or bends; twisting and winding. Page 36.

tow, in: figuratively, under discussion, as if being pulled out for examination. From the literal meaning of *tow,* use a vehicle or boat to pull (another vehicle or boat). Page 68.

track: be in perfect alignment with corresponding or related parts, said especially of a gear or similar moving parts. Page 44.

trade route(s): a route used by merchant ships to transport goods from one area to another. Between Europe and the Americas, the trade route used by Spain took advantage of winds blowing from northeast to southwest to cross the Atlantic to the Caribbean. On the return voyage, ships traveled up the coast of North America until reaching an area where the prevailing winds, blowing from west to east, enabled the ships to sail back to Europe. Page 12.

trade wind(s): a strong, steady wind that blows toward the equator. Trade winds north of the equator blow from the northeast and trade winds south of the equator blow from the southeast. For centuries sailing ships have relied on these winds for travel across the oceans. Page 10.

trained: directed, aimed or pointed in a particular direction. Page 85.

tramp: a ship that does not make regular trips between the same ports, but takes a cargo when offered and to any port. Page 3.

transmission tower: a tall structure that supports an *aerial* (also called *antenna*) that sends out radio waves carrying messages or signals. Page 58.

transmitter, Collins: a radio broadcast transmitter produced by the *Collins Radio Company,* one of the United States' foremost designers and producers of high-quality radio equipment, founded in 1933. A *transmitter* is a device that generates radio waves carrying messages or signals and sends them out from an antenna. Page 56.

trawler: 1. another name for a *troller* or *trolling boat,* a boat used to catch fish by means of *trolling,* fishing by trailing a baited line along behind a boat. *See also* **trolling boat.** Page 68.
2. a commercial fishing vessel employed in fishing with a *trawl net,* a large, baglike net that is dragged along the sea bottom behind the ship. Page 84.

trebled: made better, improved or increased by three times as much. Page 60.

tributary: a stream that flows to a larger stream or river. Page 106.

tricing up: hauling up, such as by chains around the wrists or hands, and left hanging, as a punishment. Page 103.

trimmed: adjusted (a sail) with reference to the direction of the wind and the course of the ship to obtain the greatest advantage of the wind power. Page 25.

troll: fish by trailing a baited line along behind a boat. Page 70.

trolling boat: also called a *troller,* a boat used to catch fish by means of *trolling,* fishing by trailing a baited line along behind a boat. Trolling boats often use multiple lines attached to two or four long poles. Page 69.

trolling mast: a tall pole located at about the center of a trolling boat. The mast supports from two to four *trolling booms,* long poles from which baited fishing lines run. *See also* **trolling boat.** Page 68.

trough: a long, narrow hollow or depression, as between two waves. Page 33.

truck, burst from a: (of a flag) suddenly raised to the top of a mast, just below the *truck,* a circular or square cap of wood fixed on the top of a mast, usually with small holes through which a rope can be run for raising a flag. Pirates would raise their flag on approaching a merchant ship to cause an immediate surrender. Page 19.

truck, up the: (of a flag) to the top of a mast, just below the *truck,* a circular or square cap of wood fixed on the top of a mast, usually with small holes through which a rope can be run for raising a flag. Pirates would raise their flag on approaching a merchant ship to cause an immediate surrender. *See* **up the truck** for illustration. Page 20.

tube, twenty-four-: having twenty-four *vacuum tubes,* devices once broadly used in electronics, such as in radio transmitters and receivers, to control flows of electrical currents. Called *vacuum tubes* because they are sealed glass tubes or bulbs from which almost all the air has been removed (creating a vacuum) to improve electrical flow. Page 56.

tugboat: a sturdily built, powerful boat designed for towing or pushing ships, barges, etc. Page 200.

turbine(s): a machine with blades that are turned by the movement of a liquid or gas, such as air, steam or water. Page 77.

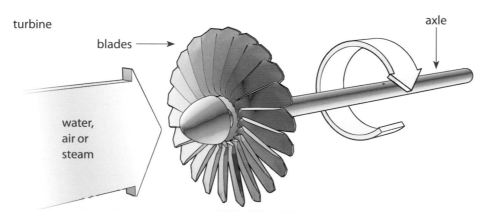

turbines, oil: ship engines that derive power from the burning of oil, which in turn heats water and creates steam that rotates one or more turbines, turning the ship's propellers. Page 8.

turbine, steam-: describing a type of ship that derives power from steam that rotates one or more turbines. The resultant rotation turns the ship's propellers and drives the ship through the water. *See also* **turbine(s).** Page 7.

turn out: 1. (of an engine, machine or the like) produce rapidly or regularly. Page 8.

2. prove to be in the end. Page 103.

'tween decks: the usual sailors' abbreviation of *between decks,* used to denote the inside deck of the ship, immediately below the main or upper deck. Page 181.

twenty-four-tube: having twenty-four *vacuum tubes,* devices once broadly used in electronics, such as in radio transmitters and receivers, to control flows of electrical currents. Called *vacuum tubes* because they are sealed glass tubes or bulbs from which almost all the air has been removed (creating a vacuum) to improve electrical flow. Page 56.

twin screw ship: a ship with two screws (propellers). Both screws can turn to move the boat forward, the one on the starboard side turning clockwise and the port side screw turning counterclockwise. Turning is usually done with one screw moving the boat forward and the other backward. Page 169.

two-fisted: of stories or writing, describing events in a way that is tough and aggressive. Page 84.

typhoon(s): a violent tropical storm having winds of or in excess of 74 miles per hour (119 kilometers per hour). Also called a *hurricane* or *cyclone.* Page 3.

U

U-boat: a German submarine, especially one used during World Wars I (1914–1918) and II (1939–1945). From German *U-Boot,* short for *Unterseeboot,* literally, undersea boat. Page 83.

uncanny: beyond the ordinary or normal; extraordinary. Page 117.

Uncle Sam: the representation of the United States Government, often pictured as a tall, thin man with white whiskers, wearing a blue coat, red-and-white-striped trousers and a top hat with a band of stars. Page 63.

under full sail: with all sails raised. Page 34.

"Under the Black Ensign": an LRH story first published in *Five-Novels Monthly* magazine in August 1935, this pirate adventure is set in the Caribbean during the seventeenth century. An *ensign* is a flag that shows the nationality of the ship it is flown on. The *black ensign,* also called *black flag,* was traditionally flown by a pirate ship and often showed a white skull and two long, crossed bones on a black background. Page 10.

under weigh: moving; advancing; making progress. The use of *weigh* is in reference to the phrase *weigh anchor,* which literally means raise the anchor (of a ship), as in preparation for moving. Page 29.

underwriter(s): a person, firm or organization that issues insurance and accepts liability for specified risks. Page 68.

undress blues: the everyday uniform of a sailor, consisting of blue trousers and shirt with long sleeves and a broad square collar hanging down in back. Page 84.

unfiltered: not fitted with a *filter,* a device for minimizing or blocking electrical interference from something (such as an electrical appliance) that causes a crackling noise or disruption of a radio program. Page 57.

unheralded: without prior announcement; unexpectedly. Page 102.

unimpeachable: not able to be *impeached,* challenged or discredited or called into question (as a person's honor or reputation, etc.). Page 12.

unit: the number one, the smallest whole number. Hence *"the speed advances but unit"* refers to the speed of the boat increasing by only (but) one step at a time (as opposed to the resistance increasing much more greatly with every single step of speed increase). Page 76.

unsmart: not brisk, vigorous or active; lazy. Page 190.

untoward: unfavorable or unfortunate. Page 173.

up sail: raise the sail or sails. Page 44.

up the truck: (of a flag) to the top of a mast, just below the *truck,* a circular or square cap of wood fixed on the top of a mast, usually with small holes through which a rope can be run for raising a flag. Pirates would raise their flag on approaching a merchant ship to cause an immediate surrender. Page 20.

truck

U.S. Naval Reserve: a part of the United States Navy that includes navy personnel who live as civilians after serving on active duty but continue to train at regular intervals. In emergencies such personnel can be called to active duty. Page 101.

USS *Henderson*: a United States naval transport vessel from 1917. During the 1920s and 1930s, the *Henderson* was primarily assigned transport duties in the Pacific Ocean. *USS* is an abbreviation for *United States Ship*. Page 8.

USS *Nitro*: a United States naval vessel used as a troop transport. The *Nitro* voyaged regularly between ports in Asia and those on the northern Pacific coast of the United States. *USS* is an abbreviation for *United States Ship*. Page 7.

utility, public-: of or relating to an organization supplying the community with electricity, gas, water, etc. Page 59.

V

Valencia: a city in eastern Spain, founded in Roman times. Page 135.

valves, grind: a *valve* is a device with a spring that opens or closes to control the flow of gas into an engine. When the valve opens, the spring pulls it closed again. Valves are used to seal a container so that a liquid or gas can only enter it and not escape. *Grinding valves* is done to smooth the surfaces of the valve by removing surface defects, carbon deposits, etc., to create a tighter seal and thus better engine performance. Page 29.

valve spring(s): a device with a spring that opens or closes to control the flow of gas into an engine. When the valve opens, the spring pulls it closed again. Valves are used to seal a container so that a liquid or gas can only enter it and not escape. Page 45.

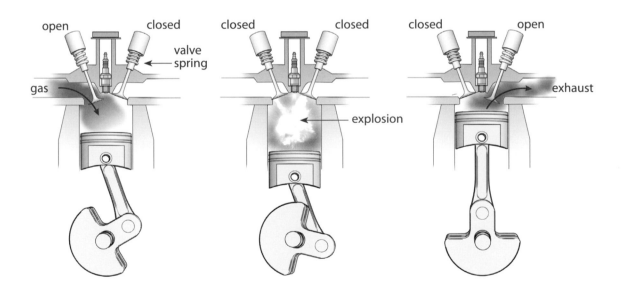

Vane: Charles Vane (1680–1721), an English pirate who robbed ships of England and France in the early 1700s. An associate of Edward "Blackbeard" Teach (?–1718) and known for his cruelty, Vane was captured and executed in Jamaica for piracy. Page 103.

vantage point: a place or position that provides a good view or, figuratively, a broad perspective (of something). Page 64.

vector(s): a quantity possessing both magnitude (size, greatness, extent) and direction. A *vector* is represented by an arrow, the direction of which indicates the direction of the quantity and the length of which indicates the magnitude. Page 185.

veddy: an informal or humorous term for the word *very*. Page 29.

V8: an engine with eight cylinders arranged in a *V* shape. A *cylinder* is a chamber in an engine in which a mixture of fuel and air is ignited, the explosion of which generates the power for moving. Page 106.

Venezuela: a country in northern South America, on the Caribbean Sea and the Atlantic Ocean. The region was claimed for Spain by Columbus in 1498. Spanish control lasted until the country became independent in 1811. Page 14.

veracity: correctness or accuracy. Page 154.

veritable: possessing all of the distinctive qualities of the person or thing specified. Page 85.

vermin-ridden: full of *vermin,* small animals and insects that can be harmful and that are difficult to control when they appear in large numbers, such as rats, flies, lice, mosquitos, cockroaches and the like. The word ending *-ridden* means full of. Page 17.

Victoria: a city and seaport on the southern end of Vancouver Island. Page 29.

Victoria Yacht Club, Royal: the yacht club of Victoria, a city and seaport on the southern end of Vancouver Island in the province of British Columbia, Canada. The yacht club was founded in 1892 and is the oldest sailing association in western Canada. Page 29.

virtue of, by: by reason of; as a result of. Page 95.

vogue, in: in general favor or acceptance; popular. Page 20.

voll: a German word meaning *full* (speed), the speed normally maintained while sailing. (Instructions on the telegraph are in German as it was German made.) Page 204.

voraus: a German word meaning *ahead* or *forward*. (Instructions on the telegraph are in German as it was German made.) Page 204.

W

wake: the visible trail (of agitated and disturbed water) left by something, such as a boat or a ship, moving through water. Page 3.

wake, hauled: moved rapidly, as if pulling the wake along behind. The *wake* is the visible trail (of agitated and disturbed water) left by something, such as a boat or a ship, moving through water. Page 39.

wake, in (one's): also *in the wake of,* a condition left behind someone or something that has passed; following as a consequence. From the literal meaning of *wake,* the visible trail (of agitated and disturbed water) left by something, such as a boat or a ship, moving through water. Page 14.

wardroom: on a warship, the dining room and lounge for the officers other than the commanding officer. Page 89.

wardroom country: in the navy, the part of a ship containing the *wardroom,* the dining room and lounge for the officers other than the commanding officer. Page 94.

war-headed torpedo: a reference to a *torpedo,* a self-propelled underwater naval weapon with an explosive charge, equipped with an internal-guidance system that controls its direction, speed and depth. *War-headed* refers to the portion of the torpedo filled with explosives, called the *warhead.* Page 64.

watch: a nautical term that means each of the periods of time into which a day is divided, especially each of the alternating periods of time for which a part of a ship's company remains on duty. Also the action of being on duty during such a period (on watch). Page 9.

Watch Officer: an officer who stands a watch on deck during which he is in charge of the ship. When on duty his title is *Officer of the Deck (OOD).* Page 94.

waterlogging: making a ship, boat, etc., unmanageable by flooding it with water. Page 55.

water, rusty: drinking water with impurities, due to not being filtered or to being stored in tanks containing rust. Page 174.

wavelength: in broadcasting, the wavelength (distance between successive crests of a wave) used by a broadcasting station. Page 56.

way, give: help to make (a ship or boat) move through the water. Page 69.

WC(s): an abbreviation for *water closet,* a small room containing a toilet and, often, a sink; a bathroom. Page 161.

weigh anchor: literally, raise the anchor (of a ship), as in preparation for moving. Used figuratively to mean prepare to start something. Page 3.

weigh, under: moving; advancing; making progress. The use of *weigh* is in reference to the phrase *weigh anchor,* which literally means raise the anchor (of a ship), as in preparation for moving. Page 29.

well deck: an open space on the main deck of a ship that lies at a lower level, situated between the upper deck in the front of the ship and the raised deck at the back. This term also means any deck that has a raised deck before and after it. Page 181.

West Indies: a large group of islands between North America and South America comprising the Greater Antilles, Lesser Antilles and the Bahamas. Page 12.

West Indies minerals survey expedition: the *West Indies Mineralogical Expedition,* an expedition organized and conducted by L. Ron Hubbard during the early 1930s. The expedition toured Puerto Rico and other Caribbean islands while conducting its primary mission, the first complete mineralogical survey of Puerto Rico under United States jurisdiction. Page 101.

Westinghouse: Westinghouse Electric Corporation, founded in the United States in 1886 by American engineer and inventor George Westinghouse (1846–1914). The company was one of the world's largest suppliers of equipment and services relating to the control, distribution, generation and use of electric power. Page 77.

what you're at: what you are engaged or occupied in; what you are doing. Page 181.

wheel: 1. a ship's propeller. Page 46.

2. short for *wheelsman,* one who handles or steers a vessel with a wheel: helmsman. Page 161.

wheelhouse: also called *pilothouse,* an enclosed place in the forward part of a vessel, containing the steering wheel, compass, charts, navigating equipment and, in larger vessels, communication systems to the engine room and other parts of the vessel. Page 160.

wherefore: the cause or reason. Page 19.

wherewith: also *wherewithal,* that with which to do something; means or supplies for the purpose or need. Page 71.

whilst: a chiefly British term meaning during the time that; while. Page 148.

whisker pole: a light pole used for extending the corner of a sail. One end of the pole fits around the mast and the other end goes through the corner of a sail, enabling the sail to be extended to catch more wind. Page 32.

whitecaps: waves with broken and foaming white crests. Page 3.

white line: rope (line) that is not coated, in contrast to line that is black due to being coated with tar. (Tar is used to preserve lines that are constantly soaked in water.) Page 36.

whole track: the moment-to-moment record of a person's existence in this universe in picture and impression form. Page 148.

whooshed: moved swiftly with a loud, rushing or hissing noise. Page 45.

Who's Who in America: a well-known reference work first released in the late 1800s and since then regularly updated. The publication gives short biographical essays on prominent persons. Page 101.

Why: the real basic reason for a situation that, being found, opens the door to (allows) handling; the basic outness found that will lead to a recovery of statistics. Page 186.

Willemstad: a seaport and capital of *Curaçao,* an island in the southern Caribbean Sea lying off the coast of Venezuela. *See also* **Curaçao.** Page 143.

willful: showing stubbornness, like a person who tends to do what he wants without regard to what is best. Page 46.

wind, across the: with the wind on the side of the boat. Sailboats can usually move faster when sailing across the wind than in any other direction. *See also* **run and reach.** Page 69.

wind catch: the action or condition of taking or receiving the impact of the wind, as a sail. Page 25.

wind charger blade: the blade from the propeller of a *wind charger,* a device that converts wind into electricity. Also called a *windmill.* Page 32.

windward: on the side that is facing the wind. *See also* **telltale(s).** Page 149.

withal: therewith; with that. Page 38.

with the flood: with the rise or flowing in of the tide. Page 35.

work parties: organized groups of workmen. Page 159.

world's his oyster, the: the world is the place to gain opportunity or success, as a pearl can be taken from an oyster, an often-quoted phrase first recorded in the play *The Merry Wives of Windsor* (1600) by English poet and playwright William Shakespeare (1564–1616). A character in the play asks an associate for a loan and when refused replies, "Why then, the world's mine [my] oyster, Which I with sword will open." Page 101.

would-be: wishing or pretending to be; posing as. Page 120.

wreckers: persons who cause shipwrecks on rocky coastlines by using false signals and then steal the cargo or other goods from the wreckage. Page 120.

wry: marked by a clever twist. Page 106.

Y

yarn: tell a *yarn,* an entertaining anecdote or story of real or fictitious adventures. Page 62.

yaws: deviates erratically from a straight course by swinging to one side of the course and then the other, as occurs when the seas are coming from directly astern and the ship is more or less out of steering control. Page 164.

yea: indeed; truly. Used to introduce a statement. Page 41.

yelping: figuratively, crying out or calling in a shrill, sharp manner. Page 44.

yowling: making a loud, wailing noise. Page 69.

YP: a designation for *Yard Patrol,* in reference to a patrol vessel, such as one assigned to escort ships in a harbor or local area. During World War II (1939–1945) a number of these boats were converted from fishing boats to serve in the United States Navy. Page 84.

Z

zurück: a German word meaning *back* or *reverse*. (Instructions on the telegraph are in German as it was German made.) Page 204.

INDEX

stockless-type anchor, 72, 73

antipiracy action

instructional programs for, 200

antiterrorist action

instructional programs for, 200

Apache, 107, 108

log, 109

Apollo

bridge, illustration, 128–129

christening, photographs of L. Ron Hubbard, Commodore, 116, 121

history of, 125

Hurricane Ten and, 122

interior photographs, 130–131, 132

photographs, 121, 124, 127, 128–129, 134, 146–147, 162, 168, 176, 179

photographs of L. Ron Hubbard, Commodore, aboard, 126, 133, 157, 165, 167, 171, 183, 187, 191

plaque of historic site in Madeira, 1, 145

ports of call, 135–147

replica of, 122–123

Royal Scotman and, 120, 135

scale model in Lisbon Maritime Museum, 1

see also **Royal Scotman**

ARC

group and raising, 178

archeological expedition

Enchanter, 188

Asia

L. Ron Hubbard called upon many a port between Caribbean and, 3

Asiatic Fleet

Harry Ross Hubbard, 7

Athena

Avon River remembered today as, 117, 118

see also **Avon River**

Author's League of America, 101

Auto Identification System, 203

aviators

swiftly determining positions, 51

Avon River

remembered today as *Athena*, 117

helm and, 169

photograph, 118

refit of, 119

Azores, 122

B

Bahamian ferry

Freewinds rescuing, 200

Baker, 40, 44

Barbarossa, 93

barometer

Magician, photograph, 32

Bella Bella, 40, 41

"best" people

teamwork and, 178

bilges

dirt in, 98

billing and drilling

Apollo and, 123

Lieutenant Harry Ross Hubbard serving in, 7

Gulf Stream

Blue Water II and, 101

H

halyards, reeving, 104

Harbor Island, 56

Harley-Davidson, 192

photograph of LRH astride a, 193

"Hat of Master, The," 189–190

Havana

sailing in *Blue Water II* to, 101

head sea

description, 163

heart in the throat navigation, 39

helm, 129

commands, 170

photograph by L. Ron Hubbard, 168

ships answer differently to, 169

Helmsman

center, locating, 169

changing watch

profitable courses and, 164

commands to, 170

expert, 169, 170

how to keep a ship on course, 165

how to steer, 169

lubber line, pushing, 170

overcontrol and, 169

poor, 169

steering without a compass, 123

Herbert Reefs, 40, 44

Hispaniola

Spain and, 12

Holland

Spain and, 12

Hope Island, 39

map, 37, 38, 39, 40

Hornigold, 105

horsepower

determining, 76

propeller and, 77

tachometer and, 76

house

boat versus, 32

Hubbard, Harry Ross

America's Asiatic Fleet, 7

United States Navy Lieutenant, 3

hull, handling, 53–55

Hurricane Ten

Apollo directly in path of, 122

Husky I, 112–113

Hydrographic Office

correcting coastal charts for United States, 25

publication strictly ballast, 31

I

Indian Island, 41

Indian village, 40, 44, 45

Inside Passage

Magician, photograph, 34

instruction

Freewinds instruction on antiterrorist and
antipiracy action, 200

incompetence remedied by discipline
and, 190

International Executive Director, 106

**International Maritime Organization
(IMO)**

Freewinds training and, 200

Ivory Island, 40, 41, 42

J

Jamaica

Henry Morgan and, 14

Kingston, 135, 142, 144

Spain and, 12

Japan

President Madison and, 7

Java

braving typhoons off a still primitive, 3

Supercargo going to, 8

John Drummond

Main Passage and, 41

Jolly Roger

pirates and, 11, 13

Jones, John Paul, 93

K

kelleting, 72, 74

Kelsey Bay, 36, 37, 38

Kelvin Hughes Radar System

fully digitized, 203

Kennedy, Walter

pirate, 18

ketch

charting North Pacific coastline in a
32-foot, 1

Ketchikan, 36, 63

arriving to Alaska, 48

electricity in homes, 59

maps, 40, 46

photograph of L. Ron Hubbard, 24

photographs, 47, 52, 60–61, 66–67

"The Voice of Alaska," 53–79

KGBU, 52–79

clean juice and, 60

only Alaskan chain broadcast station, 56

"The Voice of Alaska," 53–79

transmission tower, 58

K-gun launchers, 85

Klewnuggit Inlet, 40, 43, 44

KOL

broadcast station, 56

L

Lama Passage, 40, 41

landlubbers

difference between sailors and, 118

landsman

meticulous care of ship not understood by, 97

Las Palmas, Canary Islands, 135, 136, 141

Enchanter and, 117

Sea Organization and, 135

latitude

ded-reckoning, longitude and, 51

obtaining positions of, 51

Lawley & Son's shipyard, 84

legacy, nautical, 123, 199–207

León, 12

letters

letter from L. Ron Hubbard to a sailor's mother, 87

letters of the *PC-815*, 87–89

license

to helm any sailing ship on any ocean, 1, 26, 101, 199

lifeboats, 207

lines

serving or splicing, 104

Lisbon, Portugal, 141

Maritime Museum, famed photographic shoot, 192

photograph of *Apollo*, 134

scale model of *Apollo* in Maritime Museum, 1

log

Magician chronicles, 25–48

l'Olonnais, 11, 103

buccaneer captain, 13

Execution Dock and, 14

longitude

ded-reckoning, latitude and, 51

obtaining positions of, 51

Long Range Navigational systems (LORAN)

antecedent of, 51

testing, 25

long-stemmed glass

voyage free of "roll and pitch" and, 123

Lookout

photograph, 172

ships and, 166

Los Angeles

guns trained on, 85

Lowe Inlet, 40, 43, 44

lubber line

compass and, 170

illustration, 170

pushing, 170

luck

competence, coordinated organization and, 199

M

THE
L. RON HUBBARD
SERIES

"To really know life," L. Ron Hubbard wrote, "you've got to be part of life. You must get down and look, you must get into the nooks and crannies of existence. You have to rub elbows with all kinds and types of men before you can finally establish what he is."

Through his long and extraordinary journey to the founding of Dianetics and Scientology, Ron did just that. From his adventurous youth in a rough and tumble American West to his far-flung trek across a still mysterious Asia; from his two-decade search for the very essence of life to the triumph of Dianetics and Scientology—such are the stories recounted in the L. Ron Hubbard Biographical Publications.

Drawn from his own archival collection, this is Ron's life as he himself saw it. With each volume of the series focusing upon a separate field of endeavor, here are the compelling facts, figures, anecdotes and photographs from a life like no other.

Indeed, here is the life of a man who lived at least twenty lives in the space of one.

FOR FURTHER INFORMATION VISIT
www.lronhubbard.org

The L. Ron Hubbard Series
A PROFILE

To order copies of *The L. Ron Hubbard Series*
or L. Ron Hubbard's Dianetics and
Scientology books and lectures, contact:

US AND INTERNATIONAL

BRIDGE PUBLICATIONS, INC.
5600 E. Olympic Blvd.
Commerce, California 90022 USA
www.bridgepub.com
Tel: (323) 888-6200
Toll-free: 1-800-722-1733

UNITED KINGDOM AND EUROPE

NEW ERA PUBLICATIONS
INTERNATIONAL ApS
Smedeland 20
2600 Glostrup, Denmark
www.newerapublications.com
Tel: (45) 33 73 66 66
Toll-free: 00-800-808-8-8008